ODO CASEL

THE MYSTERY OF
CHRISTIAN WORSHIP
AND OTHER WRITINGS

ODO CASEL

❧

THE MYSTERY OF
CHRISTIAN WORSHIP

AND OTHER WRITINGS

Edited by

BURKHARD NEUNHEUSER, O.S.B.

With a preface by Rev. Charles Davis

THE NEWMAN PRESS
WESTMINSTER, MARYLAND
DARTON, LONGMAN & TODD
LONDON

DARTON, LONGMAN AND TODD LTD
29a GLOUCESTER ROAD
LONDON, SW7

THE NEWMAN PRESS
WESTMINSTER, MARYLAND

2482
C 267E
c.2

148583A

© *1932 for Part I, and* © *1959 for Part II, Verlag Friedrich Pustet,*
Regensburg.

This translation © *1962 Darton, Longman and Todd*
First published 1962

This is a translation of the fourth German edition of Das Christliche
Kultmysterium *and of the other writings of Dom Odo Casel which appeared
with it in 1960, published by Verlag Friedrich Pustet. In Part I, Chapters
2–5 are revised and enlarged versions of articles originally published as
follows: Chapter 2 in* Liturgische Zeitschrift *3 (1930/31) 39–53; 72–83;
105–115. Chapter 3 in* Bayerische Blätter für das Gymnasialschulwesen
63 (1927) 329–340, Chapter 4 in Liturgishce Zeitschrift *4 (1931/32)
37–44, Chapter 5 in the first edition of* Die Betende Kirche *(1924)
182–206, published by Maria Laach.*

*Printed by W. & J. Mackay & Co Ltd, Chatham. Nihil
obstat: Joannes M. T. Barton, S.T.D., L.S.S., Censor depu-
tatus. Imprimatur: Georgius L. Craven, Vic.Gen., Epus.
Sebastopolis, Westmonasterii, die 30a Aug. 1960. The Nihil
obstat and Imprimatur are a declaration that a book or pamphlet
is considered to be free from doctrinal or moral error. It is not
implied that those who have granted the Nihil obstat and
Imprimatur agree with the contents, opinions or statements expressed.*

CONTENTS

LIST OF ABBREVIATIONS

A.L.W.   Archiv für Liturgiewissenschaft

J.L.W.   Jahrbuch für Liturgiewissenschaft

PREFACE TO THE ENGLISH EDITION[1]
By Charles Davis

I T is difficult to know how best to present this book of Casel to English readers. Many, I think, will not be quite sure what to make of it. Their first reaction will probably be one of surprise that it is so straightforward. Made nervous—or perhaps braced in readiness—by learned talk about the theology of mysteries, they may be confused—or deflated—when given so simple an exposition. The large use made of the pagan mysteries in explaining the Christian mystery may puzzle or cause some doubts, but the rest will be found unexceptionable—even disappointingly obvious. Some, well-read in the writings of Fr Jungmann and sensitive to the pastoral function of the liturgy, will jib at some of the remarks of Casel and be put off by his apparently romantic, unrealistic approach to the liturgy. There is need, it seems, for some explanatory remarks to help people place the work, appreciate its bearing and significance and recognize both its value and its defects.

Das Christliche Kultmysterium, of which this present book is a translation, is a simple, brief and non-technical presentation of the Christian religion as a 'mystery' and of the liturgy as that 'mystery' made present. (As is well-known, Casel gave a new richness to the concept of mystery.) We have here not a technical treatise but a piece of popular spiritual writing. The miscellany, made up of fragments from the literary remains of Casel and added to the fourth edition here translated, is more erudite in character, but the work itself is astonishingly accessible. It is a statement of his major concern, not a detailed analysis and defence of all his positions. When we recognize this, we see its proper value. Increasingly complicated discussions surround Casel's thought. This is inevitable since he raises some very difficult problems for the theologian and the historian, but it would be a pity if these debates on the technical level should obscure the important message that Casel has for the ordinary Christian. He would have been the first to have deplored such an outcome, impatient as he always was with the ins and outs of theological questioning—indeed, his work suffered from an excessive indifference to the difficulties his language created for theologians. But for him what mattered was the right basic approach to

[1]The substance of this preface was published in *The Clergy Review*, Nov. 1961.

the Christian religion, the right answer to the question, What is Christianity?—and that is what he sets forth in this book. A special chapter on the Mass would have made it more adequate as a synthesis, and the lack of this is bound to cause a certain dissatisfaction or sense of incompleteness; but Casel reserved the direct treatment of this point for another work, *Das Christliche Opfermysterium,* never actually finished but due to be published posthumously under the editorship of Dom Viktor Warnach. Perhaps, however, the more general exposition offered here will drive home more effectively that basic idea of Christianity which underlies Casel's more detailed work on the liturgy.

I have already suggested that much of what he says may strike some as disappointingly obvious. Perhaps I am over-optimistic in taking for granted such a measure of agreement, but it is not opposition but an indifferent, tepid assent that I fear most. How difficult it is to gain credit for stating a truth, especially when that truth has always been implicit in the faith as held by all believers! Complacently, those who have in fact never given the truth a thought nor acted upon it declare that they always knew it to be so, and they resent any criticism of their previous mentality. People can easily overestimate the quality of their faith in these days of renewal. The impression of simple obviousness left by truths now restated is taken as proving a living and effectual grasp of those truths, whereas it often denotes blindness to their significance and implications. However unusual some of his expressions and whatever the inadequacies of his explanations and of the support he claimed for them, Casel's central insight is in my judgement undeniable, and I see it as having all the obviousness of the undeniable when once stated. But it needed stating none the less, and it still needs stating. If anyone doubts this, let him compare—honestly and realistically—Casel's concept of Christianity with the outlook of the average Catholic today. We have a long way to go before what is on paper the obvious meaning of Christianity represents the actual, conscious outlook of the mass of the faithful.

As is usually the case with pioneer thinkers, Casel was in reaction against a current mentality. In the name of the liturgy and ancient tradition he rejected what he considered a widespread, modern impoverished idea of the Christian religion. If we were to take seriously the way it is often presented, Christianity would be reduced to a matter of accepting a collection of doctrinal statements and of observing a strict moral code, assisted in this by periodical infusions of helps from God called graces. A poor substitute for the Pauline vision of God's eternal plan! It might indeed be admitted that man can do nothing without graces from God, but that does not prevent religion as thus understood from making people busy above all with themselves, or rather with their souls. It lacks an objective transcendence and becomes centred on man and his spiritual states, with the doctrines so many additional items in his intellectual baggage, so many objects for his curious scrutiny. Religion devoid of a vision of God's cosmic design becomes a different thing to different people: there are the sophisticated devout with their seeking after spiritual perfection, or even after mystical experience; there are the unsophisticated pious with their many devotions and petitions, softening the harsh fragments of their daily experience with religious sentiment but failing to unify their lives or give them real meaning; there are the coldly professional theologians so occupied with the juggling of their concepts that the realities of revelation escape their notice. But for all these and others like them religion has lost its sacredness, and with this its power to bring men to the divine. It was in opposition to this modern, anthropocentric, subjective, rationalist concept of religion that Casel declared that the Christian thing was not a religion but a mystery as the ancients understood the word.

Little purpose would be served by giving yet one more summary of all that Casel meant by this. After all, in this book Casel is speaking for himself. But I cannot resist drawing attention to certain points.

For Casel a 'mystery' was not primarily a mysterious truth beyond our reason but a reality—a divine reality, hidden yet communicated. Since a mystery is a divine reality, there is ultimately but one mystery, God Himself in His own inner reality and life. A key feature of the book is its stress on the theocentric character of a true Christian outlook. We must restore a sense of the divine, it urges, an awareness of the complete otherness of God, of the unfathomable depths—the mystery— of God. Everything in the Christian scheme goes back to the eternal love or *agape* of God—which is God Himself in His inmost essence. God, ineffable and unapproachable, has indeed communicated Himself to us; He has come to us so that He might take us to Himself and give us His life. But religion is not primarily what we do, but God's action on us by which we enter into His life. We must recapture an awe before God, a sense of His majesty and inaccessibility to man as man, and then we will appreciate the mystery of His eternal plan of love, which is the Christian revelation.

God has revealed Himself, communicated His love and imparted His life in Christ. The mystery of God has become the Christian mystery, the mystery of Christ. But notice that this mystery is not just the person of Christ but the events of His saving mission. The Christian mystery is the coming into this world of the divine life, power and love in the saving acts accomplished in the incarnate Son. And the centre of the mystery of Christ is the Pasch, the return to the Father, the passing of Christ from life in the flesh to a risen life in the Spirit.

Casel assimilated well the Pauline understanding of the paschal mystery and what he says about the mystery of Christ is now a common-place of biblical theology. But the further development of this, though claimed as equally biblical, has remained closely associated with his name and is regarded as a tenet characteristic of the theology of mysteries. It is that we must relive the mystery of Christ. We do not benefit from what Christ did while remaining outside the saving events once accomplished in Him. What was realized in Christ must be realized in us. Being a Christian does not mean just that we accept the teaching of Christ and receive graces won by Him; it means a real share in the very saving acts that constitute the mystery of Christ. Therefore the past mystery of Christ must be made present so that we can enter into it and relive it in an oneness with Christ.

It is at this point that we meet the liturgy and understand Casel's insistence that the liturgy brings present the unique, unrepeatable mystery of Christ, realized historically in the past and sacramentally re-presented in the liturgical commemoration. It is because it does this that the liturgy itself is called a mystery. Here Casel turns to the pagan mystery cults and finds in them that ritual type which can help us to understand the kind of thing the liturgy is. The Christian liturgy is unique and owes its origin to no pagan cult, but the mystery religions were a providential preparation for Christianity and the Fathers borrowed many special words and phrases from them and used these to express the new Christian reality. Even now, so Casel maintained, a consideration of these ancient cults and of the mentality associated with them can help remove the obstacles to an understanding of the liturgy that arise from the limitations and prejudices of the modern mind.

Once the liturgy is understood as a mystery in the sense that Casel explains, its essential role in the Christian life is evident. The Christian mystery is the divine reality or love communicated to men in the events of Christ. The liturgy is that mystery made present so that we may make contact with it, take part in it and be saved by doing so. It follows that the liturgy must be the central and most essential activity of the Christian religion. It is of its nature the centre and source of the life of the Church and the indispensable concern of every Christian. The statement almost wearies by its familiarity today. Some decades ago this was not so. Part of the significance of Casel's teaching is that it makes so clear the essential function of the liturgy. If the Christian life is not simply a matter of getting graces from Christ but of reliving His mystery and if we do this by celebrating the liturgy, then nothing can take the place of the liturgy or serve as a substitute for our share in it.

Casel's approach to the question of an active participation in the liturgy is determined by his concern with the nature of the liturgy. That all the faithful should and indeed must participate in the liturgy is evident from what has been said, but Casel is much more insistent on the inward quality of this participation than on the outward expression of it. A true participation is possible only if the liturgy is understood for what it is, namely a mystery—or, in other words, only if it is seen as the mystery of Christ made present and our union with this in a sacramental commemoration. This understanding is what is important. There is not much point in restoring the laity's external share in the liturgy or striving for changes in the rites, unless people are led back to a deep inner sharing in the mystery of Christian worship. Casel admits the need for an active, external participation in the liturgy, but he is far more concerned with our internal attitude.

With his stress on the necessity of a true understanding of the liturgy and of a genuine inward participation in it, all must agree. Ritual changes without a deepening in the spiritual consciousness of the faithful will do little good. There is a real danger of thinking that an adaptation of outward forms will solve all problems and at once produce a vigorous liturgical life. Such an easy expectation will bring a rapid disillusionment. So, Casel's remarks deserve pondering. At the same time, I think it is true to say that Casel was out of touch with the pastoral problems of the liturgical revival and, further, that there is a definite tinge of romanticism in his approach to the liturgy. By romanticism I mean a failure to see and admit the reality, often defective, of liturgical forms and practice in the actual life of the Church, both past and present. His view on the use of Latin and his dismissal of the desire for intelligibility—which, unfortunately, are sure to be seized upon and exploited—are only the more visible symptoms of an attitude that will be sensed elsewhere in the book. The chapters on the Church's Sacred Year and Sacred Day show him alive to the beauty of the liturgy and with a deep understanding of its spiritual riches, but it is difficult to shake off an impression of unreality. Why ? Because the liturgy he describes does not seem to be the growing and changing thing that it actually has been. He has fixed it in an imagined moment of classical perfection and isolated it from the ups and downs of its history—both from the enriching additions and healthy changes and from the distorting accretions and unhealthy rigidity. Fr Jungmann, with his genetic method of study, has spoiled us for any account of the liturgy that abstracts from its concrete reality.

An interesting essay could be written on Fr Jungmann and Casel as two of the great men of the liturgical revival. Casel gained from the patristic tradition an unsurpassed depth of insight into the meaning of the liturgy; his work has the greater doctrinal significance. He gave the movement a theological seriousness that has done more than anything else to ensure its permanent influence. But he lacked the breadth of outlook necessary to appreciate the concrete problems of the liturgy in the life of the Church. With Fr Jungmann, on the other hand, one is never out of touch with the liturgy as it has been and is actually celebrated. An historian, he has an unequalled mastery of the complex changes in liturgical forms, but he has as well a wonderful sense for the abiding values of the liturgy. With fine discrimination he is able to assess the gains and losses through the centuries and to suggest reforms that will restore to traditional values their pastoral efficacy. A deep pastoral concern pervades all his work. If Casel is the deeper thinker, Fr Jungmann is the wiser counsellor.

These remarks must not be taken as denying the pastoral importance of Casel's work. The testimony of so practical an apostle of the liturgical revival as Pius Parsch shows how it can give the inspiration necessary for solid pastoral work. The present book will endure as a classic statement of the meaning of the liturgy—indeed, of the meaning of Christianity. Its influence is particularly needed to combat a harmful superficiality in liturgical thinking. The dialogue Mass is not the acme of liturgical achievement; more important is what the liturgy means to the average participant. This book will continue to bring a new spiritual vision to priests and lay people. Its power to do so explains its historical importance.

PREFACE BY THE EDITOR

EASTER 1958 was the tenth anniversary of the day on which Odo Casel left us in a death which movingly, one might say enviably, closed a life dedicated to the meaning and vision of the mystery of Christ. It was in the chapel of the Benedictine nuns of Herstelle, for whom he had laboured twenty-six years, that, after he had sung the threefold *Lumen Christi,* he suffered an attack. In the dawn of Easter day he went into the eternal day of Christ.

Odo Casel's death brought to an end the great theological work which he had carried out for friends, for the academic world, and indeed for the whole church; a work of bold, sweeping vision, serious research and interpretation, of criticism and defence. Recently a book by Theodore Filthaut[1] has given a disinterested presentation of the whole discussion of the Mystery idea and its results up to the present; this book won Casel's approval. Casel's death has meant only the end of his personal share in the discussion. He was the explorer, the man of intuition, first conception, and all-embracing synthesis. This vision of his is preserved above all in the fifteen volumes of the *Jahrbuch für Liturgiewissenschaft* which he edited,[2] and in the practical fruit of the growth of liturgical life, to which his work gave birth.[3] But critical voices have been raised; opponents have rejected the whole of his work, and friends have wished for fresh examination of individual elements, indeed have felt such an examination really necessary. The same thing is suggested by the encyclical *Mediator Dei,* which appeared in November 1947. Casel saw in it from the first nothing but approval and confirmation. None the less, a more exhaustive consideration of the encyclical, particularly of its section on the Church's year[4] and of the letter which the Holy Office issued rejecting an interpretation of this section rather

[1]*Die Kontroverse über die Mysterienlehre* (Warendorf 1947; French translation: *La Théologie des Mystères. Exposé de la controverse.* Paris-Tournai 1954)

[2]For this matter all the volumes are important; first consideration should be given however to the longer articles which Casel himself mentions in note one on p. 9.

[3]Characteristic of this is the testimony of so tested a practical worker and master in popular liturgy as Pius Parsch; he has always acknowledged the great stimulus which the idea of liturgy as mystery celebration was to him. Cf the preface to the liturgical calendar issued by Klosterneuburg for 1926; also the *Jahr des Heiles,* tenth edition, 1932.

[4]Cf my article 'Der positive Sinn der päpstlichen Grenzsetzung in der Enzyklika *Mediator Dei*' in *Vom Christlichen Mysterium* Patmos Verlag (1951) 344–363, in particular p. 354 ff.

one-sidedly favourable to Casel,[1] showed that an examination of the whole position, of its foundations and various aspects, working from a thorough analysis, was really needed. Yet just such critical work as this has shown in a most marked way how fruitful Casel's vision remains. Although it may be found desirable to re-fashion his views in one way or another, to allow for a more nuanced perspective of some matters, his main position remains strong, and of the greatest importance for an all-embracing interpretation of the work of Christ and its out-growth in the worship of the church. A brief report on the extent of this abiding contribution to theology, as well as of the movement of theological discussion of it over the past ten years, largely freed now from any personal element, has appeared in the volumes of the *Archiv für Liturgiewissenschaft*[2] and in a paper delivered at the Conference for Patristic Studies at Oxford in 1955.[3] The matters which have been discussed are in particular: the interpretation of St Paul's theology of Baptism in Romans 6;[4] and the support Casel finds in St John Chrysostom[5] and in most other fathers before Ephesus.[6] From this point of departure further work has gone forward in a specifically theological and speculative direction. One is a work by the Abbot of Neuesheim;[7] another is the latest effort to form a speculative structure for the mystery conception of Casel in the

---

[1]A treatment of this work will be found in 'Mysteriengegenwart, ein Theologoumenon inmitten des Gesprächs', A.L.W. III/1 (1953), 106–110.

[2]The article mentioned in note one, and 'Ende des Gesprächs um die Mysteriengegenwart?' A.L.W. IV/2, 1956, 316–324; a further report is to appear in the same journal.

[3]'Mysteriengegenwart: das Anliegen Dom Casels und die neueste Forschung'. *Texte und Untersuchungen* 64, pp. 54–63; *Studia Patristica*, Vol. II (1957) and *The Downside Review* (translation), Spring 1958, pp. 266–273.

[4]The first stimulus was given by Schnackenburg in his book *Das Heilsgeschehen bei der Taufe nach dem Apostel Paulus* (1950). One should also mention the paper of Stommel on Romans VI and its relation to the rite of Baptism: *Römisches Quartalschrift* 49 (1950), pp. 1–21. An answer to these criticisms has been made in the tradition of Casel by Victor Warnach in two papers: 'Taufe und Christusgeschehen nach Römer VI' in A.L.W. III/2 (1954), 284–366, and 'Tauflehre des Römerbriefs in der neueren theologischen Diskussion': A.L.W. V/2 (1958), 274–332.

[5]G. Fittkau *Der Begriff des Mysteriums bei Johannes Chrysostomus*. Eine Auseinandersetzung mit dem Begriff des Kultmysteriums in der Lehre Odo Casels (1953); also my review of this book in A.L.W. IV/2 (1956) pp. 406–412 and the works mentioned in note seven above.

[6]J. Betz, *Die Eucharistie in der Zeit der griechischen Väter*. Vol. I, p. 1: Die Aktualpräsenz der Person und des Heilwerkes Jesu im Abendmahl nach der vorephesinischen griechischen Patristik. (1954). This book is reviewed in A.L.W. V/2 (1958) and discussed in the work mentioned in note 7.

[7]I name only one of his many works, *Das Wesen der Eucharistiefeier und des christlichen Priestertums* (1953) Cf the review of it in A.L.W. IV/2 (1956), p. 417 and the reference to A.L.W. III/1 (1953), 183–187.

tradition of St Thomas, the work of a monk of Laach, Polycarp Wegenaer.[1] The question of the church's year has also been taken up.[2] The group of questions centering round the theological interpretation of the word *mysterium*,[3] to which Casel had given much stimulus, has fallen somewhat into the background, as well as his position on the relationship between Christian and Hellenistic mysteries,[4] a matter for the historian of religions. These last matters are not of outstanding importance for the theological problem proper; but they should not be forgotten; there is room for new consideration and research in them.

All of the work which has been done shows in various ways that the editors of the memorial volume of studies dedicated to Dom Casel[5] were correct when they wrote in their preface that 'historical and theological work is still necessary for a final, valid and systematic view of the work of Casel, before the whole content of his vision will be understood and given firm shape, before all its lines and contours will be seen in their clearest light, and all it has to offer be realized and brought to fruition'. This volume was intended as a 'provisional and diversified work on the deep and widespread activity arising from the stimulus Dom Odo gave to studies'. The editors, of whom the present writer was one, were not unconscious that Dom Odo's work had been challenged, nor that he himself was always seeking to obtain a deeper grasp of his material as the controversy progressed. He was still young when he died; his death need not mean an end to the discussion. Much has been done in continuing it in the past ten years; much still remains to be done.

It is for this reason that, with renewed interest, we take up the works of Casel, the labourer of the first hour, the path-finder and path-breaker, and present with all the care and reverence possible new editions of them. Criticism may well be raised at this or that particular point; but the works of Dom Odo have won for themselves a

---

[1]*Heilsgegenwart:* Das Heilsgegenwart Christi und die Virtus Divina in den Sakramenten unter besonderer Berücksichtigung von Eucharistie und Taufe. Liturgiewissenschaftliche Quellen und Forschungen, Heft 33 (Aschendorf, 1958).
[2]Cf *Liturgie und Mönchtum* 5 (1950): Beitraege zur Theologie des Kirchenjahres; L'année liturgique selon Dom Casel, *Questionnes Liturgiques et Paroissiales* (1957), 286–298.
[3]J.L.W. 15 (1941), p. 269.
[4]There is a critical work in this sense by R. Padberg which nonetheless regards Casel's main intention with good will: 'Verkündigung und Religionsgeschichte': *Theologische Quartalschrift*, (131 (1951), 272–287).
[5]Edited by A. Mayer, J. Quasten, B. Neunheuser: Patmos, 1951.

classical position, and deserve therefore to be re-issued as they came from his hand. This principle, which the editors of his posthumous papers have adopted,[1] is even more necessary in the case of works which appeared during his lifetime, of which the first part of this book is one. The third edition was seen to press by Casel shortly before his death. Dutch, French, and Spanish translations have been prepared.[2]

The relatively large success of the little book is understandable; it is the best short presentation of the mystery theology from Casel's own hand; in it are found united a solid theological formulation, reference to the New Testament foundations of this synthesis, an adequate orientation for the textual and historical background of his views, yet without such a technical apparatus as to burden the reader unnecessarily; above all a fine style and a language which is more than that of a mere investigator. The book looks beyond its narrower base to its implications for the life of the Spirit centred on the worship of the Church.

We had no wish, nor even felt able to change anything in this classical text of a brilliant scholar and thinker. This edition, then, gives unchanged the text of the third edition, which in turn was very little different from the second. All that we have thought fit to add by way of commentary or correction from our present-day point of view has been put at the end in notes clearly distinguishable from the text, which however is marked with an asterisk at the points concerned. In addition, we have hoped to do a service to our readers by adding, from the papers of Dom Odo, two new chapters which complete and close the original work, although they were not of course originally written for it. These chapters, 'The Meaning of the Mystery' and 'The Church's common life in Mystery', are fragments from the author's papers, including notes taken at his conferences, book reviews and letters. It was first intended to include them in the forthcoming edition of another book which Casel planned but did not finish: 'The Mystery of Christian Sacrifice'. The editor of that volume, Victor Warnach, agreed with me that these two chapters would be a fitting addition to the present work. We owe their preservation to the devotion of the nuns of Herstelle, and this is the place to express the gratitude of the editors to that community for their great work on behalf of Odo Casel's writings. At the same time,

---

[1] *Mysterium des Kreuzes*, 1954; *Vom wahren christlichen Menschenbild*, 1953; *Mysterium des Kommenden*, 1952.

[2] Het Christelijke Kultmysterium (1943); Le Mystère du Culte dans le Christianisme (1946); El misterio del Culto cristiano (1953).

it must be made clear that Part II of this book was not finally corrected by the author himself.

It is our hope that the new edition of this book may win new friends; but above all that it may serve to deepen the understanding by Christians of the church's worship, and to help them in their zealous participation in it; for in it we find Christ and his saving work; in it we make Christ's one sacrifice our own; we build up the church, his body, find healing, and adore the Father in Spirit and in truth.

Maria Laach,
Feast of the Assumption of Our Blessed Lady 1958.
BURKHARD NEUNHEUSER,
Monk of Laach.

PART I

THE CHRISTIAN MYSTERY

I

THE MYSTERY AND MODERN MAN

'THOU sparest all things, Lord, lover of souls, for they are thine: in all is thine imperishable Spirit. Therefore it is that thou dost chastise but tenderly those who wander from the way, and make them mindful of their sins, reproaching them, that, freed from evil, they may have faith in thee.'[1]

God indeed allows men freely to go their way, for he has made them free. But his living breath, his holy spirit, his action, are in all: man is never wholly alone. This is the ground for that astonishing fact of history, that mankind is always being re-*generated*, that is re-acquiring a new spirit. We can observe this renewal today when changes in human life are occurring as perhaps never before; certainly at no time have men stood so in need of a 'turning', of *conversio* in the original meaning of the word, of the new life, as in our day. For never have they wandered so far away from the Mystery of God, or stood so near to death.

'The fool hath said in his heart "there is no God".'[2] This foolishness has reached its height in the millions who call themselves 'godless', and who, by the very use of this purely negative word, show the emptiness and insecurity of their revolt.

The Mystery of God, who dwells above all creatures in limitless majesty, whose action influences the most insignificant human event, whose wisdom is all surpassing and boundless, whose power cannot be overcome; this God of mystery has become a burden to man, a burden of which he would gladly be quit, in order to go his own way unhindered. He will have no eternal law or independent will above himself; he wants to be free of every tie not of his own making, to be his own last end, his own ruler, servant to no-one, subject to no-one. Nature is his to master, it is to become his empire and the subject of his scientific, merely rational, investigations. There is no world of the irrational, no 'other'. There is only matter, which is to be subjected to factual investigations.

So it has come about that nature, too, has lost her mystery. The cosmos is emptied of its spiritual content, or rather emptied of it in such a

[1]Wisdom 11, 26–12, 2. [2]Ps. 13, 1; 52, 1.

I

measure as never before; nature is no longer symbol, a transparency of higher realities. She breathes no secrets which make man cry: 'Such wisdom as thine is far beyond my reach, no thought of mine can attain it'.[1] Man has explored the deepest reaches of nature; every day the earth loses size and depth. Now, just as he has broken into the smallest atom, he is prepared to step off into space and win for himself the secrets of the stars. Nature, dethroned and stripped bare, has nothing left to it except the business of making man's life easier and more pleasant; vast sums of money are amassed and spent in order to make every material thing quickly available to all; applied science works its miracles, and lays the earth at the feet of man for him to use and to control. That strange curse which God pronounced after the Fall, that men should make their daily work a mystery of reparation and give it meaning for another life seems to have been extinguished. Poverty, sickness and pain, which were also to remind man of that other realm, have been fought with undreamed-of success; death itself is put off as long as possible; the life-span is almost double that earlier generations expected. The mystery of death is so far as possible kept covered and out of public sight; there are those who dream of doing away with it altogether, or proclaim its end as an ideal for the 'golden future'.

Still, though the outer world had been deprived of its secrets, there might have remained the unsearchable depths of the human soul. But these depths, too, have been probed and subjected to the searchlight of psycho-analysis; what glimmers there has been revealed as a confused mass of half-suppressed, sensual desires and wishes, more inspiring repulsion and fear than any other reaction. Love, religion, friendship, ideals—all have been exploded as mere nervous twitchings. With this, reverence for the mystery of the other person, or for the community disappears. How can any man exercise public functions as an instrument of divine authority, how can he hope for love and respect from those in his charge? How can the community demand the service of the individual, to include, on occasion, the sacrifice of his life? Society cannot stand for anything greater than the individual himself. No, man is an atom among other atoms; let him enjoy his span of life, and that to the fullest extent possible. There is no 'love' which can, by the gift of itself to another person or to the community, raise the individual into a new dimension of existence. It is usual nowadays to talk a great deal about the brotherhood of nations and service to humanity; but behind all this

[1]Ps. 138, 6.

there is not that deeper love which is a sharing in the very love of God himself, his *agape*, but instead the self-divinization of mankind, which sees in itself the god it means to worship. Community means nothing except individuals lumped in a mass, joined together for the sole purpose of fighting off, by their collective weight, any power which might make a claim to rule over them: a spectacle of brute power.

Modern man thinks that he has thus finally driven out the darkness of the Mystery, and that he stands at last in the clear light of sober reason and self-conscious, autonomous will, for the first time truly master of the world. But what happened at the dawn of history has repeated itself. Then, too, at the moment when man believed that he had obtained godhead by his own power, that he could recognize by the light of his own understanding what was good and evil, that he had come of age and needed no parental care, in that moment he 'saw that he was naked'.[1] He recognized his shame, saw himself as a king in disgrace, a monarch without a throne. The sin of our first parents becomes not merely an infectious poison in successive generations; it is repeated over and over again in each. And every time the result is the same: the revolutionary becomes a slave. Today this slavery is perhaps at its worst, when the revolutionary imagines he has freed himself from all bonds whatever. He is in fact not subject to individual human tyrants, but rather to much worse and more cruel impersonal powers, whose rule he can never shake off. The last road to freedom, which in antiquity was open even to the slave, modern man has closed up to himself: the road to God. He remains wholly circumscribed in the bounds of the material world. By imagining he is the ruler of this world, he is forced more and more to do its will; soulless machine and dead money master him, and demand blood offerings, the sale of his heart and mind: a pitiful end to the great age of individualism which had seemed to have begun with so much attraction and promise for the future.

For, if the last results of an age of individualism inspire us with something less than admiration, we must not forget how deceptively attractive those beginnings were. The men of the early Renaissance seem to wander through a lovely countryside in the full bloom of springtide; the age of Gothic was proudly conscious that it had climbed out of the shadows, away from the weary ponderousness of the Romanesque, out of the secret atmosphere of the crypts, and into the clear light of day, and of a reasonable, bright human culture.

[1]Gen. 3, 7.

No mystery hovered over that era captivating the minds of men, hiding the nature of reality. Reason, *ratio*, made itself felt in every sphere of life, stripping creation of its quality of wonder to the curious eyes of man, with the result that there seemed to be ever less and less place in the universe for the action of God. Since that time 'science' has had the effect of more and more breaking the bonds of faith, and has run on from triumph to triumph. For its part, the emancipated will has strained itself to even greater titanic efforts, and, in Promethean pride, worked marvels of invention.

Nor did the new spirit leave the sphere of religion and the church untouched.* The West, of course, did on the whole remain faithful to the old religion. But the attempt was made, nonetheless, to exhaust the secrets of God's revelation with reason; to dissect it, and to 'demonstrate' its truth. Mathematical thought, the most typical product of man's abstractive faculty, was set to work among the humanities, and even in theology. Natural science, disinterested in the action of a higher being, was discovering laws of evolution in all living beings, and sought to apply this principle to the dogmas of the church, as well as other things.

Then, too, emphasis on the autonomy of will showed itself in a departure from the traditional theology which had made God the Alpha and Omega of being, his will all-active, and human will and perfection his gift. In the piety of this period, next to God stands man, free, independent, seeking his own way to God, no longer raised up by God to himself. The lone individual fights in solitary battle for the heights; the church as the mother of graces moves into the background. Thus a new conception arose in the life of piety with a carefully adjusted psychology adapting itself to each individual, and methods of interior life calculated to stimulate each individual's gifts.

The clear consequence of this was a withdrawal of emphasis on the church's mystery. It put too much emphasis on the secret activity of God's grace, on the involvement and co-operation in action between God and man, in which man was the receiving partner, too much emphasis on the *ecclesia* as mother, bringing the individual into the common life. It was too little open to the view of 'reason' and to proof; its content was too difficult to grasp and yielded too few measurable results; laid too great a task upon the purpose of 'personality' and the 'greatest happiness

*The asterisks which occur in the text or the notes refer the reader to the Editor's notes on pp. 206–9.

of men', being all for God and the holy fellowship. In short, it was too simple, too uncomplicated, too much God's affair to suffice for the man who had come to such consciousness of his own powers. Rationalism and mystery do not go well together.

Our time has brought the fall of rationalism and a new turning to the mystery. The humanization of religion had progressed so far that, finally, there was no religion left. For this reason many doubted religion, which no longer held them with any inward grasp, did not bind them, was no longer something greater than they. Others, with more justification, have returned to a richer belief. They are seeking once more the ancient image of God in majesty and boundless greatness, the God who leaves human things far behind him, and 'raises man up when he crushes him'. The God of power, whom the prophets showed, and the unfathomable *agape* which made itself known on the cross, to mankind's amazement reveal anew the glory of this Godhead. Man comes once more to see that God is all in all, that his power fills all things, his will rules over them, his love penetrates them. He realizes that he himself first acquires greatness when he becomes nothing before this mystery. He senses once more the deep harmony between God and creation; the world becomes for him once more a stage on which God's drama is being carried out, a symbol of thoughts which reach beyond it. God's mystery once again inspires dread, attracts and calls us.

The mystery means three things and one. First of all it is God considered in himself, as the infinitely distant, holy, unapproachable, to whom no man may draw near and live; in likeness to whom everything is impure, as the prophet said: 'I am a man of unclean lips, dwelling in the midst of a people with unclean lips; and I saw the Lord, the King of battles, with my own eyes.'[1] And this all-holy one reveals his mystery, comes down to his creatures and reveals himself to them; yet once again, *in mysterio*, that is to say, in a revelation by grace, to those whom he has chosen, the humble, the pure of heart, not to the proud and the self-important. Hence his revelation remains a mystery, because it is not open to the profane world, but hides itself, shows itself only to the believers, the ones whom he has chosen.

God's being, then, is infinitely above the world; yet by grace he dwells within his creatures, within mankind: he is at once transcendent and immanent. In essence he surpasses all he has made, yet penetrates it everywhere, by his presence and his action.

[1] Isaiah 6, 5.

The ancient world had a shadowy foreboding of the mystery. It knew that all the things of earth are only the reflection and creation of a glory that surpasses them. This foreboding of the mystery brought forth the temples of the Sumerians and Babylonians and the pyramids and sphinx of the Egyptians with their air of eternity. In Greece the deep things of platonic wisdom speak of it; the mystery-cults in the Classical and Hellenistic age approach it. Everywhere there is longing to bring heaven down into the world, to bring man nearer to God, and marry the two hemispheres.

In the case of the Jews, God himself gave approval to this longing by his revelation. It is true that the Law strongly sharpened the boundaries between God and man. It was the barrier around the holy mountain where God ruled. But the prophets went on speaking in new and ever more detailed pictures of God's approaching kingdom, of the time when he would pitch his tent among his own people and his Spirit would penetrate all flesh.

God's coming in the flesh fulfilled and more than fulfilled all longing and all promise; this event gave the word *mysterium* a new and deepened meaning. For St Paul μυστήριον is the marvellous revelation of God in Christ. God, the one who hides in everlasting silence, 'who dwells in inapproachable light, whom no man has seen nor can'[1] has revealed himself in the flesh; the *Logos*, his Son, has become man, and in a way which escapes our grasping, has shown the wholeness of his Father's love on the Cross. 'God gave proof of his love for us: it was while we were still sinners that he died for us.'[2] John says the same thing in other words: 'No man has seen God; the only-begotten Son who is in the Father's bosom, he has declared it to us.'[3] In the Son of God made man and crucified we look upon the mystery of God which was hidden before the ages, but through Christ is made known and revealed to the ecclesia, the body of those whom he has called.

Christ is the mystery in person, because he shows the invisible godhead in the flesh. The deeds of his lowliness, above all his sacrificial death on the cross, are mysteries because God shows himself through them in a fashion which surpasses any human measurement. Above all else, his resurrection and exaltation are mysteries because God's glory is shown through them in the human person of Jesus, although in a

[1] I Tim. 6, 16.
[2] Rom. 5, 8.
[3] Jn. 1, 18.

manner hidden to the world and open only to the knowledge of the faithful. This mystery of Christ is what the apostles proclaimed to the Church, and what the Church passes on to all generations. Yet just as the saving design is not merely teaching, but first and foremost Christ's saving deed, so, too, the church leads mankind to salvation not merely by word only, but by sacred actions; through faith and the mysteries Christ lives in the church.

Thus the mysterium acquires a third sense, which, however, is most intimately connected with the first two; since Christ is no longer visible among us, in St Leo the Great's words, 'What was visible in the Lord has passed over into the mysteries.'[1] We meet his person, his saving deeds, the workings of his grace in the mysteries of his worship. St Ambrose writes: 'I find you in your mysteries.'[2]

The meaning of the divine mystery, three-fold yet one, is the subject of this little book. The mystery is ἄρρητον, ineffable; beyond utterance, not only in the original meaning, that it might not be spoken, but further that its content cannot be exhausted by words. Everything we say of it will fall short of the mark; but just because it is ineffable, there is always occasion for saying something of it. The *pneuma* which comes from the Lord will reveal all the rest to those whose wills are ready, while the man without faith will gain no hint of its depths.

The book will speak first of the position which the mystery of worship has within the Christian scheme; then of its relationship to the mysteries of antiquity, which lend it their language; and finally of the mystery as it acts throughout the sacred year and sacred day.[3]

The turning to the mystery is a present fact; the task for each individual is to find his way to the spring of healing. For it is only the mystery of God which can heal the world again; in it the *pneuma* of God acts, the blood of Christ flows to restore the world and give it holiness, to reconcile it to God, transfigure it. Today the world outside Christianity and the church is looking for mystery; it is building a new kind of rite in which man worships himself. But through all of this the world will never reach God. Let us hold fast to the mystery of Christ, the gift the Father sent among us in the incarnate Word. To this mystery the Church with the Spirit's breath upon her has given visible countenance by the work of many hundreds of years, has made a form which,

[1] Sermo 74, 2, P.L. 54, 398A.
[2] *Apologia prophetae David*, 58.
[3] [Casel's book on the Mass is to be published under the German title, *Das Christliche Opfermysterium*. Ed.]

unchanged in essence, yet gives the mind its freedom. We need not go looking for it, we need only give ourselves to it, go about the celebration of the bridegroom's mysteries with the church, Christ's bride; in this we shall ourselves be transformed in him, and go his way with the Son to the Father.

2

THE MYSTERY OF WORSHIP IN THE CHRISTIAN COSMOS

IF we would learn what the mystery's place is in the Christian scheme of things, we must first ask, what is the Christian scheme.

i *The Mystery of Christ*

Christianity is not a 'religion' or a confession in the way the last three hundred years would have understood the word: a system of more or less dogmatically certain truths to be accepted and confessed, and of moral commands to be observed or at least accorded recognition. Both elements belong, of course, to Christianity, intellectual structure and moral law; but neither exhausts its essence. Still less is Christianity a matter of religious sentiment, a more or less emotionally toned attitude towards 'The divine', which binds itself to no dogmatic or moral system whatever.

St Paul thinks of Christianity, the good news, as 'a mystery'; but not merely in the sense of a hidden, mysterious teaching about the things of God, a sense the word already bore in the philosophy of late antiquity.[1] Rather for him *mysterium* means first of all a deed of God's, the execution of an everlasting plan of his through an act which proceeds from his eternity, realized in time and the world, and returning once more to him its goal in eternity.[2] We can express the mystery, so

---

[1] Cf my book, *De philosophorum Graecorum Silentio mystico* (1919); J.L.W. 6 (1926) p. 138; 8 (1928) p. 145 ff, 225 ff; 13 (1935) p. 99 ff; 15 (1941) p. 155 ff. Also *Theologische Revue* 24 (1925) 41–47. [*Archiv für Liturgiewissenschaft* I (1950) contains a posthumous article by Dom Casel on Paul's mystery language, Ed.]*

[2] . . . 'He made known to us the mystery of his will, according to the decision which he took in him (Christ) for the design of fulfilling the ages, to sum up everything in Christ, in heaven and on the earth' (Eph. I, 9).
'You have heard of God's saving design of grace given to me for your sakes, how revelation made known to me the mystery, as I briefly declared to you. When you read it, you will be able to see my grasp of the mystery of Christ which was not made known to the sons of men in other generations, as it has now been revealed to the holy apostles and prophets in spirit: that the nations

9

conceived, by the one word 'Christ'[1] meaning by it the Saviour's person together with his mystical body, the church. It embraces first of all God's incarnation, which is his last and final revelation to the world. Paul says this mystery was 'hidden' or 'unspoken before the ages', because it lay in the womb of the godhead, unknown even to the multitude of angels; hence it is called *mysterium, arcanum, secretum*. But this mystery was revealed in time, by God's taking flesh from mankind, and appearing visible to it. It is a 'revelation', an 'uncovering' in the highest and ultimate sense. Before, God spoke 'in divers ways and in divers manners, through the prophets', 'now . . . in his Son'.[2]

Yet the incarnation as such, however, does not exhaust the mystery of 'Christ'. Because of the sin of man the mystery took on the shape of economy: God's love and wisdom, planning salvation. 'The Word was made flesh, and pitched his tent among us, and we saw his glory. . . .'[3] Here John gathers together the whole saving plan. The Lord's glory was not everywhere equally recognizable and visible. Jesus became saviour, redeemer for sinners. Therefore he did not take flesh immediately in a glorified state, but rather came in 'the likeness of the sin of flesh',[4] in order to kill sin through this flesh of his. So he came in lowliness, unrecognized,[5] bearing the burden of this sin, with those of its consequences which his godhead could allow. He had no sin of his own, nor inherited any sin, for he was born of the Virgin, by the Holy Ghost. But he took up the burden of the law, bore the sorrow and the

---

are of one calling and one body and one share of the promise, in Jesus Christ, through the gospel. . . . To me the least of all the Saints this grace was given to proclaim to the heathen the unsearchable riches of Christ and to illumine all as to the design of the mystery, hidden from the ages in God the creator of all; so to the principalities and powers in heaven was to be made known through the church the manifold wisdom of God . . .' (Eph. 3, 2 ff). Cf. the parallel passages in Col. 1, 25–27 where the mystery is said to be 'Christ in you' (2, 2) and yet 'Christ' himself is 'the mystery of God.' 'We utter the hidden wisdom of God in mystery, which God predestined before the ages, for our glory' (I Cor. 2, 7). Romans 16, 25 speaks of 'the revelation of the mystery shrouded in silence for all time.' Cf. also Romans 11, 25.

[1]Col. 2, 2. For understanding the mystery of God: Christ.

[2]Heb. 1, 1 f.

[3]Jn. 1, 14.

[4]Rom. 8, 3. Cf. II Cor. 5, 21: 'He who had no knowledge of sin made himself sin so that we might become God's justice in him.'

[5]'Jesus Christ who was from the beginning by nature God, did not see in the rank of godhead a prize to be coveted; he dispossessed himself and took the nature of a slave, fashioned in the likeness of men, and presenting himself to us in human form; and then he lowered his own dignity, accepted an obedience which brought him to death, death on a cross.' (Phil. 2, 5 and 8.)

bitterness of persecution and at last the cross and death, guiltless as he was, Love brought him onto the wood, for the sins of men,[1] and when this body of his died on the cross, sin was killed with it; Satan was undone, because an innocent man has suffered pain for the guilty. Now, a new man rose, all whole and sanctified; by his obedience he had earned the right to sit beside God, and to be one with the Father forever. 'That is why God has raised him to such a height, given him that name which is greater than any other name; so that everything in heaven and on earth and under the earth must bend the knee before the name of Jesus, and every tongue must confess Jesus Christ as Lord, dwelling in the glory of God the Father.[2] The Son of man is raised to be Lord, he is no longer in the flesh of sin, but has become wholly Spirit (*pneuma*);[3] his manhood is utterly transformed by its glorification in the godhead. Everything which was merely human is past. 'Henceforward, we do not think of anybody in a merely human fashion; even if we used to think of Christ in a human fashion, we do so no longer', says St Paul.[4] This god-man, raised to be over-lord and priest, filled with glory, is the summit of God's revelation under the New Alliance.

Yet God's revelation of himself in this way is not communicated to the world at large: the world as such is not fit to see things which belong to him[5]; rather is it given to the chosen, to the saints, first of all, to 'the apostles and prophets in *pneuma*'[6] and then to all who really believe, and so to the *ecclesia*, the common body of all whom God has called.[7] To them the mystery is revealed; yet it remains a mystery because it is something which of its very nature belongs to God and is, therefore,

---

[1] I Peter 2, 22: 'he did no sin, and no lie was in his mouth: he was ill-spoken of, and spoke no evil in return, suffered and did not threaten vengeance, gave himself up to the hands of injustice. So, on the cross his body took the weight of our sins; we were to become dead to our sins and live for holiness; it was his wounds that healed.'
[2] Phil. 2, 9–11.
[3] II Cor. 3, 17: The Lord is Spirit: ὁ δὲ Κύριος τὸ πνευμά ἐστιν.
[4] II Cor. 3, 17 ff.
[5] Jn. 16, 3: 'they will do this, because they have not recognised me or the Father.' Jn. 17, 25: 'Just Father, the world has never acknowledged thee; but I have acknowledged thee, and these (the disciples) have acknowledged that thou hast sent me . . .' I Jn. 3, 1: 'the world does not know us (Christians) because it did not acknowledge the Father.' Acts 13, 27: 'the people of Jerusalem and their leaders gave to him no recognition, nor to the voices of the prophets. . . .' I Cor. 2, 8: 'No princes of the world have acknowledged it (God's wisdom in the mystery), refers to the ruling spiritual powers of this *aion*'.
[6] Eph. 3, 5.
[7] Eph., 3 10.

closed to unaided human reason, something God's grace must reveal if it is to be made known.[1]

The content of the mystery of Christ is, therefore, the person of the god-man and his saving deed for the church; the church, in turn, enters the mystery through this deed. For Paul, Peter, and John, the heart of faith is not the teachings of Christ, not the deeds of his ministry, but the acts by which he saved us.[2] 'We can see one who was made a little lower than the angels, I mean Jesus, crowned now with glory and honour for the pains of his death. . . .'[3] Through his death and resurrection, through his blood the Lord has found 'everlasting redemption'.[4] Through it he has entered the holy of holies and mounted up to God's throne; and he has made the way for us to go there also.[5] There he is high-priest[6] who gives the grace of the Spirit and creates his church.

The Christian thing, therefore, in its full and primitive meaning of

[1] I Cor. 2, 9 f: '(we proclaim): what is written, what eye hath not seen, nor ear heard, nor has it entered into man's heart, what God has prepared for those who love him. And God has revealed this through his *pneuma*.' The translation of *mysterium* by 'secret' leads to error even where it refers more to God's hidden truth, and most certainly when it clearly means God's act or the ritual action; for to the initiate to whom it is revealed, it is a secret no longer. It remains a secret to the unbeliever: to *mysterium* belongs the *revelatio* (unveiling), which still keeps the intrinsic veil of divine things. [Cf. J.L.W. 15 (1941), p. 269 ff. ed. Cf. also J. A. Robinson's note on mysterion in his Commentary on the Ephesians, Trans.]*

[2] This is particularly marked in Peter, who had been the Lord's constant companion. According to him, the *pneuma* proclaimed through the prophets, 'sufferings in Christ and the glory following upon it' (I Peter 1, 11); Christ's blood is the centre of the gospel: 'in obedience and the sprinkling with the blood of Jesus Christ' (1, 2). Christians are redeemed 'through the precious blood of Christ, the pure and spotless lamb' (1, 9). Christ is known before the creation of the world, revealed at the end of time, through Christians who believe in God through him 'who has awakened them from the dead and given them glory' (1, 20 f). The Lord's suffering is mentioned again, (2, 21 ff; 3, 18) 'with the life-breath of the Spirit', the resurrection and place at God's right hand. II Peter 1, 16 tells of Christ's transfiguration on the holy mountain, but in a form which has the whole 'epiphany' in view; the letter here stresses the second coming.

John tells in his gospel, quite naturally, of the actions of Jesus on earth; but he looks at everything in the light of the incarnate Logos' divine sonship, and selects signs which will illumine it. At the first of these we find, 'he shewed his glory and his disciples believed in him' (2, 11). At the end, 'these signs are written down, that you may believe that Jesus is the Christ, the Son of God' (20, 31). The idea of *Kyrios* in St Paul is replaced in John by the dignity of Messiah and sonship which began with the incarnation, and was made plain by the exaltation of Christ after the passion. Hence, the first epistle of St John speaks of the revelation of eternal life through the incarnation, and of the blood of Jesus which cleanses us from every sin' (1, 1). 5, 5 f sums up: 'who overcomes the world if not the one who believes that Jesus is the Son of God?' He it is who came through water and blood, Jesus Christ. In 5, 20 the *parousia* is mentioned: 'We know that the Son of God comes'.

[3] Heb. 2, 9.   [4] Heb. 9, 12.   [5] Heb. 10, 20.   [6] Heb. 9, 5 f.

God's good Word, or Christ's, is not as it were a philosophy of life with religious background music, nor a moral or theological training; it is a *mysterium* as St Paul means the word, a revelation made by God to man through acts of god-manhood, full of life and power; it is mankind's way to God made possible by this revelation and the grace of it communicating the solemn entry of the redeemed Church into the presence of the everlasting Father through sacrifice, through perfect devotion; it is the glory that blossoms out of it. At the mid-point of the Christian religion, therefore, stands the sacred *Pasch*, the passage which the Son of God who appeared in the flesh of sin, makes to the Father.[1] The pasch is a sacrifice with the consecration of the person that flows from it; it is the sacrifice of the God-man in death on the cross, and his resurrection to glory: it is the Church's sacrifice in communion with and by the power of the crucified God-man, and the wonderful joining to God, the divinization which is its effect.

Both of these sacrifices flow together; they are fundamentally one; the Church, as the woman of the new paradise and the bride of Christ, acts and offers in his strength. Christ living in time made his sacrifice alone on the cross; Christ raised up by the Spirit makes the sacrifice together with his Church which he has purified with the blood from his own side, and thus won her for himself.[2] It is not as if the Lord, now in *pneuma*, were making a new sacrifice with the Church: through the one sacrifice he has reached the term of offering, and reigns now forever at the Father's right hand; he is himself the glorified sacrificial gift. The church, not yet brought to her completion, is drawn into this sacrifice of his; as he sacrificed for her, she now takes an active part in his sacrifice, makes it her own, and is raised thereby with him from the world to God, and glorified. Thus Christ becomes the saviour of the body, and the head of the Church:[3] God has given Christ 'to the ecclesia as the head which towers over all, given him her who is his body'.[4] *

Bridegroom and bride, head and members act as one. If the man, the head is the leading actor, the stimulus to action, his bride, his members' work with him, use the power which is theirs. Christ is saviour, the one who accomplishes salvation; the church for its part

---

[1] Rom. 8, 3; Jo. 13, 1.
[2] Eph. 5, 25 'Husbands love your wives as Christ loved the church and gave himself up for her.'
[3] Eph. 5, 22 f.
[4] Eph. 1, 22.

M.C.W.—B

shares in the act of Christ, receiving the influence of every act he does, but receiving actively; healthy members share in the action of a body. Indeed, just this makes the body a live one: a living bride, a loving bride and spouse, sharing in the actions of Christ. Every Christian is a christ, as St Augustine says,[1] 'We are to be joyful and give thanks that we are not only become Christians, but Christ'. And Methodius of Philippi in *The Banquet of the Ten Virgins*[2] says: 'The Church is with child, and lies in labour until Christ be formed in us and born in us; every one of the saints is to become Christ by participating in Christ.'

How does this participation come to be? How does a man become member of Christ? In the last analysis every participation is the work of God's grace and of eternal predestination. Upon this grace rests the first beginning of salvation's way, faith. But there is not yet the incorporation into Christ's mystical body; baptism gives this; at baptism, for the first time, the Christian meets the mystery of worship.

Christ in his human nature went through the passion and became Spirit (*pneuma*): glorified Lord (*Kyrios*), High-priest, the dispenser of the *pneuma*, and thereby head of his Church. By his sufferings he was healed[3] glorified;[4] he put aside, along with the earthly condition of his flesh, the 'sin' he had freely taken up, when he 'became sin for us' by carrying sin's weight in the manner just mentioned. This way of salvation was to be ours, too, but in Christ. He became the perfect type for us, not merely in the realm of moral action; he is the model we are to liken ourselves to in everything so far as creatures may. But we cannot do this of our own power; only through a saviour; Christ's salvation must be made real in us. This does not come about through a mere application, with our behaviour purely passive, through a 'justification' purely from 'faith', or by an application of the grace of Christ, where we have only to clear things out of the way in a negative fashion, to receive it. Rather, what is necessary is a living, active sharing in the redeeming deed of Christ; passive because the Lord makes it act upon us, active because we share in it by a deed of our own. To the action of God upon us (*opus operatum*) responds our co-operation (*opus operantis*), carried out through grace from him. How is it possible to do this great work where God and man are fellow-actors (each according to his own proper fashion; God as the master craftsman, man receiving

---

[1] *Tractatus in Joan.* 21, 8.
[2] Symposium 8, 8.
[3] Jn. 17, 19.
[4] Jn. 7, 39. 12, 23 (Cf 28).

what God does, yet sharing in the workmanship)? For this purpose the Lord has given us the mysteries of worship: the sacred actions which we perform, but which, at the same time, the Lord performs upon us by his priests' service in the Church. Through these actions it becomes possible for us to share most intensively and concretely in a kind of immediate contact, yet most spiritually too, in God's saving acts.

St Paul depicts for us the substance of the mystery of worship with great clearness and depth in the sixth chapter of his Epistle to the Romans* (3 ff), 'You know well enough that we who were taken up into Christ by baptism have been taken up, all of us, into his death; we have, then, been buried with him through baptism, in death, in order that as Christ rose from the dead by the Father's glory, thus we might walk in newness of life. For if we have grown up in the pattern (ὁμοιώματι) of his death, we shall share also in his resurrection. We know this, that the old man in us was crucified with him, in order to annihilate the body of sin, in order that we should no longer do slave-service to it. For the man who has died is quit of fault; if, then, we die with Christ, we believe that we shall share his life. We know that Christ, risen from the dead, dies no more; death has no more rule over him. The man who has died, has died once; the man who lives, lives for God. So you are to consider yourselves dead to sin, living for God in Christ Jesus.' To such men as these are his words directed in Colossians 3, 1–4: 'if, then, you are risen with Christ, seek the things which are above, where Christ is, sitting at God's right hand. Think of the things above, not those of earth. For you have died, and your life is hidden with Christ in God. When Christ, your life, be revealed, then you, too, will be revealed in glory.' An excellent commentary to the passage is found in Cyril of Jerusalem's second mystagogical Catechesis (5 ff*): 'O rare and paradoxical fact: we did not die as things of nature die; we were not buried in the fashion of them, nor risen after crucifixion in that way; rather it was a likening in image; but the salvation was a fact. Christ was really crucified, really buried, really rose; all this he has given us, so that we might win a real share in the likening of his sufferings. Here is surpassing love for men: Christ took the nails in his sacred hands and feet and suffered the pain; allowed me salvation through a share in its salvation without pain and without effort. Let no one, then, think that baptism is only the grace of sins' forgiveness and acceptance as a son, as John's baptism was. Rather we know that baptism was indeed the purification of sins, and the gift of the *pneuma,* but also the off-set of the sufferings of Christ; therefore St Paul has just called out to us, "you know full well" (Romans 6, 5 supra). He said this in connection with the opinion that baptism indeed gave the remission of sins and acceptance to sonship, but communion with the real sufferings of Christ by imitation of them. In order that we might all know that Christ did everything he undertook for our sakes, for the sake of our salvation, and suffered in fact not in appearance, and that we become sharers in his pain, St Paul has called out with such clarity: if we have grown up in the pattern of his death, we shall share also in his resurrection. The word "grown up" (σύμφυτοι) is meaningful; for as the true vine is emplanted here, we too are engrafted into it through sharing in the death by baptism. Give full attention to the apostle's words: he did not say, "if we have grown up in his death", but "in the pattern of his death". Christ's death is real in him; soul was really separated from body; his body was wrapped in a linen winding sheet. But with you it is the likeness, the pattern of this death and suffering; still you have not received a likeness of salvation, but rather its reality.' The mystery of Christ which was completed in our Lord in all reality in time is, therefore, fulfilled; fulfilled on us first of all in representative, symbolic forms, not purely external ones, but rather images filled with the reality of the new life which is communicated to us through Christ. This special sharing in the life of Christ, both symbolic and real, is what the ancients called mystical;* it is something mediate between a merely outward symbol and the purely real. Thus the Apostolic Constitutions say[1] of the martyr who dies for Christ without baptism 'he dies by experience of Christ, the others in type (τύπος)'. That does not mean that the baptised bears merely an image of Christ's death upon himself, but that in him the Lord's death is fulfilled mystically, that is, in the manner of the sacrament, while the witness in blood shares the complete, natural reality of the Lord's dying. That the sacrament does not simply give the grace of new life, but preserves 'the community of real sufferings by imitation', is what Cyril is emphasizing, in full agreement with St Paul. So we are right to call mysteries those sacred rites which imitate and pass on the mystery of Christ.[2] When St Paul calls the apostles

---

[1] V, 6, 8.

[2] In this we abstract from the analogy of the ancient mysteries, which is fundamental for terminology. On this matter see, in the next Section, that Christian terminology is in fact (not linguistically) completely intelligible within its own framework. To the texts from St Cyril we may add the detailed and very clear Catecheses of Theodore Mopsuestia, the most important of which I give in J.L.W. 13, 99 ff.

(I Cor. 4, 1) 'stewards of God's mysteries', he means first of all the mystery of Christ which he proclaims, and then, in addition, the sacred actions by which we are taken up and engrafted into this one mystery.

By his passion the Lord became *pneuma*;* accordingly, we too have been filled with *pneuma* through the mystical passion in baptism and the spiritual resurrection which flowed from it: we have become spiritual men. *Pneuma* means the life of godhead, which the Lord gives us, now that he is raised up to it, become it, his human nature uplifted now to God, and his place at the Father's right hand. Possession of the *pneuma* is, according to Peter,[1] Paul,[2] and John,[3] the mark of the Christian[4]. It is expressed in a particularly positive fashion within baptism through the rite of breathing, as the washing primarily expresses purification from sin.*

Through the *pneuma* the Christian is made like Christ, the *pneuma* in person and thereby is himself anointed with this *pneuma*, as Cyril of Jerusalem tells us (Mystagogical Catechesis 3, 1): 'After you were baptised in Christ and had put on Christ, you were formed too in the likeness of the Son of God. Because God predestined that we should have acceptance as his sons, he made us also of one form with Christ's body of glory. Because you are now sharers in Christ you are rightly called christs, anointed ones, and of you God said, "touch not my anointed ones" (Ps. 104, 15). You were anointed as you received the image of the holy *Pneuma*, and everything was done in image upon you, because you are images of the anointed one. He bathed in the river Jordan, and gave the water the good odour of his divinity, so that when he rose out of it, the *pneuma* came bodily upon him, like resting upon like. In just the same way the chrism was given to you as you stepped out of the spring of waters, the off-set of that chrism with which Christ was anointed. But

[1]Acts 2, 38: 'do penance, and be baptised, every one of you in the name of the Lord Jesus, for the remission of your sins and you will receive the gift of the spirit'.

[2]Romans 8, 9: 'You are not in the flesh but in *pneuma*, if God's *pneuma* dwells in you. But if anyone has not Christ's *pneuma*, he is not Christ's.' I Cor. 3, 16: 'do you not know that you are God's temple, and that his *pneuma* dwells in you?'. 12, 3: 'No one can say Jesus is Lord [recognise him as the Christ] except in the *pneuma*.' More precise treatment, ibid, 2, 10–16.

[3]Jn. 3, 24: 'We know that he dwells in us by this token: the *pneuma* he gave to us.' John, too, has the true Spirit recognized in confession of Christ: 'You know God's Spirit by this: every spirit is from God which acknowledges that Jesus Christ has come in the flesh . . .' And 2, 20: 'You have the chrism (the anointing with the Spirit) from the holy one. . . .'

[4]By their common share in the Spirit, all Christians become one body of Christ: 'for in one spirit were all baptised into one body.' (I Cor. 12, 13.)

this is the holy *pneuma* of whom the blessed Isaias spoke in the person of the Lord, "the Spirit of the Lord is upon me, and he has anointed me to bring the gospel to the poor; he had sent me on his business". With no tangible oil or myrrh was Christ anointed at men's hands; the Father who has chosen him out as saviour of the whole world anointed him with the holy Spirit (Acts 10, 38), and the prophet David cried out, "Thy throne, O God, stands firm from everlasting: a wand of uprightness is the sceptre of thy kingdom. Thou didst love justice and hate wrong; therefore, O God, thy God has anointed thee with the oil of joy before all thy companions" (Ps. 44, 7 ff). As Christ was crucified in fact, buried and raised up again, so you gained your high estate at baptism, crucified with him in likeness, buried with him so as to rise with him, so is it, too, for you with the chrism. He was anointed with the oil of spiritual gladness, with the *pneuma*, called the oil of joy because it is the spring of joy in spirit. And you were anointed with myrrh, and in this way became co-sharers, companions of Christ.' The Christian is, therefore, a second christ, *pneuma*. Christ is *pneuma* by the hypostatic union with the divine *Logos* who is *pneuma*;* but this union works an upraising of his human nature which is wholly fulfilled and revealed in the resurrection. The Lord came first in the humbled flesh, because his will was to redeem sinners; this flesh had to be nailed to the cross in order that sin and death should die. But in the very moment when sin was brought down on the cross, the slave Jesus, the humbled Son of Man, appeared in the glory of Kyrios and Son of God. The whole God-man is now *pneuma*. *Pneuma Christi* then denotes the whole Lord as glorified: the divine *pneuma* together with the glorification of the man Jesus. If the mere man is christed after the model of the *kyrios* raised up in the *pneuma's* fashion, it means that this man's being is exalted, too, through God's grace, and the in-dwelling of the Trinity which follows upon it.[1] Not as it were the *Logos* alone, for in the redemption and incarnation all three persons act together and Father, Son, Holy Spirit are of one indivisible substance. Therefore we read in John 14, 23: 'if any man love me, he will keep my word, and my Father will love him, and we shall come to him, and take up our abode with him', and verse 26 speaks immediately of the advocate, the Holy Spirit, whom the Father will send in my name.

Through initiation, therefore (baptism and confirmation), man becomes a living member of Christ, a 'christus'. Now he is no *mere* man,

---

[1]Better, by the in-dwelling of God and the exaltation of human nature which flows from it: both things, created and uncreated grace are not to be separated.

but man transformed, divinised, new-begotten out of God to be God's child.[1] He carries the life of God within him.[2] As a member of the High-Priest, Christ, he is himself *christus*, an anointed one; he is a priest who may sacrifice to God the Father, a sacrifice which through Christ becomes uniquely acceptable and accepted.[3]

There is no religion without sacrifice. Religion is the ordering between God and his creature; God bends down to man, and man climbs up toward God; by his taking it and passing it into his possession God makes the sacrifice holy and consecrates it. If the offerer is stained with sin, and thereby retarded in his sacrifice, the act must become first of all one of reparation. In this case it is carried out first in the form of a purification to make the sacrifice proper acceptable. 'Without bloodshed there is no forgiveness'[4] and no sacrifice of sinful man. The sacrifice made pure by reparation can find its way up to God. The last and most proper offering is man himself: the offering to God of man's free choice of love; this is the only sacrificial gift which does not already belong to God in this fashion.[5] Man wants to go up to God and be healed by him. But where he cannot or will not himself be the sacrifice, he finds a

[1]Jn. 1, 12 f 'to those who received him he gave the power to become God's children, to those who believed his name . . . were begotten of God.' According to 3, 5, the Christian is born anew of water and the Spirit, and what is born of Spirit is Spirit. I Jn. 3, 9: 'no-one who is born of God sins, because God's seed abides in him'; 5, 18: 'we know that no-one who is born of God can sin, but the divine origin protects him and evil does not lay hands on him'. St Paul writes to the Galatians: 3, 26 'you are God's sons by faith in Jesus Christ.' And 4, 4 ff: 'when the fulness of time came, God sent his Son, born of a woman, subject to the law, to pay the price for them who were its subjects, and to give us the acceptance sons have. But that you might be sons (it follows) God has sent the Spirit of his Son into our hearts to cry out, Abba, Father.' Romans 8, 14 ff: 'They who are moved by the Spirit are God's sons, For you have not received the spirit of slavery for fear, but the spirit of acceptance as sons, in which we cry out, "Abba, Father".'

[2]Jn. 1, 4 'In him was life and the life was the light of men.' 6, 57: 'As the living Father sent me and I live through the Father, so he who eats my flesh will live through me.' 11, 25: 'I am the resurrection and the life; the man who believes in me will live, even though he die.' 5, 24 ff: 'The man who hears my word and believes the one who has sent me, has eternal life . . .' I Jo. 1, 1 ff ' . . . of the Word of life . . . life was revealed and we have seen it and given witness to it; we tell you of everlasting life which was with the Father, and was revealed to us . . .'

[3]I Peter 2, 4 ff. 'Coming to him (Christ) you will be formed as living stones into a spiritual dwelling, a holy priesthood, to make spiritual offering well pleasing to God through Jesus Christ. . . .' 'You are a chosen race, a royal priesthood. . . .' Cf Hebrews 13, 15: 'through him we make continual sacrifice of praise to God.'

[4]Heb. 9, 22.

[5]cf M. ten Hompel, *Das Opfer als Selbsthingabe und seine ideale Verwirklichung im Opfer Christi* (1920) 35 ff.

substitute: this was the case with Jews and pagans. In Christianity the primitive idea of sacrifice was restored, when the greatest representative of all mankind, the god-man Jesus Christ, made a total offering of himself to God on the cross.

In God's eyes, Christ is mankind's spokesman; but because at the same time he is God, the Son of God, he is the Father's messenger to mankind. A mere man could have made no sacrifice to please the Father; even in paradise Adam's sacrifice of love was pleasing to God only because the *pneuma* was in him, and gave back to God, in this way what was his. After his sin, man could bring no proper sacrifice.

God, of course, did accept the sacrifice of Abel and the other holy men of the Old Testament, but only in the light of Christ's sacrifice to come. Man could not now go up to God of his own power. God had first to make the way for him, give him reconciliation, come down to him, so that the individual might dare to approach God once more. God's descent came in the incarnation and the sacrifice of Christ. So we read in the Epistle to the Hebrews, 'What the law contains is only the shadow of those blessings which were still to come (i.e. in the new alliance), not the full expression of their reality.' The same sacrifices are offered by the priests of the Old Testament year after year without ceasing, and still the worshippers can never reach, through the law, their full measure of growth. If they could, must not the offerings have ceased before now? There would be no guilt left to reproach the consciences of those who come to worship; they would have been cleansed once for all. No, what these offerings bring with them, year by year, is only a remembrance of sins; but that sins should be taken away by the blood of bulls and goats is impossible. As Christ comes into the world, he says: 'No sacrifice, no offering was thy demand; thou hast endowed me, instead, with a body. Thou hast not found any pleasure in burnt sacrifices, in sacrifices for sin. See then, said I, I am coming to fulfil what is written of me, where thy book lies unrolled; to do thy will, O my God . . . through this will we have been made holy by the offering of the body of Jesus Christ once for all.'[1] Christ therefore has made this sacrifice in his human nature, but with the power godhead gave him. So it was God himself who performed the reconciliation in Christ's sacrifice as St Paul says to us: 'one died for all; all then, died. And he died on behalf of all so that those who live should live no longer for themselves, but for him who died and rose for them . . . so that if any

[1] Heb. 10, 1–10.

one is in Christ he is a thing new made; older things are past (look!), all things have become new. All this from God who has reconciled us to himself through Christ who, in turn, ministers reconciliation to us; in this way, God was in Christ, reconciling the cosmos to himself, not taking into account its faults . . .'[1] At the deepest level, it is God who has offered the sacrifice; for 'God did so love the world that he sent his only-begotten Son into the world', that we might live in him.[2] This was the fashion of his life: 'not that we loved him, but that he loved us, and sent his Son as a sacrifice of reconciliation for our sins'.[3]

How Christ carried out this sacrifice, we have seen when we sketched the economy of it; there, we showed, that this will to sacrifice was accepted and completed through an obedience to death, and the glory and transfiguration of Christ which flowed from it. His rise to the state of kyrios first gives the Lord his consecration as priest. 'He has reached his fulness, and is author of everlasting salvation for all who give him obedience.'[4] 'Through his eternal priesthood he can continually save those who make their way to God through him; he lives forever to make intercession on our behalf.'[5] 'We have such an high priest who has taken his place at the right hand of the throne of majesty, in heaven; one who performs the rites of the holy place and of the real tabernacle, which no man, but rather God has made.'[6]

Because of the inmost oneness of being, and the realm of action following upon it, which grows up between bride and bridegroom, between head and body, it follows that the church must take a share in Christ's sacrifice, in a feminine, receptive way, yet one which is no less active for that. She stands beneath the cross, sacrifices her bridegroom, and with him, herself. But she does so not merely in faith or in some mental act, but rather in a real and concrete fashion, in mystery; she fulfils the 'likening' of that sacrifice through which the Lord offered himself in the presence of earth and heaven, in utter openness, in the total giving of his body, to the Father.* Here again we meet the essential meaning of the mystery of worship: without this mystery, the church would be an offerer without sacrifice, an altar with no gift, a bride cut off from her bridegroom, unconsecrated, knowing no way to the Father.

Then, too, Christ would be priest without people, no high-priest, nor

[1]II Cor. 5, 14–19.   [2]Jn. 3, 16.
[3]I Jn. 4, 9 f.   [4]Heb. 5, 9 f.
[5]Heb. 7, 24 f.   [6]Heb. 8, 1–3.

'prince of salvation'.[1] He might not call his members 'brethren' as the apostle has him do: 'the one who sanctifies and the ones who are sanctified are of common origin, all of them; he is not ashamed, then, to own them as his brethren. I will proclaim thy renown, he says, to my brethren; with the assembly around me I will praise thee; and elsewhere he says, "I will put my trust in him", and then, "Here stand I, and the children God has given me". And since these children have an inheritance of flesh and blood, he too shared that inheritance with them. . . .'[2] Christ has gone before us into the holy of holies; 'has become high-priest forever according to the order of Melchisedech'.[3] We must follow him. Over and over again in different ways the oneness of priest and people is emphasised. But as Christ, not by inward devotion alone, but by his own blood,[4] became the minister of the Sanctuary,[5] and a minister all the more exalted as the mediator of the alliance;[6] so, too, his people must make true, outwardly recognisable liturgical sacrifice, From this, too, follows the necessity of the mystery of worship: a visible community can only express its inward oneness and its harmonious action in God's service through a common ritual act. An act common to God and his human community can only be properly carried out in a symbolic action where priesthood (as mediator) takes both God's part and the people's, and gives outward expression by words and gestures to the will of both; thus the invisible action of God upon man is made known through the symbolic action of the priest, as is the deed of the worshipping community in the words and gestures which the priest employs.

These requirements are fulfilled for the Church's sacrifice, the Mass. In it the consecration of the elements by God's deed, which the priest performs in God's power again sets out the sacrificing death of the Lord in *mysterium*. Christ, therefore, offers himself in a sacramental manner: 'in his mystery he suffers for us anew'.[7] But the church 'through the priests' ministry'[8] carries out the mystery and so offers her bridegroom's sacrifice; it is then, at the same time, her sacrifice. It becomes her sacrifice, too, by a most personal participation; mystically engrafted into Christ as his body and spouse the church joins herself by the most intensive self-giving to his offering, so that she becomes one

[1] Heb. 2, 10.   [2] Heb. 2, 11–14; Rom. 8, 29.
[3] Heb. 6, 20.   [4] Heb. 9, 12.
[5] Heb. 8, 2.   [6] Heb. 8, 6.
[7] Gregory the Great, Hom in Evang. 3, 7. J.L.W. 6 (1926), p. 173 f.
[8] *Sacerdotum ministerio*, Council of Trent, Session XXII.

sacrifice with him. Here the mystical Christ (Christ and his church) reveals itself as the true high priest of the new covenant.[1] Here once more we may see the essential and necessary position of the mystery of worship within the mystery of Christ. Without it, the mystery of Christ could not become a reality age after age, from one generation to another, until the whole body shall be saved and its glory revealed with the glory of the head.

We present here a passage on the theme of the mystical body's growth and maturity through the mystery of worship, from the penetrating work of Methodius of Philippi.

'It is entirely consistent with this,[2] that the church should have risen from his (Christ's) flesh and blood; for her sake the Logos left his Father in heaven, and came down to cling to his spouse, and fall asleep in pain, going out of himself by dying freely for her. By this, after he had purified her by bathing, he made the church glorious and without spot, to receive the spiritual, holy seed which, with mild words, he sows and plants in the mind's deep places; but the church takes it, in woman's fashion, and forms it, to bring forth virtue and let it grow up. Thus is carried out the word, "increase and multiply yourselves", when she grows in stature and loveliness each day, through contact and communion with the Logos, who, even now (at the memorial of the suffering), comes down upon us, and passes out of himself.

'In no other way could the church receive the faithful and bear them through the bath of new birth. Christ had to divest himself so that we might take hold of him again when his sufferings were represented; he had so to die again, come down from heaven, and, to join himself to the church his spouse, to make her able to gain strength from his side; thus all who have their foundation in him, who are born of the bath, were to grow, by increasing of his bone and his flesh, that is to say, of his holiness and glory. Flesh and bone of wisdom are the right names for prudence and virtue, but they come from the Spirit of truth, the advocate who gives to the illumined new birth and everlasting life. But

---

[1] The co-offering of the faithful rests first of all on the objective sacramental engrafting of every Christian into the body of Christ by baptism. What the body does, the members do in company with it. The more conscious this participation is, the more deeply it is experienced, the more intensive the participation. This explains the necessity of active participation in the liturgical celebration and in its external form; the external strengthens what is within. See Section iii.

[2] Namely with the allegorical explanation of the first human pair as Christ and his church.

it is impossible that anyone should share in the holy *pneuma* and be called a member of Christ if the *Logos* did not first come down upon him and fall asleep in holy distraction, so as to bring him once more to the resurrection from sleep, and make him able to share, filled with the *pneuma*, in the refreshment and renewal of youthfulness. This *pneuma* of truth, sevenfold, according to the prophet, is called the *Logos*' right hand; God takes from him, after the holy distraction, that is the incarnation and the passion, and from him makes the helpers, the souls which are bound up to him and entrusted to him.'[1]

From the ritual memorial of the passion, therefore, the church is always growing, is being filled by the *pneuma*, is growing up to the full age of Jesus Christ.

But its sacrificial being does not exhaust the mystery of the eucharist; it has a side which is more sacramental in the narrower sense. The sacrifices of the Old Testament were partly offerings of food, presented to God and consecrated by this fact; those who shared the communion of the sacrifice ate them and so were themselves raised to communion with God. The sacrifice of the New Testament is also a food-offering, but in a much higher, more *spirital* sense. Christ has given himself as the food of the world, the bread of life[2] and the drink of eternal life.[3] 'If you do not eat the flesh of the Son of Man and drink his blood, you have no life in you. The man who eats my flesh and drinks my blood has everlasting life.[4] The incarnate *Logos* is really the nourishment of the world, because through his utterance and his *pneuma* he gives it life beyond nature and preserves that life for it. Christ has made this fact a mystery, too, because he wanted to express the real union between himself and the church in a communion of flesh and blood in the most concrete fashion possible. The explanation which he gives in John 6 becomes ever more 'mysterious' and sacramental as it progresses. Its darkness becomes light, through its concrete and holy fulfilment at the Last Supper, when the Lord gave his body and blood to the disciples in the forms of bread and wine, that is to say in the form of sacrificial food. This makes clear that not only the incarnate *Logos* but the *Logos* murdered is the world's food. If we want to express that in ritual, there is no better or simpler way than the one which the Lord chose, namely to give his sacrificial body and blood to his disciples in the form of food and

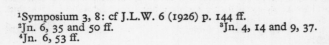

[1]Symposium 3, 8: cf J.L.W. 6 (1926) p. 144 ff.
[2]Jn. 6, 35 and 50 ff.   [3]Jn. 4, 14 and 9, 37.
[4]Jn. 6, 53 ff.

drink, and so to show in the most palpable way that the *Kyrios*, killed and raised up on high, is the inward power of his church which penetrates its whole being, fills it with the force of God's own life.

The three mysteries we have mentioned, baptism, confirmation, eucharist as food are the stages of complete engrafting into the body of Christ. Baptism cleanses from sin by plunging us into the cross; confirmation breathes the new god-life of *pneuma* into us, and communion strengthens and preserves it, makes the members grow up to their full measure in the body. They form, then, Christian initiation, the beginning of Christian life. Those who are so consecrated to it can go on immediately with the greatest act of the mystical Christ, his offering of himself and his love to the father. Through this sharing in his act, the Christian grows once more into the body; the blood purifies him again and again, the Spirit of resurrection enlivens him and strengthens him, while the sacrificial food incorporates him more and more fully into Christ, the Lord. These three mysteries are therefore the most important and most necessary for the life of the church and each Christian.

Still, the body of Christ is a living organism, not a dead heap of similar atoms: it has a variety of members with different functions, both in its final form and—which is of more concern to us—in the accomplishing those of its tasks on earth which will come to an end with the end of this world's time, that is to say when the whole body has grown to the fullness of its age and it will have no more need of human works.[1] In the first place the members need a representation on earth of the invisible head: men—for woman represents the church's bridal nature— who will act for Christ in a special fashion as leaders, teachers, priests. The mystery of priestly ordination assimilates the men Christ has called to those characteristics of his. The *pneuma* comes down upon them in a marvellous fashion, and through the laying on of hands by bishops, successors of the apostles, acts upon them; this rite represents and carries on the connexion with the apostles, and hence with Christ himself. In addition to those in authority the church also has other men and women—here sex makes no difference—who are to shine out before the whole body as models of holiness and consecration to God. They are to put on in a special way the likeness to Christ, crucified and risen in *pneuma*. Hence, the mysteries of the consecration of monks[2] and of virgins, and of the abbot and abbess as leaders of this life.

---

[1]Cf Eph. 4, 11–16.
[2]Cf J.L.W. 5, p. 1 f on Solemn Monastic Profession.

These states were counted from the beginning as states of immediate consecration to God. In the course of time they were marked by an act of ritual consecration; they retained their character as spirit-informed men, with, of course, no place in the hierarchy. The meaning of what they did was total consecration to God. The consecrated widows come into this category too. In these dedications a part was also played by the hierarchy of heaven: it is as the Church's spiritual states that these men and women are called: apostles, martyrs, confessors, virgins, widows. As the office of the church shows, they become the names of classes of saints in the choirs of heaven.[1]

With the state of marriage we return to this *aion*, for 'the children of this world marry and are given in marriage; but those who are found worthy to attain the other world, and resurrection from the dead, take neither wife nor husband'.[2] But it, too, is wonderfully exalted in the new alliance, for now it is an image of the spiritual marriage in the new covenant between Christ and his church, just as Paradise pointed towards this alliance yet to come. When, in Ephesians, St Paul gives Christ and his church as the model for Christian married people he says, 'this mystery is a great one; I speak of Christ and the church'.[3] The primaeval mystery is, therefore, the spiritual bond between Christ and his *ecclesia*, and the marriage of two Christians is a grace-giving image of that bond. The sacrament of marriage, too, has its ultimate meaning and its blessing from the mystery of Christ; and the same mystery works its effects in all the other reaches of life. Paul says, 'the unbelieving husband is sanctified in the wife and the unbelieving wife in her fellow Christian; otherwise your children would be unclean, but now they are clean';[4] in the last instance baptism will heal them. Sickness and death require a special measure of the strength of Christ's grace. 'Is anyone sick among you, let him call the priests of the church, and they will pray over him, anointing him with oil in the Lord's name; and the prayer of faith will save the sick man, and the Lord will rouse him, and if he have sinned, it will be forgiven him.'[5] For the sinners who are not ill there is also forgiveness of sins in the power of the mystery of Christ; no second baptism, but rather the return of the Spirit which had been lost, through the laying on of the bishop's hands.[6] Nor does the

---

[1] High regard for episcopal office is shown in that confessors are distinguished as bishops and other confessors.
[2] Lk. 20, 35. [3] Eph. 5, 32.
[4] Cor. 7, 14. [5] James 5, 14 ff.
[6] The practice today is for absolution with the priest's upraised hand.

dead man lack the helping and saving power of the church's mysteries; according to ancient custom in the church he is anointed and prayed for; the eucharist is offered for him.[1] It is not possible to show here how the mystery goes about its work in the many rites and prayers which accompany every step of the life of Christian man and community, and bring the *pneuma* of Christ into every sphere and relationship of living. Christians know this from their own experience.

This short exposition should show that the religion of the gospel, the piety of the New Testament, and the worship of the Church cannot exist without the mystery of worship. We are to think of liturgy (λειτουργία) in its pure and ancient meaning: not an extension of aesthetically-minded ritualism, not ostentatious pageantry, but the carrying out, the making real of the mystery of Christ in the new alliance throughout the whole church, in all centuries; in it her healing and glory are made fact. This is what we mean when we say that liturgical mystery is the most central and most essential action of the Christian religion.

ii *Mystery and Ritual types*

The New Testament taught us that Christianity is Christ's good news; it is a mystery, which contains the incarnation, the invisible God's visible appearance among us, the act of redemption on the cross, culminating in the resurrection through which the Lord showed us his glory, not indeed to the whole world, but to those few witnesses 'whom God had chosen out',[2] and through them to the Church (*ecclesia*). The parousia at the end of time will end this plan of salvation. In the time between, the church lives by faith and in the mysteries of Christ's worship. These mysteries are a working out and an application of Christ's mystery. God, who revealed himself in the man Christ, acts now, after this man has been glorified, acts now properly for the first time. He works through Christ the high-priest and the usual ordering of the Church's means of grace in the mystery of worship, which is nothing else than the God-man acting on earth from age to age. For this reason, it, like him, shares God's majesty and action and is hidden beneath symbols,[3] taken from the world, which both hide and point to

[1] Cf *Altchristliches in der Totenliturgie* Lit. Ztschrift 3 (1930/31) 18–26. In Dionysius the Aeopagite, burial belongs to the mysteries.

[2] Acts 10, 40 f.

[3] Cf Irenaeus of Lyons, *Contra Haereses* IV, 18, 5 'As the bread which comes from the earth receives God at the epiclesis (calling upon his name) and is ordinary bread no longer but eucharist, with two elements, earthly and heavenly; so our bodies when they take the eucharist are corruptible no longer, but possess the hope of everlasting life.' (Cf V 2, 3.)

its reality. Thus it is possible that the Lord, though eternally glorified in heaven and visible to all, should be still hidden in the world, and go on revealing the whole strength of his glory. The Lord's manner of presence in the mystery therefore, holds a position between that in his life on earth before the resurrection, and his glorified life in heaven: the divine power is fully in action, yet faith must be there to see it; there is not yet simple vision. 'We go our way in faith, not seeing.'[1] So in the mysteries is fulfilled what we heard: 'blessed are they who see not, and yet believe'.[2] On this St Leo the Great comments, 'In order that we might share in this blessedness our Lord put an end to his bodily presence among us. First of all he performed what was necessary for the preaching of the gospel and the mysteries of the New Testament; then he rose up to heaven before his disciples, forty days after he had come back from the tomb. There he will remain, at the Father's right hand, until the time is past which God has allotted for his children to be multiplied, and comes again in the flesh in which he rose, to judge the living and the dead. What was visible in our redeemer has passed over into the mysteries; and, that faith may be nobler and more firm, after vision came teaching, whose influence the faithful are to follow, illumined by the rays of light from heaven.'[3] The Saviour then, adapts himself entirely through the mystery to his church's state; and by so doing, he carries out the great saving design, the *economy*, which was not meant merely for those who walked with him on earth, but for all generations, and all ages until the end of this world's time. The church still walks in faith's darkness, not the light of vision; yet, she is already redeemed, she already possesses the 'pledge of the Spirit',[4] lives 'in Christ'[5] glorified; she is his body, and his bride. Therefore she gives herself to him with all the high-priestly strength he has given her; but under the veil of the symbols. She is not yet utterly redeemed and united inseparably with God; she has still in her members to fight with sin and with the world; she is not recognized, but persecuted, and she must weep at the number of her own children who fall. She is more like the crucified Lord than him risen and carried up to glory, although she bears within herself the riches which are the reflection of it; riches which flash out secretly from time to time. So the *mysterium* also shines with God's own

[1] II Cor. 5, 7 cf I Cor. 13, 12.   [2] Jn. 20, 29.
[3] Sermo 74, 2 Migne 54, 398; cf J.L.W. 8 (1928) p. 154.
[4] Romans 8, 23.
[5] The well-known formula of St Paul. Cf Wikenhauser, *Die paulinische Christusmystik* (1928).

jewels, but hides them beneath a veil which at once covers and portrays them; what it portrays is first of all the cross of Christ, his dying and his blood, and through these the glory which comes after. The mystery is like the stones on an ancient jewelled cross, which do not change its shape, yet clothe the bareness of the wood with loveliness. Baptism points first of all to the killing of the old man; the fragrance of its ointment breathes the good smell of resurrection. The mass is a memorial of Christ's death; his body, sacrificed and his blood poured out are shown to us. But that this body and blood should become food and drink for life is fruit and symbol of the resurrection to everlasting life. Through these mysteries the church takes her share in the passion of Christ, the passion by which 'he died to sin', and through this dying she takes her share in his life which 'he lives for God'.[1] Through the cross she is filled with the *pneuma*, made holy, brought to glory, deified.

The mystery, then, becomes a bridal gift which is of extraordinary fitness for the church; it is her espousals, her very life which the mystery gives her, a deep communion with Christ in living and acting. Here is the fulfilment of the mystical marriage of which St Paul sees a shadowy image in human marriage: the mystery which is completed to full measure 'in Christ and the church'.[2]

Thus we come upon another light shed on the need for the mystery, from the church's point of view. As the spouse of the new spirital Adam it is she who receives of him, and yet is 'like him';[3] she shares in his work in the cultivation of the very gift she has received; she makes it a thing of beauty, and gives it back to her lover. The church has nothing of her own, for 'what hast thou which thou hast not received?'[4] Even after Christ's great sacrificial deed she could bring nothing new to the Father; Christ fulfilled the sacrifice for all time: 'through one gift of sacrifice he has perfected forever those to be made holy';[5] 'there is no other offering for sin'.[6] Over and over again the New Testament teaches us that Christ completes the divine plan of salvation, and the new *aion* is here among us[7]; after him there is no new kingdom, no new sacrifice or healing. His sacrifice was the evening offering of the world, and his resurrection the dawn of a new and everlasting morning.[8] Yet the church still wants to

[1]Rom. 6, 10. [2]Eph. 6, 22–32.
[3]Gen. 2, 18. [4]I Cor. 4, 17.
[5]Heb. 10, 14. [6]Heb. 10, 26.
[7]Cf for example Heb. 1, 2; 9, 26. I Peter 2, 20.
[8]This is the mystical sense of the supper and of Christ's dying in the evening and rising in the morning.

give testimony of her love, through a sacrifice; she wants to make the gift of her love to the Father, in a tangible, symbolic form, now, while she is still a pilgrim; she will be doing, not merely taking something. For this, again, she has the mysteries and in them she can express her love and meaning: their symbolic elements are taken from the earth,[1] just as their words are a part of human speech; these sacred acts are men's acts, acts the church can make its own, can perform again and again,[2] surround with warmth and beauty; in this way she turns them into eloquent signs of her own mind's devotion. Yet, in all of this, she does not separate herself from her bridegroom, for from him she receives continually the heart of these mysteries, and it is his life she lives in them.

Ever more clearly, then, we see that the rite-form 'mystery', that definite form of worship which the word and concept *mysterium* denote, is wholly necessary in the worship of the new alliance; it is not merely for the exterior service which is due to God from a visible community, but also, precisely for the inmost and essential self-gift to God which is the last end of all Christian worship. For in this new alliance God has revealed himself to be love, and love it is he seeks, not honour, from his creatures. A Christ-mysticism is the real centre of New Testament ritual, the physical or realistic uniting of the church, as the body or the bride, with Christ the glorified God-man, and with him to the trinity, so that God is all in all.[3] The other two forms (εἴδη, species) those of prayer and sacrifice, meet in the New Testament in the mystery form. Only conjoined to its head can the body of Christ pray in *pneuma*;[4] the only sacrifice the Church can make is that which Christ, her head and saviour, has made.

Every act of worship, every act towards God under the new covenant, is joined essentially with the mystery, and is stamped by it with the mark of Christ; God receives nothing without this mark, under the new alliance. The mystery belongs to those unspeakable riches which God has given us in Christ. The old covenant had no mysteries;* in it God had not yet appeared as man among us, not yet died for us on the cross;

[1]Note 3, page 27.
[2]*Frequentare* in liturgical prayers.
[3]I Cor. 15, 28.
[4]Romans, 8, 26 f: 'the Spirit comes to the aid of our weakness when we know not what we ought to pray for, to pray as we ought the Spirit himself intercedes for us with unutterable groanings, and God who can read our hearts, knows well what the Spirit's intent is; for indeed it is according to the mind of God that he makes intercession for the saints.'

the other hemisphere was not yet open to man, for Christ had not yet come to open it. Fear still ruled, the law of love had not yet been preached. The everlasting covenant of *agape*, that love of God's, with no works as its condition, was not yet formed; there was only a bond for a certain time, built on the law. The shared work of God and man belongs to the mystery; its author can only be a God-man, and this work gives entrance into the eternal, divine, life, here already 'in promise', while its fullness is reserved for the time to come. The mystery gives a most intimate, most real union with God; the Father begets, the *Logos* joins himself to us as bridegroom; *Agape*, God's own love, is the mark of this mystical union. Only the new alliance could bring the mystery and through it reveal the inmost heart of God, his love.

Jewish worship, of course, had the forms of 'memorial' along with prayer and sacrifice. Because God showed himself to the Jews in historical events, these events were to be kept continually before the people's minds; first of all, the liberation from Egypt, upon which the existence of Israel as God's sacred people turned, was celebrated in the annual feast of the Passover. God's prescriptions were carried in exact ritual: the paschal lamb eaten in travelling clothes; the history read recalling how they left the land where they were slaves. So Israel's salvation and the founding of God's people was celebrated each year in ritual, and God's preserving of Israel in the promised land secured anew.[1]

But the passover use was not properly a mystery because it was related first of all to human events, and a human deliverance.* It was the Pasch of Christ, his bloody death, which saved the world from its sins and fed it with food of everlasting life, god-life. On the eve of the earth's pasch, the saviour made of this pasch a complete mystery; he anticipated his death in the mystical rite, and made food of his sacrificed body, gave his blood as the foundation of a covenant. Here an historic event was celebrated but one which had its end beyond time, in God, in the passage from this *aion* to the world to come. It was not only an action of God's upon his people, but an action he carried out among them in human form. Now men were given the power of imitating and following

---

[1] On the paschal meal see Strack-Billerbeck *Kommentar* IV, 1 (1928) 40 ff, esp. p. 68: 'In every generation man is obliged to act as if he had come out of Egypt, for it says, "for the sake of what Jahwe did for me as I came out of Egypt" ' (Ex. 13, 18). (Pes, 10, 5). Billerbeck comments (p. 69): 'Here is the plainest expression of the idea that the paschal meal is meant to be a memorial meal.'

in what God made man had done among them, and so of sharing in his life by means of their own concrete deed.

This pasch of Christ was, therefore, something completely his own, with no expression in the old covenant; hence it was such an abomination to Judaism, with its own single mind. The Jews, like all Semitic peoples thought of God as a powerful, terrible ruler, separated from mankind by an unbridgeable gap, whom one approached fearful and adoring; here was no room for a close relationship. Even the language of these peoples could not express the new god-life of the new alliance.* But God, in his providence, had seen to the growth of certain religious forms which, while not approaching closely to Christian reality, could offer words and forms to express this new, unheard-of thing in a way open to men's understanding.

The Indo-germanic peoples in their striving for deeper union with God had gradually fashioned richer and more refined forms of worship. These, particularly in the Hellenistic age, following the campaigns of Alexander the Great, entered a period of fruitful mixing of Greek and near Eastern ideas, and led to the mystery cults. This synthesis, which in many respects was to give its language and form to the coming Christianity—the Gospel is written in its common language, and dogma, too, used its superb power of expression—developed the ritual-form *mystery* to its classical height. Its fundamental idea was participation in the lives of the gods, who in some way or other had appeared in human form, and taken part in the pain and happiness of mortal men. The believer acted with them by sharing their suffering and deeds portrayed in the rite, and performed in it once more by ritual imitation. Thereby he entered into an intimacy with them which was expressed through various images taken from human life; he became a member of the race of gods.[1] This gave him the assurance that after death he would not share the general fate of mortals in Hades' darkness, but attain the blessedness of light; already on earth it cut him off from the mass of uninitiated, and made him a 'holy man', a consecrated person; sometimes it gave moral impulses as well. The *Mystai* formed among themselves a close, sacred community, under a selected, ruling priesthood. Worship in this community was carried out with rich and dramatic symbolism in which the divine actions were performed in a hieratic and formal manner with a rich use of natural symbolism. We hear for example that the high-point of the Eleusinian mysteries was the showing to the μύσται of a newly-

[1] In Eleusis for example.

cut ear of corn: a symbol of the newly burgeoning life, to men striving for it, a pledge of life after death.[1]

We may not, of course, carry over our elaborate concepts of Christian symbolism into the ancient mysteries. They remained the prisoners of unredeemed nature, in the slavery of the 'world's elements' as St Paul says of a Jewish-hellenistic cult;[2] they did not lead to the supernatural life of the true God. They were only a shadow, in contrast to the Christian mysteries; but they were a longing, 'a shadow of things to come'; the body whose shadow they cast was 'the body of Christ'[3] which showed itself beforehand in the types of the old Testament too. An analogy existed for them, as it did for the whole of nature and supernature, and so they were able to lend words and forms to the mysteries of Christ which belonged to that supernature. They did not give existence or content; how, indeed, were the weak and poor elements of the world[4] to attain of themselves the mystery of Christ? But they made it possible to give a body to the new and unconceived elements of the New Testament's revelation. When St Paul speaks of the 'things wrapped in silence for the ages' or of the 'hidden mystery', everyone in the ancient world knew immediately what this was: the familiar language of the mysteries, its purpose to make clearer to them, that as these mysteries were surrounded by a terrible majesty which claimed reverence, so, too, God's saving design came out of the hidden depths of his vast silences; and that these silences were now revealed. The whole new way of worship in the Christian community could no longer be expressed in the old language of Jewish or pagan ritual. We have only to call up the picture: on the one hand, the vast temple, with its huge altars, covered with the blood of slaughtered animals and smoky from countless burnt offerings, served by a throng of priests to kill the animals; choirs and shouts of the people: here was prayer and sacrifice in the old fashioned way, a reverence to all-powerful divinity. On the other hand, the Christian community without temple or altar, in simple houses around a table, with bread and wine. A leader says the *eucharistia*, the memorial renewed of Jesus crucified and risen; a family meal is held, bringing the community together. Was this cult of any kind in the ancient sense? Yes, said the Christians; here was the only true sacrifice: the mystical Christ

---

[1]For details, my *Liturgie als Mysterienfeier* (1923) also *Mysterium in Gesammelte Arbeiten laacher Mönche* (1926) particularly p. 29 ff.

[2]Col. 2, 8 and 20. Jewish cult is slavery to the elements of the world. Gal. 4, 3 and 9.

[3]Col. 2, 17.   [4]Gal. 4, 9.

sacrificing with and for his church, filling her with his Spirit. This is where the official ritual language of the Jews and pagans gave up; this mystical common work of Christ and the church could, if at all, and then only to a limited degree, find expression in the language of the mysteries, purified of everything merely natural, and made resplendent. In any case we observe that even quite early expressions from the mysteries are used for the Christian mystery; Christian writers like Justin Martyr, Tertullian, even Cyprian, note with astonishment the analogy of the mysteries, and comment on them. Moreover this takes place at the same time as the church held these mysteries in detestation —it was a period of their flowering—and fought them with all her power. From the peace of Constantine, the church's triumph over paganism, the language of the ancient mysteries was used even more unhesitatingly to express the unfathomable content of what she herself possessed, as far as this was possible at all; indeed many ancient forms and customs were taken over to enrich and adorn Christian simplicity. The gold and silver of Egypt, to use one of the fathers' favourite images, was melted down to embellish the vessels of the church.

In the course of time, the language of the mysteries, as a glance into the Roman Missal[1] shows us, became so much the church's property, that all consciousness of its ancient origin was lost. Who thinks of the word sacrament as resting in last analysis on the language of the ancient mysteries?[2] But this is no simple loss of memory through the usualness of the thing, but rather the consequence of the fact that Christianity is of its own very essence, as we saw above, a mystery religion, and the mystery language its own most rightful possession. The ancient church lived in mystery, and needed to construct no theory about it.*

The situation became different after the beginning of modern times, and the growth and development of modern thought which entered into ever sharper opposition to the thinking of the church. Ancient thought, considered as a whole, had a great reverence for all being: the individual felt himself to be a member of the great cosmos, and willingly submitted to its order. The self-seeker was taken for a rebel; his deed was ὕβρις which brought down the anger of the gods. Behind the visible world the

---

[1] On the ancient Roman sacramentaries whose texts have been partly preserved in the Roman Missal, Cf J.L.W. 2 (1922) p. 18 ff. For the mystery language of the Greek rites see P. Hendrix *Der Mysteriencharakter der byzant. Liturgie* (Byzant. Ztschrift 30 (1929) p. 333–339).

[2] Cf *Theol. Revue* 24 (1925), 41–47 and J.L.W. 8 (1928), p. 225–232 where the word *sacramentum* is discussed, and the passage from Greek μυστήριον to Latin *sacramentum*.

deep sight of ancient man saw a higher kingdom of spirit and godhead, of which the things we see are symbols; reflected reality, and at the same time mediators and bearers of spiritual things. Ancient thinking was at once concrete, because concerned with objects, and spiritual, because these did not remain confined to material objects. To men like these, it did not seem difficult to believe that God could communicate his life through symbols, or that their own religious acts could leap up into the circle of God's life; it was no different whether they conceived these things as more cosmic or as more spiritual; in either case it was a symbolic action which rose to the height of the god's mode of living. The symbolic, strength-giving rites of the mysteries were real for the ancients; when the church of Christ entered the world she did not end, but rather fulfilled their way of thinking.[1] Christ, of course, put nature out of its exclusive rulership, when he revealed God, as transcending the universe, taught us of the Spirit of life, and gave it to us. In his preaching, beside the community is the irreplaceable value of the individual soul. But he left the unconditional rule of God and the community all their pride of place; he gave them their final reason and highest development. It was symbolism which was sanctified and divinized when the *Logos* appeared in human flesh, and 'we saw the glory of God in the face of Christ'.[2] It cannot seem strange to us, then, when at his going away, Christ leaves the mysteries as signs of his divine presence, or when John, deepest of the evangelists, in his 'Spirit-informed' gospel,[3] makes so much of them. On the other hand it is also an historical truth that the Hellenes sometimes found it easier to grasp and to grasp more deeply the truth of the gospel than did the Jews with their purely Semitic, imageless, legal thinking. The Christianity of the ancient world appears to us as the fulfilment and glorification of what Greco-Roman antiquity was.

It became something quite different in the Germanic peoples who had given themselves to Christianity. A new kind of thinking arose when they received the culture of antiquity.* In it man was a lone individual, cut loose from the divine wholeness, moving always towards making himself his own midpoint, constructing for himself his own law and his own world, with no God outside him as an over-lord, no God

---

[1] Cf Mt. 5, 17. For the relationship of ancient culture to Christian worship cf J.L.W. 3, (1923) 1, ff. Also Chapter III.
[2] II Cor. 4, 6.
[3] Clement of Alexandria in Eusebius *Historia Ecclesiastica* VI, 14, 7.

with whom the creature enters into real relations. It followed immediately from this that the things of nature become subjective. They could at best be regarded as arbitary images; images, that is, of human, subjective apprehension; they were emptied of objective, independent value, and could no longer convey God's power. How this destroying, atomising notion took God out of the world and brought down every kind of community, we need not set out in detail; everyone with any vision can see now with dismay where Europe and the world she influences have come, thanks to individualism, old fashioned liberalism and Marxism.[1] The Catholic church has done something miraculous by holding fast to the cosmos of God's values in the midst of general chaos and by keeping for us, in the mystery of worship, symbols full of God's true power and presence. The liturgical renewal in our day is nothing but a new recognition and stress upon these values in the church, and an attempt to make them once more the common property of all the faithful. For there is no doubt that something of man-centred ideas has come into the minds of many Christians, and that this has gradually shown itself, in the life of faith, as rationalism, and in the life of piety as a tendency to introspective self-indulgence. Prayer has been moving away from consciousness of the mystical body of Christ, falling into the isolated feeling and thinking of the 'God-seeking' individual; sacrifice has been taken for nothing more than a mental attitude, and given 'ascetic' value, if not completely subordinated to external activity. The mystery itself, with its objective ordering of things according to God and real union with him disappeared beneath a mass of more or less personal devotional exercises which left more freedom to individual feeling. *Devotio*, a word which to the ancients[2] meant the church's worship, became the devotion of a purely interior state of individual consciousness. This modern spirit pushed its way even into the domain of theology, despite its dogmatic safeguards, and showed itself in a weakening of the great, deep thinking of the older theology, emphasizing man, his reason and his self-rule, to the detriment of God, Christ, church and sacrament. It is quite understandable, then, that the mystery teaching, as the logical outcome (in the sphere of worship and its mystical insight) of the old notions of faith, should be considered by many theologians, to be a foolish, unfounded, and even dangerous doctrine; rejected and fought by them as

[1] Cf Ch. I.
[2] A. Daniels, *Devotio* J.L.W. 1, p. 40 ff.

a deceitful *fata morgana*, it is yet championed by the followers of the old theology who take the Fathers and Aquinas as their models.[1]

This makes it clear that the renewal and revival of the traditional teaching is not due to a whim for touching up long out-dated ideas, nor to aestheticism, or some other arbitrary fancy; it proceeds necessarily from the spiritual state of our time. After the ebb and failure of anthropocentrism, once more the tide of a deeper divine life begins, a striving for God as he really is, for his dreadful majesty revealing itself in the New Testament, not merely as terror as it did in the Old, but as the deepest, incomprehensible love: the abyss of love which would plunge us into itself. This longing to penetrate once again the whole of life with God's lively Spirit, not merely at the 'times of devotion' but in all being and action, is the response to the mystery; its very name shows that it denotes the inconceivable, the power of God's action which surpasses all thinking. Here man can only tremble; not in reverence and terror only, but in love.

New ideas always live first of all in small circles. In this case they first grow out of the heart of the church; but it is surely a work of providence, too, that even in the world outside the church, de-christianized, a new kind of thinking gradually rises. The spirit of rationalism, of self-sufficient science, is more powerful than ever in

---

[1]For details I note the most important references. J. B. Umberg S.J. assembles the doubts of many theologians in his articles on 'Mystery-piety?' *Ztschrift für Askese und Mystik* 1 (1926) p. 351–366, and 'Mystery-Presence' *Ztschrift für kath. Theologie* 52 (1928) p. 357–400. His operational base is the difficulty, in the mystery-teaching, of conceiving how Christ's past saving act should become present; this is supposed to be philosophically impossible. Yet the difficulty is ill-conceived, because the presence here brought to be is not a natural and historical, but sacramental one. For the notion of sacramental presence cf particularly Vonier's book, *A Key to the Doctrine of the Eucharist* 1925. My answer to Umberg in *Bonner Ztschrift f. Theologie und Seelsorge* 4, 1927, p. 101–117 and J.L.W. 6, 113–204, 8, 145–224, where I seek to show the propriety of the mystery-idea from scripture, patristic tradition and dogmatic theology. The teaching of tradition is further given in J.L.W. 13, 99–171. Gebhard Rohner shows correspondence to Thomistic teaching in *Divus Thomas* (Freiburg) 8, p. 1–17 and 145–174. Some French Jesuits near to Thomism have given the ideas friendly treatment, the patrologists Jules Lebreton and J. de Séguier in *Nouvelle Rev. de Théol.* 61 (1929) p. 289–299, where they attempt to prove the thesis from the Thomistic notion of transubstantiation. Of course it is always well to speak cautiously of proof, as we are here in the realm of the *mysterium stricte dictum*. I have replied to the work of Joseph Dillersberger, *Eine neue Messopfertheorie?* (*Theologie u Glaube*, 22, p. 511–88), which accepts the thesis with some essential differences, in the same periodical (23, p. 351–367). More literature in the literature section of J.L.W. under 'Mass' (Fourth section of the reviews in each volume). B. Neunheuser gives an introductory survey of the speculative work in this area over the last few years: *Lit. Leben* 2, 1935, p. 189–217.*

the masses, but among the better-educated there is the dawn of strivings
to new consciousness of symbolism, to a grasp of the need for depth.
Mankind today is sick with the rationalism of exact science and longs
once more for the symbols of God's world. It can find them, where
they have always remained, in Christ's church, where his mystery is
proclaimed by the true God and shows the way to him. The church's
faithful, however, must learn once more the greatness of their treasures;
they must cleanse away the rust of neglect, and let them shine once
again in the light which love and knowledge brings to bear, so that
they may show the world once more the only true and saving mysteries.

The recent popes have called once more for active sharing in the
mysteries of worship;[1] there is the flowing spring of Christ's life. This
active sharing will only then be really and truly fulfilled when the
Liturgy is known again for what it is at the deepest level: the mystery
of Christ and the Church.*

iii *Mystery and Liturgy*

Christ's mystery in God's revelation in the saving action of his
incarnate Son and the redemption and healing of the church. It
continues after the glorified God-man has returned to his Father,
until the full number of the church's members is complete; the mystery
of Christ is carried on and made actual in the mystery of worship.
Here Christ performs his saving work, invisible, but present in Spirit
and acting upon all men of good-will.[2] It is the Lord himself who acts
this mystery; not as he did the primaeval mystery of the Cross, alone,
but with his bride, which he won there, his church;[3] to her he has
now given all his treasures; she is to hand them on to the children she
has got of him. Whoever has God for his father must, since the incarnation, have the church for his mother.[4] As the woman was formed
in paradise from the side of the first Adam, to be a helpmate, like to
him[5], the church is formed from the side of Christ fallen asleep on

[1]Cf J. Pinsk in *Lit. Zeitschrift* 3, p. 63.
[2]Lk. 2, 14.
[3]Eph. 5, 14 ff.
[4]Cf St Cyprian, *de Unitate Ecclesiae* 5 f. We are born of the church, drink
her milk, are enlivened by her Spirit. . . . She keeps us for God, leads those she
had born to his kingdom. The man who cuts himself off from the church and
joins an adulteress is separated from the church's promise. He will not attain
Christ's reward, if he deserts Christ's church. He is a stranger, an uninitiate,
a foreigner. No one can have God for his father who does not have the church
for his mother.
[5]Gen. 2, 18.

the cross to be his companion and helper in the work of redemption. At the same time, the fathers teach us[1] the mysteries flow in water and blood from the Lord's side; the church was born from Christ's death-blood and the mystery with it; church and mystery are inseparable. This is the last ground for the fact that the mystery of worship becomes liturgy.

The Greek word Liturgy[2] originally meant the act of an individual in the service of the city; for example fitting up a ship for war, or sponsoring a choir for the tragedies in honour of Dionysus; service generally, and in particular the service of God in public worship. In this sense it is used by Old and New Testament. Thus, Zacharias, the father of John the Baptist, performed his liturgy in the temple.[3] St Clement of Rome speaks in his letter to the Corinthians (40 ff) of the liturgy of the Old Testament which he puts before them as the model for the service of the New. And if in the New Testament the whole of life is sacred and a service of God, the fathers' directions have particular application to the common worship of the Christian community. The rulers of this community 'perform liturgy' for it;[4] they conduct it in the service of God, particularly in his worship. The layman, too, performs his liturgy: the high-priest has received his liturgy, the priest his proper place, the Levites have each their special duties: 'the layman is bound by the prescriptions for the people. Every one of us, brethren, is to please God in the place God has appointed for him, with a good conscience and due dignity, not going over the bounds of his own liturgy'.[5] Here the liturgical order of the temple is carried over into Christian ways; in Hebrews[6] Christ himself is named

---

[1]As one of many we present Augustine's *Tractatus in Joannem* 120, 2: 'it is a pregnant word the evangelist has used; he does not say the soldier thrust into his side, or wounded him in his side, or anything else, but that he opened his side. Thus, so to speak, the doors of life were to be opened through which the church's mysteries proceed, without which no one goes into the life which is true life. This blood was poured out for the remission of sins, this water was preparation for salvation's cup; it made the cleaning water and the good drink. An image of it was the door which Noah made in the side of the ark; through it the animals were to enter, which were not to die in the flood: they signified the church. Therefore the first woman was made from the side of a sleeping man and called life, and mother of the living. She signified a great good thing, before the great woe of sin. And the second Adam fell asleep here on the Cross, with head bowed, so that his spouse might be formed from what flowed out of his side. . . .'

[2]λειτουργία—old Attic λῃτουργία: λάος, ἔργον: public work, public service.

[3]Luke 1, 23.

[4]I Clement 44, 4.

[5]I Clement 40, 5–41.

[6]I Clement 8, 2.

as the performer of liturgy in the New Testament, the liturgist of the true holy place and the true tabernacle, which the Lord and no man fashioned. Here we recognize clearly that the primaeval mystery of the New Alliance is no liturgy in the usual, ritual sense; the expressions about the liturgy of the old covenant are being used in a higher sense concerning the purely spiritual facts of the new. Christ's sacrifice is not a liturgy in the old, ritual sense, but plain and noble reality, the ultimate and greatest fulfilment of what the old covenant had given in type. But when the church carries out the mystery of Christ in her own mystery of worship, in ritual, forms and expressions of the old covenant find a new and higher kind of reality, and fulfilment in the new rites. Here a liturgy arises which is first of all an exterior form, but does not carry 'a foreshadowing of good things to come';[1] rather it is the grace-filled reality, the redemption itself.

When we place the words 'mystery' and 'liturgy' side by side, and take mystery as mystery of worship, they will mean the same thing considered from two different points of view. *Mystery* means the heart of the action, that is to say, the redeeming work of the risen Lord, through the sacred actions he has appointed: liturgy, corresponding to its original sense of 'people's work', 'service', means rather the action of the church in conjunction with this saving action of Christ's. We saw above, that Christ and the church work together inseparably in the mystery; but we can none the less characterize mystery as more the act of the bridegroom, and liturgy the act of the bride, without thereby making too great a division. For when the church performs her exterior rites, Christ is inwardly at work in them; thus what the church does is truly mystery. Yet it is still proper to use the term liturgy in a special fashion for the church's ritual action. And this gives rise to the question, how has the mystery of the new covenant become liturgy?

The deepest ground for it lies in the fact we have already mentioned, that Christ has given the mysteries to his church. The Council of Trent teaches (Session XXII) that the new high priest, Jesus Christ 'was to offer himself to God once and for all on the altar of the cross, and there to accomplish everlasting salvation. But since priesthood was not to be extinguished through his death he left to his beloved bride, the church, a visible sacrifice, as human nature requires. Through it that bloody, unique sacrifice completed on the cross, was to be made present,

[1]Heb. 10, 1.

to continue the memorial of him until the end of time, and to apply his saving power to the remission of the sins we commit daily. After he had celebrated the ancient passover, which the multitudes of the sons of Israel sacrificed for a memorial of their coming out of Egypt, he instituted the new pasch for us, the slaughter of himself, handed on through the church by means of her priests, through visible signs, in memory of his passage from this world to the Father.'

The content, and so the essential form of the mysteries have been instituted and commanded by our Lord himself; he has entrusted their performance to the church, but not laid down to the last detail what is necessary or desirable for a communal celebration. By leaving the Spirit to his church, he has given her the ability as well, to mint inexhaustible treasure from the mystery entrusted to her, to develop it and to display it to her children in ever new words and gestures. Her bridegroom's love moves her to make of his gifts a praise to his love; her motherly goodness leads her to explain it to her children with all care, so that they may make it their own. So the liturgy, born of her fullness of the Spirit, and love, becomes a work of beauty and of wisdom.

It would be worthwhile to make clear this development of mystery into liturgy, with examples. But we must be content to point out some of the main lines of development. The Lord demanded a rebirth for entry into his kingdom; the natural man cannot reach God unless he first be changed. The old man must die, the new man, begotten out of God, must rise. 'If a man be not begotten of water and *pneuma*, he cannot enter heaven.'[1] *Pneuma* is the breath of God, from which supernatural life flows; it is God himself,[2] and his life dwelling in the new man. This word shows clearly that it is not a change of will that makes the Christian, but a completely new being, a 'sharing in God's being'[3] as St Peter says: we are then in the pure realm of grace and the invisible life of God. But the Lord says that the new man must be born again of water; thus the mystery of worship arises; for in the realm of God's supernatural action this birth from water can only be the exterior and visible expression of the inward, real birth from *pneuma*. It has therefore no natural worth of its own, but only symbolic value; this symbolic value is what the Lord says is absolutely necessary. For without this exterior act we could not recognize God's act. The plain, objective, sensible, tangible act of plunging into water is the pledge for the reality of God's new begetting; at the same time the community gives the

[1]Jn. 3, 5.   [2]Jn. 4, 24.   [3]II Peter 1, 4.

necessary witness that a new member has been added to it. It would be an error to think that it was enough to have a dumb dipping into water to form a picture of God's grace: water, matter from below, has no capacity for that. It must be complemented by something higher, formed and fashioned by it: the Spirit which comes from above. But what is better suited to express Spirit than the lightness and refinement of the Word, as the Lord speaks of it in the third chapter of St John's gospel? It gives motion to what thought would express; the ancients called it *Logos*, spirit-shaped, and thence it was so connected with *pneuma* that the two words are often interchanged. The element of sense and tangibility which the word indicated is clear. The fullness of the mystery comes from both: 'take away the word, and what is water except mere water. Word comes to the water, and the *mysterium* is there, itself like a word to be seen. Where does water have so great a power that when it touches the body, it should wash the heart? All of that from the mere word.'[1] The Lord called for a rebirth: the death of the old man. He himself showed us how it was to be done by dying on the cross and rising for God. Christians must be plunged into this death and resurrection, so that Christ's life, the life of the Trinity, revealed through him in the new alliance, might dwell in them. Therefore the candidate is stripped bare, as God made the first man, and as the second Adam hung on the cross.[2] The old man is to die and a wholly new one come out of the waters. The name of the Trinity is spoken over him; according to ancient Christian faith this meant that the whole power of the present Godhead came down upon this man and fashioned him anew by grace to God's own likeness. This plunging into Christ's death, and resurrection with him to God's life, as the words of Christ in St John's gospel (Chapter 2) describe it, is approved by St Paul as the meaning of baptism in his deep discourse in Romans (6). An extraordinarily rich store of meaning is contained in the simple words which St Matthew uses to tell of baptismal institution: 'go out, then, and teach all peoples to be disciples, baptising them in the name of the Father and the Son and the Holy Spirit, teaching them to observe all things which I have entrusted to you.'[3] How simply

---

[1] St Augustine *Tractatus in Joann*, 80, 3 cf 15, 4. The translation 'Word' does not give the full sense of λόγος; in later times this sentence of Augustine's was misused to make the sacrament a mere kind of sermon. This would have been impossible if there had been a proper understanding of λόγος—*verbum*.

[2] Cyril of Jerusalem, *Mystagogical Catechesis* II, 2.

[3] Mt. 28, 19.

this command is to be carried out is related in the story of the chamberlain's baptism by Philip.[1] They came to water, and the eunuch said, 'what is to keep me from baptism?' Both go into the water, the eunuch is put under, and made a Christian. Here we see the mystery in its simplest form, as it had to be under the circumstances.

With deep understanding and love the church has gradually expanded this simple rite and formed it into a rich service, without neglecting the mystery-centre. All the variety of texts, rites, and objects only serve to express the one content and do God honour, to bring it as close as possible to all the faithful. The candidate comes to the church; he is taken through repeated instruction in faith, which is the door to this new life; the blessed salt, wisdom's symbol, is given him; again and again the hand of the priest is laid on to bless him; exorcism is pronounced to drive out the evil enemy, and break the power of the demon over him; the secrets of the Christian way, the Our Father and the Creed, are given to him, yet only orally; written they might come to profane hands. He first hears nothing of the mysteries proper, baptism and eucharist, because he is not yet initiated, and as yet has no capacity to understand such things. We see how the church prepares and expresses ever more clearly the one side of baptism, the death of the old man, fallen to demons, and on the other gradually leads him into the region of holiness. Shortly before baptism the candidate has to repeat what he has learnt before the bishop: once more he is solemnly exorcised to make room for the coming of the Holy Spirit. Then comes the vigil. Out of the darkness of error, and of demons, out of the womb of life the divine light streams, and the new life in the Spirit is born. With a good teacher's insight, the church leads her children through the rites into their new life, of which they knew nothing before, shows them wonders of which they had only seen the shadows. The impression made on these men was all the more tense from waiting.[2]

First of all the radical turning away from the life they had lived before in paganism, found gripping and vivid symbolic expression in renouncing the devil, his pomps and his works. Candidates held out their arms to the West, towards the kingdom of darkness, blew, and with a sign renounced the devil eternally. Then they turned to the East, to the holy light and life, to Christ, the dawning from on high,[3] promised everlasting faithfulness to him, confessed him their master and acknowledged faith in him. Then they were stripped; nothing of human

---

[1] Acts 8, 26.   [2] Ambrose *De Mysteriis* I, 2.   [3] Lk. 1, 78.

making was to go with them down into the water; no work of man's mind: a wholly new man was to emerge. Then the whole body was anointed; this was a sign that the divine Spirit was to give them strength in the fight against the devil. Then they went down the three steps into the baptismal well; the water had been made holy beforehand by the bishop's *epiclesis*, invocation of the *pneuma*, and made fruitful for the new life, an image of the church's sacred womb. Three times they were plunged beneath the waters, and the name of the Holy Trinity called down upon them again; now the Trinity came and possessed them, sealed them with its own seal. From this point the positive aspect of the new life came out more and more.

Plunged under three times, the candidate came out on the other side of the well, three steps up; now, as initiate and new-born son, he was clothed in the white garment of light and immortality, and a burning light placed in his hands. He comes before the bishop who lays hands upon him, anoints him with the fullness of the god-life, first given in the waters. The new man, streaming with God's own light and glowing with love of him, goes up to the church where the baptised receive him with a kiss, and pray with him in fellowship for the first time. Now he may take part in the Eucharist, eat of the divine food and drink the blood of Christ which has become life for him. Milk and honey are given to him, the new-begotten child of God, who has entered the promised land and there sings songs of praise to the Lord. He is fully initiated, a fellow-subject with the saints and sharer of God's house, a member of Christ, a beloved son in the likeness of God's own Son; he awaits everlasting life.

Our brief description gives only a weak image of the rich liturgy which has grown out of the mystery of baptism. The sources, too, from which the church drew when she made the liturgy cannot be given here in detail, indeed can hardly be mentioned. Therefore we shall say a few words about them. The proper content of the mystery is given by the actions and words which the Lord has himself laid down. Still, he did not intend to create something completely new, to teach or fashion a new salvation. He used the age-old forms mankind had always known, changing them and improving them. The idea and even the form of some kind of baptism is a live thing among most of mankind, when purification from sin and passage into a new and holier life is to be expressed and realized. In particular the exterior rites and the objects used, because they are bound up with the natural movements of life and the things nature makes, are already, to a high degree, settled; water is water, whether it is used for natural rites of cleansing or highly elaborate rituals. The word is freer and more mobile; but it, too, is bound up with a language as it has grown to be. For his revelation God uses the word of human speech; it is thus that men are to understand him. The liturgy, too, uses human expressions and human formulae to make the mystery of God known. For the texts of its celebrations there is an extraordinary pattern in the Word of God in Scripture; here the Holy Spirit itself proclaims the gospel in the tongues of men, but with the power of God. Much is passed unchanged from the scripture into the liturgy, taking on a new form, a new dimension; from mere writing it has gone back to its first life.[1] In one special way this is true of the Old Testament word which receives a last light and a great richness in the liturgy of Christ's mystery. When, on Christmas night we read from Isaias, we read what is no longer prophecy but present fact. Here is the deepest ground for the allegorical or spiritual interpretation of scripture: since Christ appeared, we have the key to the Old Testament, the key which opens all doors: now we see not only the letter which kills, but the Spirit that gives life.[2] Nowhere have we a clearer recognition of the Spiral character of scripture than in the liturgy, where all its words are turned to praise of the mystery of Christ, or the life of the Christian in Christ.[3] The scriptural word is, as it were, born again from the heart of the church, and receives a new dimension; it becomes the voice of Christ crying out through the prophets and the church's voice, too. God's word has this about it, that unlike man's words it does not rise with the moment and disappear; it descends over and over again into the souls of God's people in the church, and while it continues there, it grows up again new, fresh and youthful. It comes to man begotten of the Spirit of God. The accusation so often heard, that you cannot pray spontaneously from the heart in age-old formulae, does not apply; this word rises spontaneously from the heart of the church our Mother.

[1] Cf Ildefons Herwegen in *Lit. Ztschrift* 3 (1930–31), p. 8 ff.

[2] II Cor. 3, 6; cf 14 f 'Until this day this veil remains with the Jews at the reading of the Old Testament. There must be a turning to the Lord first and then the veil will be taken away. . . .' This is true of the reading of the Old Testament in general, and the solution of all the difficulties brought against such reading.

[3] Cf Nicetas of Remesiana *De Utilitate Hymnorum* C.6 (In Psalmis) *Christi sacramenta canuntur.* All the mysteries of Christ from the incarnation to the second coming are mirrored in the Psalms.

The ceremonies of the law were unfit for use in the Christian liturgy in Christ's sacrifice; they had been fulfilled, and thus brought to an end. We should note that the Lord held his supper in connexion with the paschal meal, but that from the rite proper of the Jewish passover nothing went into the Christian eucharist; the ordinary table prayers were the first foundation of the Christian 'thanksgiving'.[1] Similarly, Christian baptism cannot be traced to the Jewish baptism of proselytes, although it has certain parallels with general human customs, from which that ceremony grew up as well.[2] In general we can take it that the Christian religion, as the fulfilment of all mankind's longing in the religious sphere, as the *catholic*, the common religion of mankind, takes to itself as of sovereign right and with sovereign freedom all that mankind has developed in truly great religious forms. If the Church were to shut herself off in fear from the world about her, she would not be the catholic church, but a sect. But she has accepted everything she found, into the world of her thinking, and thereby transformed everything; in her furnace she has cleansed everything from what was all too human, and left only the gold behind.

The 'plenitude of time'[3] when Christianity came into the world was peculiarly well-suited to give form to the liturgy. It was the mark of the entire ancient world that it had shaped the indwelling symbolism of the natural world into an elaborate yet simple language; this was particularly true of religious forms, and the mysteries we have just been speaking of. It was a custom in antiquity to anoint oneself after a bath with fragrant oil, for strength and beauty. The church has made this custom a rite of the new life by anointing the baptised, for an image of the sweet odour of the Spirit. Another custom was for a new-born child to take milk, mixed with honey. In many mysteries the 'new-born' received a cup of sweet milk: in just the same way, the Christians give their newly-begotten in Christ a drink of milk and honey; St Peter tells the young Christians, that like new-born children, they are to feel longing for the Spirit's milk, so they may grow in salvation.[4] It was similar with clothing. In the Greco-Roman world, clothing was not a casual or indifferent matter; with a new garment went a new manhood. In the mysteries a garment or a sign of the God was put on, and the

---

[1] Cf Strack-Billerbeck IV, p. 627 ff.
[2] Cf J. Leipoldt *Die Christliche Taufe im Lichte der Religionsgeschichte* (1928) and, on this book, J.L.W. 9, 203 ff.
[3] Gal. 4, 4. Eph. 1, 10.
[4] I Peter 2, 2.

initiate became that god. In connexion with these customs, Paul cries out, 'all of you who have been baptised in Christ, have put on Christ';[1] in Easter week the church sings this of the baptised who stand about the altar in their white clothing. This last example shows us once more that some customs which signify a mystical uniting with the godhead, were particularly well-appointed to serve the Christ-mysticism of the liturgy. Thus the age-old idea of representing the embodiment of divine strength with food and drink is brought up to its highest pitch of reality by the eucharist: a real meal with God, representing our deepest union with the god-man and rendering it fact, as the Lord himself says of it in John 6.

In these ways the whole of mankind, the whole creation has 'done service to the mysteries' as the blessing of water in the Roman Ritual says of it.[2] Similarly different elements make their own contributions, as do different peoples, races, and ages. Christendom, then, is Catholic, common to mankind; despite all unity in faith and moral teaching, it can and must express itself in a variety of ways. The liturgical forms of the sober, serious, lapidary Roman is one thing; the mystical depth and warmth of the orientals, the agile-minded, poetical Gauls, the dreamy and passionate Celts, or the cloudy, emotional Germans quite other things—to name only a few currents. Every people has expressed its pecularities in the liturgy, and made of them a sacrifice to God.[3]

But even within the one church different conditions have taken changing roles in the development of the liturgy. The clergy's part was a leading one, but laymen, too, have contributed with poetry, music, and the other arts; the liturgy of the seculars was not that of the monks, and the liturgy of cathedrals not that of village churches.

The whole church, therefore, and all conditions of men in her have worked together, and shaped the liturgical ornaments of the mystery, each man in his way, each according to his *charisma*, all on the ground of their inner sharing in the mysteries. The whole church is its bearer, as the Council of Trent says when it declares, 'Christ left behind the priesthood to his beloved spouse the church, so that by their service the church might carry out the mystical death'. Within her structure, every member acts his role in his appointed place, conjointed to all the rest; this is what Clement of Rome says. The God-appointed,

---

[1] Gal. 3, 27.
[2] *Creatura tua mysteriis tuis serviens.*
[3] A. Baumstark, *The Growth of the Liturgy* (Mowbray) 1957.

consecrated hierarchy holds the immediate and authoritative place of
Christ as the actor of the mystery and high priest; the rest of the faithful,
each according to his rank, form part of the church as Christ's bride.
From thence it comes that the whole church, not merely the clergy
is to take an active part in the liturgy, each according to sacred order,
in his proper rank, place, and measure. All members are truly, sacramentally conjoined to Christ their head; every believer, because of the
sacramental character he received in baptism and confirmation, has

part in the priesthood of Christ the head. This means that the layman
does not merely assist with private devotion and prayer at the priest's
liturgy, but is, by his objective membership in Christ's body, a necessary
and real sharer in the liturgical fellowship. It belongs to the perfection
of this participation, of course, that this objective priesthood should
be made real and brought up to its highest pitch by a personal sharing
of life. As psychology teaches us, the inner life grows stronger to the
extent that the external act corresponding to an interior one is consciously made: we hear a song, but the inner participation in it will be
greatly heightened and made easier if we sing it ourselves. So with the
liturgy, the decisive thing is inward participation which does not
require unconditionally to be made external; but external participation
does belong to the intense sharing of the experience, and to the completion of its symbolic expression.

In this, we must hold to the fundamental laws of the mystical body,
as we have stated them: every member in its place, according to its
duty and the measure of its grace. Laymen can never assume the service
of the consecrated priesthood; every rank must keep its place. Everything is not for everyone, and not everything is immediately open to
all. The mystery remains a mystery, and shows itself gradually to the
eyes of the pure and the humble. So there is no esoteric cult of the
liturgy, no aesthetic sampling; humility and purity of heart and openness to Christ, disclose the way to Christian mysteries. The meaning of
the mystery is in a high degree something which belongs to ordinary
people, precisely because they love the whole, and at the same time
recognize that the things of God are hidden. But, as the fathers teach
us, there are steps in knowledge; the outward expression of this is the
reservation of sanctuary for priests, the choir for monks and virgins,
and the people. Many of the difficulties of the liturgical renewal would
disappear with a careful observance of the ancient notion of hierarchy.
Is it not wisdom on the church's part to have put the *veil* of a ritual

language over the liturgy, precisely because the mystery is not to stand in the fierce light of every day? Is it necessary to turn all texts into the vernacular, make every detail of every rite visible? Does not this take away something irreplaceable, the glow of veneration which means more to the people than understanding every detail? The obviously praiseworthy intention of bringing people back to active participation in the liturgy should not fall into the democratic heresy.[1] Hierarchy, that is to say, holy order and graduation of value must be maintained in the liturgy; in this way the true common life of the whole ecclesia arises; every order shares what belongs to it with the other. Common life does not mean everyone having the same, but each giving from his riches to the other to fill up that other's lack. Love is founded on mutual giving, and St Paul's word is fulfilled: by the mutual bond of aid in the strength of each member, the growth of the body is brought to fullness; the body is built up in God's love, *agape*.[2]

The sacred mystery is the visible expression, and at the same time the highest living activity of the mystical body of Christ: head and members are one in the sacrifice to the Father, to whom all honour goes up through the Son in the Holy Spirit, and from whom all grace and blessing come down through the same Word and Spirit. So ever deeper knowledge, and live sharing in the mystery become the central Christian theme of the sacrifice to God which pleases him, as Gregory of Nazianzen tells us in the Easter sermon:[3]

'We would bring a gift to him who suffered for us and rose. You might imagine I was thinking of gold or silver or precious fabric or stones; but all of this is passing earthly matter of which evil men usually have the greatest amount; no, we will bring ourselves as a gift, the thing most precious and most proper to God. We would give back the copy to its original, recognise what we are, give honour to our type, penetrate the meaning of the mystery, the reason of Christ's dying. Let each of us give all, give away all to him who gave himself up for us as the price of our freedom, for him who took our place. No one can give something greater than when, knowing the mystery, he gives himself, and, for Christ's sake, becomes all that Christ became for ours.'

[1] L. Verwilst O.P. has called attention to this false motive: *De stand van den priester aan het Altar* (Lit Tijdschr II, p. 321–327), directed first of all against the attempt to place the altar in the middle of a church and thus remove a proper sanctuary. Verwilst sees this as a result of the levelling spirit, whereas the church has always striven to protect holy things for the sake of reverence.
[2] Eph. 4, 16.   [3] *Oratio I in Pascha*, P.G. 35, 397 ff.

3

THE ANCIENT WORLD AND THE
CHRISTIAN MYSTERIES

It is a disheartening fact, that the wave of mysticism which is now passing over our age after the high tide of rationalism neither moves toward nor is in any way formed by the norms of Catholic Christendom. For the greatest part it loses itself in every kind of shallow bog and muddy pool, or foams away its power uselessly. This is not the fault of Christianity. On the contrary the religion of the *Logos* whose Spirit acts in the church and his appearance as a man among men, can show the only sure way and clear end to this longing. But Christianity, particularly in the centuries since the Renaissance and the Reformation has been looked upon so much as a mere juridical institution, a moral activity, a function of popular education, that the highest and finest desires and capacities of the human mind have only too often sought satisfaction elsewhere. At the very least mysticism became a special compartment in religious life, open only to a few, and by means of a special method. If today authority has to give warnings about occultism, theosophy, the 'Russian soul', and Oriental thought generally, it looks with high regard upon the German, Spanish and French mysticism of the late Middle Ages and the Counter-reformation. Yet it might be more suggestive to turn attention to that mysticism which blooms in the heart of the church herself, which belonged to her very being from the first, and which is therefore open to all Christians. It grows out of the common life, and gives the individual full satisfaction: Christ himself made it the way without which no one comes to the Father. It is therefore essentially Christian, essentially of the Church. We mean liturgical mysticism, the mysticism of the ordinary worship of the church, carried out and regulated by its priests; a mysticism, therefore, of sacred action, Spirit-informed, the property of the congregation led by proper authority, where the Lord himself shares its work with his bride and leads her to the eternal Father.

If we ask why this pure Christian ritual and congregational mysticism receded, the final answer will be found without any great difficulty in the modern decline of awareness of the God-given, objective mould which dominated the ancient world and the early middle ages. The theocentric attitude of mind was exercised, at least in shadowy form, in the ancient world by the humble subjection to nature, which was of divine fashioning; some enlightened minds, with Plato as their head, developed this view of nature and taught it. In Christianity the theme was brought to its splendid climax in the utterance: God is *agape.* This humble and therefore exalted attitude was broken, by another fall as it were, the self-emancipation of the age of Gothic and the Renaissance. In the latter period this revolution led to a self-divinizing heathendom. In their Reformation, the Germans, who, as St Clement Hofbauer said 'wanted to stay pious', produced a movement of personal piety, but destroyed consciousness of God as mystery. The first thing Luther rejected was the Canon of the Mass, containing the eucharistic sacramental mystery; he kept the communion, 'the Supper', as an expression of faith. In Catholic Christianity the mystery was kept in fact and protected by prescription; but it lost altogether too much ground in the piety of the people, giving place to the more subjective devotions which appeared, partly left over from the Gothic age, partly new creations.*

What the Christian of the ancient world brought with him from his old way of life, he had only to deepen and make more spiritual; he had a sense for objective norms and ideas, such as the modern man has to learn with effort and to make his own. Of course grace can take up the empty space, and compensate for what nature lacks; but in general the rule is true *gratia supponit et perficit naturam*: grace builds on and perfects nature.

From this point of view classical education which, because it was so bound up with nineteenth-century Liberalism and is therefore threatened by the latter's decline, takes on a new meaning for our future. It ought not to give merely formal and logical schooling; ancient form grows out of its own kind of consciousness. It is this consciousness which is a matter of life and death for our time more than any other. 'The powers which God sent to form the Christian thing made their entrance into history in the mighty framework of ancient culture, and in the works of the church fathers the well-springs of European culture brought to ripeness their most precious fruit.'[1] These 'powers which God sent' could develop even more intensively today if men's

[1] Proposition I of the Regensburg Diocesan Synod, 1927.

spontaneous ways of thought were better oriented towards the ancient ideal of an objective order of things which places the whole man, not just reason or emotion, into the cosmos of relations to God, his author and his end; and this is true not least for the life of piety.

When we consider ancient piety, we are struck by its strong sense for norms, its bonds to firm, traditional forms which lead to its expression in an objective, peaceful clarity and in communal action; we notice this even in apparently detached individual phenomena of a mystical type, which burst out of all firm and definite shapes. These characteristics are in no way true of more recent mystical life; their concepts have arisen from observation of more recent phenomena. This mysticism, rooted in the Orient and developed in most recent times by the Germanic peoples after the emancipation of the individual, is fundamentally different from ancient, formal, communal mysticism which gave shape particularly to the hellenistic mysteries, and then found its crown in Christianity.* The one sought a lone road, of purification and concentration, flying from the world, practising ascesis, turning aside from the common life: this was its way to God, its way into the godhead. The other acted in concert with God, as he graciously revealed himself, appeared on earth, and shared his saving act, his suffering, and new life with the initiate. The follower becomes one with the cult god of the fellowship, and with all its members, yet does not pass the boundaries of creaturehood. The origin of this mysticism is with God, not with merely human longing; it is bound up with authoritative form; the community gives it assurance, independent of its receiver, orderliness and rest, greatness which passes beyond the lone individual. Not merely upward-striving *eros* for the divine but Christian *agape* (the *caritas* of the Western fathers) which comes from above and gives itself in graciousness, holds and penetrates everything from the divine centre; it develops in humble self-giving to God and the brethren. From it alone a common life can grow: not from the striving of equal men, but from a principle which stands above all them, and preserves for personality its special worth.

Let us now consider this ideal vision of the whole in some detail, and the ancient mystery first of all. Of course it is not possible at this point to give a full treatment of even one of the mysteries; we must be content to show the main features of the ritual-type mysterium. In this we are on firm ground as well, since the discipline of silence has only left us a few unclear ideas about details. A relatively detailed description of an ancient initiation is to be had in the eleventh book of Apuleius' *Metamorphoses*. The author does, of course, omit the secret portion of the initiation proper, but he brings us extraordinarily well into the mood of the mystery religions and their piety in late antiquity. If we do not have exact information about any one mystery, we have a very clear concept from various reports of what the mystery was, especially the hellenistic mystery, in which Greek form joins an oriental other-worldliness. Whereas prayer would bring the thoughts and wishes of the mind before God, and sacrifice is essentially a gift to the gods, the mystery seeks to place itself in a still deeper relationship to them. The *Kyrios* of a mystery is a God who has entered into human misery and struggle, has made his appearance on earth (epiphany) and fought here, suffered, even been defeated; the whole sorrow of mankind in pain is brought together in a mourning for the god who must die. But then in some way comes a return to life through which the God's companions, indeed the whole of nature revives and lives on. This was the way of pious faith and sacred teaching (ἱερός λόγος), of society in the earliest mythical age. But the world, society is always in need of life; so the epiphany goes on and on in worship; the saving, healing act of God is performed over and over. Worship is the means of making it real once more, and thus of breaking through to the spring of salvation. The members of the cult present again in a ritual, symbolic fashion, that primeval act; in holy words and rites of priest and faithful the reality is there once more. The celebrant community is united in the deepest fashion with the Lord they worship; there is no deeper oneness than suffering and action shared. Thereby they win a share in the new life of God; they enter his chorus, they become gods. The mysteries' way is, therefore, the way of ritual action as a sharing in the gods' acts; its aim is union with godhead, share in his life.

The mystery, therefore, embraces in the first place the broad concept of ritual 'memorial'—ἀνάμνησις, commemoratio—the ritual performance and making present of some act of the god's, upon which rests the existence and life of a community. The sacred action becomes a mystery in the full sense when it is concerned not merely with strivings in this life, keeping the worshipping assembly in health and life, making nature blossom and thrive, but rather with union with the godhead which it honours and the blessed continuation of life after death as the centre of religious strivings. Ritual communities of this kind are brought together through the call of individuals with especially high aspirations; they form a class apart, close themselves off from the profane, and receive members by secret initiation. Their aim is σωτηρία, salvation, in the full fellowship of the god after death.

We can, then give a brief definition:

> The mystery is a sacred ritual action in which a saving deed is made present through the rite; the congregation, by performing the rite, take part in the saving act, and thereby win salvation.[1]

It is easy to recognize these characteristics, and the piety which belongs to them. In the first place the mystery is defined by a revelation (epiphany) from God; it is settled and prescribed by him; its piety is therefore theocentric. Next, the mystery is not concerned with race or nation, but with the individual, yet in such a fashion that this individual comes immediately into a community, under a religious authority. The act of separation from the profane, and the solemn initiation, give him a great insight into the new life; its mysticism finds practical application, not in purely individual, interior strivings, but in actions which all share; they lead to vision, not of a quietistic interior sort, but to the real showing of God. In them all the soul's faculties are engaged; the rite is sacred art of great stylistic value: rich drama, deep symbolism hold individual and congregation. It puts the individual into a gripping and upraising circle of divine action, carries him up beyond himself. In this kind of piety the danger associated with lonely prayer, of sinking down to self-contemplation, the possibility of outward sacrifices becoming mere show are easier to avoid.

I emphasize again that here I am only picturing the type. It will be asked in reply: where in antiquity will you find such a pure phenomenon? My answer to this is, we can nowhere exactly reconstruct the religious life of the ancient world; there was every degree of religious attitude; the ideal we have pictured above was nowhere fully realized. Yet that is so because in most cases ancient culture remained bound to the worship of nature, and the mystery rites often became purely animal rites, simply repulsive to a spiritually-minded man. But none

---

[1]E.g. my article 'Mystery-Piety' *Bonner Zeitschrift für Theologie und Seelsorge* (1926, 101–117) p. 104. Historical material is completed in J.L.W. 6, (1926) 113–204). See also Chapter II, ii above and the literature given there. For the relationship of *mysterium* to art and social history see Ildefons Herwegen, *Kirche und Seele* (1926); *Christliche Kunst und Mysterium* (1929) and the articles of A. L. Mayer in J.L.W. 5, 80–96; 6, 68–97; 8, 67–127; 10, 77–141; 14, 123–171; 15, 67–154. Finally Johannes Pinsk, *Germanentum und Katholische Kirche*: Abendland 2, (1926) p. 360–362 and 3, (1927–8) p. 17–19.

of that can prevent us from recognizing in the mystery a type of high religious worth;[1] a worth, to be sure, which only received its full merit in Christianity. St Paul says of the rites of the Old Testament, 'the law held only the shadow of those blessings which were still to come, not the full expression of their reality'.[2] How much more true that is of antiquity. Yet an artist's first sketch is often of value to us in learning more about his finished composition.

Yet before we pass over to the full picture, I want to give a summary of the rich possible meanings which the word *mystery* had acquired in the ancient world; it will serve to make its Christian use more intelligible.[3] Mysteries are originally the secret celebrations and consecrations of the ancient mystery cults, the δρώμενα as a whole; next they are the individual parts and elements of the mysteries: thus the sacred λεγόμενα, the *symbola* and different formulas by which the initiates recognized each other (sacred pass); then they are δεικνύμενα the things shown, sacred objects in the *cista mystica*, symbolic and typical objects which were shown at the high point in the visionary rite, the food of the initiates, etc. All of these had holy dread about them and a fearsome command of silence for their protection.[4] The mystically directed philosophy uses the terminology of the mysteries to point up the divinity, the hidden element in the theological δόγματα. Thus mysteries especially in the visionary language of Plato, become the greatest and deepest doctrine about godhead; godhead itself is the primeval mystery, hiding itself in silence. When we speak of it at all we do so in symbols which cover as much as they disclose. Heraclitus says, 'the master at Delphi does not speak and does not conceal; he hints at things.'[5] With this symbolic language for the things of God goes allegory, not of the rationalist, Stoic kind, although it was happy to lay claim to this splendid garment, but the mystical, platonist one. The visible things of creation, the myths and sagas, the venerable rites whose meaning is now often lost to us are treated as symbols of

---

[1] Only as a *type* can the ancient mystery point to the Christian mystery, which reveals God's *agape*, since according to the myth a God is the Saviour of his cult followers. In the realm of religious consciousness the mystery belongs more to *eros*, the soul of the individual striving upwards to God. Cf Nygren, *Eros und Agape* (1930) 140 ff.

[2] Heb. 10, 1.

[3] Cf *Theol. Revue* 24 (1925) 41–47: J.L.W. 8, 225–232.

[4] Vow to silence under oath has been found recently in a papyrus: Cumont, *Un fragment de rituel d'initiation aux mystères*, *Harvard Theol. Review* 26 (1933) 151–160.*

[5] Diels Fr. 93.

theological wisdom. They point to the divine source which cannot be grasped or uttered in its wholeness. Theology becomes mystagogy, whose aim is to return to the primeval mystery. As such it remains ever connected in some way with worship, for it wills to be not simple abstraction, but the way to God. Theology and theurgy are part of the mystery.

The sober, practical religion of the Romans had neither concept nor word for mystery. It did possess a consecration to God, *devotio*, which was expressed particularly in oath-taking, above all the military one. This was called *sacramentum*. How easily an oath of this kind could be made into a kind of *mysterium*, a ritual obligation of the greatest force to the powers below is shown by Livy X, 38f, in his impressive picture of the oath recruits took in the 'Samnite legion' because of the flax about the place where they were sworn (*sacrata*). They were, as Livy says, initiated (*initiati*) according to the ancient rite of consecration (*ritu sacramenti*). The whole panoply of ritual was used; there were sacrifices and terrible oaths, so that the whole proceeding seemed more like initiation into a mystery than a military oath-taking; in particular he remarks on secret dedication (*occultum sacrum*) at the beginning, also of an oath of silence. This is clearly the beginning of the notion of *sacramentum* as consecration, mystery. This is even clearer in the report of Livy on the suppression of the cult of Bacchus by the Roman state in the year 186, when the consul in his accusation associates mysteries and military oath closely in the common term *sacramentum*: 'Do you imagine, citizens, that the young men who have been initiated with this rite (*hoc sacramento initiatos*) can be made soldiers?'[1]; how can the man who has been initiated take the sacred oath to the state? On the other hand Apuleius speaks of the military oath (*sacramentum*) which the *mystes* takes in the service of his God.[2] One sees the way which brought the word *sacramentum* into the terminology of the religious mysteries, a way full of meaning for Christian theology. Christians, even in the oldest translation of the Scripture, used the word *sacramentum* where μυστήριον could not be translated. So *sacramentum* took on the whole range of meaning μυστήριον had had. The whole ancient terminology passed into Christian usage, but in keeping with the higher spiritual level of the new religion it was made the bearer of higher and more

---

[1]Livy, Book XXXIX 15, 13; cf Reitzenstein, *Die hellenistische Mysterien-religionen* ed. 3 (1927) p. 192.
[2]Metamorphoses XI, 15.

spiritual concepts. The spiritualising process did not, however, lead to an evaporation of content; the word remained concrete, and kept its constant relationship to worship. The modern translation 'secret' in no way yields the deep, rich, concrete sense of the ancient word, but only on one side, mystic hiddenness, and this insufficiently. We recognize this immediately when we consider mystery in its Christian context, if only briefly.[1]

The last and supreme mystery of Christianity, the foundation and ultimate source of all Christian mysteries is the revelation of God in the incarnate *Logos*. God, who was hidden in timeless silence, advances into the world by a wonderful epiphany, showing himself in order to save mankind. This mystery is, therefore, an act, but an act which flows from God's depths and is therefore an endless plenitude of being. God 'made known to us the mystery of his will, according to the decision he took in Christ for the saving design in the fullness of the ages to sum up all things in Christ'.[2] St Paul has the task 'to illumine everyone as to what the design is of the mystery revealed from all ages in God, the creator of all things, so that the manifold wisdom of God may be made known to the principalities and powers through the church, according to the counsel of the ages which he took in Christ Jesus our Lord. . . .'[3] Here we see the Church brought into the mystery. St Paul praised God, 'who has power to set your feet firmly in the path of that gospel which I preach, when I herald Jesus Christ, a gospel which reveals the mystery, hidden from us through countless ages, but now made plain, through what the prophets have written; now published at God's eternal command, to all the nations so as to win the homage of their faith'.[4] John, without using the word mystery says the same thing: 'the Logos was made flesh and pitched his tent among us, and we had sight of his glory, glory such as belongs to the Father's only-begotten Son, full of grace and truth. . . . No one ever saw God; but now his only-begotten Son has himself become our interpreter.'[5] 'Life dawned; and it as eye-witnesses that we give you news of that life which ever abode with the Father and has dawned, now, on us.'[6] This everlasting life is Christ himself; therefore the epistle to the Colossians calls him the mystery: God's design to save is contained in the person of Jesus, and Christian being is: 'knowledge of the mystery of God, of Christ in whom are all

[1]Cf detailed presentation Ch II supra.
[2]Eph. 1, 9 ff.   [3]Ibid 3, 9 ff.   [4]Romans 16, 25 ff.
[5]Jn. 1, 14 and 18.   [6]I Jn. 1, 2.

the hidden treasures of wisdom and *Gnosis*'.[1] The epiphany of Jesus Christ in which godhood, manhood, heaven and earth, spirit and matter meet and unite, through which the holy Spirit came down to bring the world healing: this saving act of God is the real mystery for the Christian. 'The birth of Christ and the whole saving design, then, are one great sacrament, since in the visible man the divine majesty did that inwardly for our consecration which took place in a secret invisible fashion through its power. Therefore the incarnation is rightly called a mystery or sacrament.' Thus, in summary of patristic teaching, the monk of Corvey, Paschasius Radbert (860).[2] But the high-point of the whole saving drama is the death and crown of resurrection, when Christ entered the inmost heart of God in all his manhood, and found everlasting redemption. The pasch of the Lord, his death and exaltation is the mystery of redemption proper, the high-point of God's plan. The saved church comes out from it; the new covenant is built on it, the eternal covenant of Christ's blood. Upon it rests all salvation.

It is Christ's will that this spring should always be running in the church. Not just faith in the once dead prince is to save the faithful; his saving act is to be a continual, lasting, mystical and yet concrete presence in the church, from which the power of his blood is to flow daily to give life and healing to the faithful. The promise, 'I am with you all days until the end of the world'[3] is to be fulfilled not merely by the moral or spiritual protection of grace in abstract, but in a concrete yet Spirit-filled presence and objective nature. Therefore the Lord left behind him for his church not merely faith and Spirit but his mysteries; or rather, he ordained that the life of faith and grace should find continual new stimulus and expression in the church through the common celebration of the mysteries. The words of Christ, 'where two or three are gathered together in my name I am in the midst of them' were to be quite literally fulfilled.[4]

For this reason the Lord instituted the mystery as the last act of his life in this age. On the evening of his betrayal, in expectation of his dreadful passion and in the confidence of the victory which his obedience to the Father would bring, he gave to his disciples this mystical celebration of his redeeming deed: *tradidit corporis et sanguinis sui mysteria*

---

[1] Col. 2, 2: εἰς ἐπίγνωσιν τοῦ μυστηρίου τοῦ θεοῦ, Χρίστου. The vulgate *in agnitionem mysterii Dei Patris et Christi Jesu* completely destroys the sense.
[2] *Liber de Corpore et Sanguine Dui*, ch. 3. Migne PL 120, 1275 ff.
[3] Mt. 28, 20.
[4] Mt. 18, 20.

celebranda.[1] The bread becomes his body, the chalice his blood; the body is offered in sacrifice, the blood flows as the sacrificial blood of the new covenant: clear, symbolic yet real presentation of the death of Christ. The mystical bread and the mystical wine are at once food and drink for life; yet life can only come out of that death which leads to resurrection. Even the invitation, 'do this in memory of me', shows that the Lord did not die for ever, but lives on. In the mystery marvellous things are joined: death and life, pain and blessedness, human sorrow, and the delight which only God knows. Through death to this age he leads the way to everlasting salvation and the riches of the age to come. This sacred rite with its full divine content is what the disciples are to 'act in memory'; they are to make real again the passion of their divine master. As the church grew out of the Lord's blood, she is to live and grow in his strength. Still in heaven with his Father, each day he wills to sacrifice himself with her fighting and suffering on earth, wills to celebrate his death with her in the world by a mystical and symbolic act, and so to waken her to a new life, in and with God. Christ has given his mystery to the church's care; she acts it out, and thereby fulfils his action, which has become hers. So Christ and the church become one in act and passion: the mystery is made a new and eternal covenant. The saving act continues and is crowned in the oneness of everlasting love, until the symbol comes to an end and only the pure reality shows itself to the seeking eye in eternity.

From the mystery of redemption flow the other mysteries as does all grace; the cross which overcame sin and death, gave everlasting life. First there is baptism, a mystical-real sharing in the Lord's death for this world of sin and his new life for God. It is completed and fulfilled by anointing with the new, supernatural principle of life, the *pneuma Christi*. By this every Christian becomes a true Χριστός, an anointed one, who now has a share in the spirit of God: θείας κοινωνοὶ φύσεως.[2] As Christ is by his nature Spirit ('the Lord is pneuma'[3]) and has revealed himself in glory since the resurrection, so, too, the Christian, risen in baptism, has a real share in the divine Spirit by grace. He carries the seal of Christ, the supernatural likening to the Lord through grace; the new life is nourished and strengthened in the Spirit by the eucharist, the Spirit's food. The Christian's initiation is carried out in these three

[1]Roman Canon on Holy Thursday: 'He gave the mystery of the body and blood to his disciples, for them to celebrate.'
[2]II Peter 1, 3.
[3]II Cor. 3, 17.

mysteries. Washing, anointing, and food bring him to his Christian's fulness. As a mature Christian, he can actively participate, taking his share in the offering, celebrating it with Christ. For all the anointed are a 'holy, royal, priesthood, appointed to make offering in the Spirit, to please God through Jesus Christ'.[1] How the mystery develops among the various conditions of life and situations, cannot be gone into here.[2] All the church's blessing and consecrations are a communication from the cross, or in liturgy, a redemptive grace proceeding from the mystery of the mass. St Leo the Great writes:[3] 'thy cross is the spring of all blessing, the cause of all graces. Through the cross power is given to him who believes in place of weakness, glory in place of shame, life in place of death. Now the variety of fleshly sacrifices is ended; all the many sacrificial gifts lead up to fulfilment in the one offering of thy body and blood. For thou art the true lamb of God, who puts out the world's sin; thou dost fulfil all mysteries. As there is now one sacrifice for all the sacrificial gifts, there is now only one kingdom, formed of all peoples.'

When Leo says the crucified Lord is the 'fulfiller of all mysteries', of the typical sacrifices and rites of the Old Testament, that is true in a sense of the ancient mysteries. They, too, as the fathers and St Augustine in particular say of the heathen sacrifices, were shadows, if misleading ones, of the true mystery to come. We can understand, then, that the fathers with advancing clarity discover the true mystery in Christianity and seek in some way to express divine truth by using the terminology of the mysteries, (purified and raised), for the Christian rites. Cyprian talks of *dominicae passionis et nostrae redemptionis sacramentum*:[4] the mystery of the Lord's passion, at the same time the mystery of our redemption. And there he merely summarizes clearly the meaning of what was taught before him. But from the 3rd century onwards this teaching is always clearer, expressed in greater detail and better formed in the liturgy; we have not space for more details here.[5]

And really what the ancient world longed for but only attained in so shadowy and imperfect a form is now fulfilled by Christ's coming in grace, fulfilled in an over-powering fashion; it is so wonderful that men

[1] I Peter 2, 5.
[2] Cf II, i above.
[3] Sermo VIII *de Passione Domini*, PL 54, 339 ff.
[4] Epistle 63, 14.
[5] A detailed collection of the most important texts in my *Das Mysteriengedächtnis der Messliturgie* J.L.W. 6, p. 113 ff and 13, p. 99 ff.*

can have had no inkling of it. This is the point where divine love and divine life come down upon the poor earth, take a share in the poverty of mankind, overcome sin which has once more brought chaos into the world, create the sacrificial deed to conquer worlds by the death of an incarnate God, restore the oneness of God and man, heal and glorify the creature. Out of the blood of the dying God-man and the glory of his transforming light (δόξα) eternal salvation flows, divine life for those who belong to him. All of this was at work in the new alliance, the *ecclesia*, in the vast simplicity of her Spirit-informed rites filled with symbolism and reality beyond the scope of worlds. In this form the noblest possession of mankind's religious strivings was concentrated, purified from animal and sordid elements, given shape in the school of Greek aesthetic teaching, the breath of oriental mysticism upon it, and ennobled by its service of God. Its content was totally new: the gift of divine grace: *de tuis donis ac datis*.[1]

The best of the ancient world did service to Christendom. The service was extremely desirable; in Christianity the mystery-type gained a wholly new meaning. The sacrificial service of the old alliance was done away with, or better, fulfilled with the sacrifice of Christ. With this came the new age: the old was past. In the Church of the new alliance there could only be one sacrifice, the sacrifice of Christ. If it was to act through the centuries, it could only do so by its mystical presence in the sacrament, *in mysterio*, in the worship of the Church which the new alliance had made. In the mystery, Christ lives in the Church, acts in her and with her, preserves and enlivens her. In the mystery we too already breathe the air of the coming age of God's Kingdom and have our conversation in humble faith. For the mystery is the mystery of faith; faith alone grasps the *virtus sacramenti*, the grace contained in the mystery. When faith passes over into vision, the veil of the mystery will fall and we shall see the godhead it contains.

The sacred rites belong to this veil. Antiquity shared in its creation, and so has deserved of Christ; without the form there would be no knowledge of its content. Thus, Hellenism wins a God-given meaning for the whole history of the world.

Clement of Alexandria, the great scholar and Hellenist, said that through the Logos the whole world had become Greek; he once compared the ancient mysteries with those of Christ (his first thoughts were on the spiritual vision, but the symbolic action in worship came in too).

[1] 'Of thy gifts and presents', Roman Canon.

He saw in paganism only deep shadows, after which light rose which he greeted, full of happiness: χαῖρε νέον φῶς: welcome, new light![1] But those shadowy contours helped him in some way to express the new, inexpressible wonders:[2] 'O marvellous, holy, mysteries, O pure light. By torch-light I shall be brought to see heaven and God. I shall be made holy by the consecration. The Lord is heirophant: he brings the initiates to the light and puts his seal upon them. He presents the believers to the Father, that they may be kept for eternity. This is the thunder of my mysteries. When you wish, you may be initiated; then you will join the circle of angels which surrounds the unbegotten, unchanging, the only God; God's Logos will be our guide.'

[1]Firmicus Maternus, *De Errore profanum religionum*, 19, turns the mystery formula, 'hail, bridegroom, hail young light', on Christ: 'There is one light, one true bridegroom whose name Christ has kept.'

[2]*Protrepticus* 124, O. Stählin I, p. 84 cf there the whole passage which is clearly inspired by the *Bacchae* of Euripides.

4

THE CHURCH'S SACRED YEAR*

With every first Sunday of Advent we begin another church year. The cycle begins anew, and starts from the beginning. Is its only meaning didactic? Repetition, they say, is the mother of all learning. We have, perhaps, not drawn the value out of the old year sufficiently; does not the church therefore give us occasion to live through the whole once more? Of course this motive is present; the church knows how to teach. We are to go on celebrating the same events, so long as life lasts, exhausting the whole content of the church year and making it our own. What was neglected last year can be made up in this, the gaps filled in. And when we have lived all to its full we can still deepen what we have won and come to know. Like a path which goes round and up a mountain, slowly making the ascent to the height, we are to climb the same road at a higher level, and go on until we reach the end, Christ himself.

But didactic reasons alone cannot exhaust the meaning of return and cycle in the church's year. For we imperfect men are not properly its bearers: rather in it we join a higher sphere of action. The real actor in the church year is the mystical Christ, the glorified Lord Jesus, together with his bride the church, who in her inmost being is with him in heaven already. John has seen her: 'the holy city of New Jerusalem, come down from heaven and from God, ready like a bride adorned for her husband.'[1] St Paul in his letter to the Galatians calls her 'the Jerusalem above, the free woman who is our Mother'.[2] The fathers, therefore, speak of 'the church of heaven' (Tertullian for example, *On Baptism*, 15: *una ecclesia in caelis*.) And where else can the bride be except where her bridegroom is, at God's right hand? 'God has called us to life in company with Christ, raised us up and put us at his right hand in Jesus Christ.'[3] This *ecclesia*, bound up so intimately with her Lord does not celebrate the mystery in a negligent or half-awake fashion. She has his own strength and power; he is present in the fullness of these mysteries. The Church whose head towers into eternity, while

[1] Apoc. 21, 2.   [2] Gal. 4, 26.   [3] Eph. 2, 5 ff.

63

part of the body remains on earth—its still imperfect members—has no need of the continual change which is a characteristic of physical nature. Nature is always in flux, always changing: things rise and fall, are brought to birth and perish. But Christ and his church stand above nature, in the realm of abiding Spirit; they do not require continual flow and change; the phrase 'church-year' should not lead us to bring naturalistic notions into the realm of God.[1]

When, therefore, the church speaks of a 'year' or as the ancients did of a yearly cycle (*anni circulus*) it is in connexion with other ideas. The circle for the ancients is precisely the opposite of all development: as something completely round it is the symbol of eternity, of God. In the circle there is no before or after, no greater or less; it contains the highest point of likeness and oneness. The circle has neither beginning nor end. It returns upon itself and stretches out to all directions; it is the deepest rest and the highest exercise of power. The circle is, then, an image of life, but of life without development, without growth; of eternal life and fullness (πληρῶμα). Circle and sphere are the sensible images of eternal perfection. The sacred course of the liturgy is to speak of eternity not of nature, which comes, blooms, puts forth its fruit, then fades and dies. So there is no dying in the church year, only life, even in the way through death. Nature has a shadowy eternity in her capacity to come back to life after fading and sinking away; but death always comes again; how short the bloom is, how long the dying and the death. There is no winter in the church's year; if in spite of that, it starts up again, circle forming on circle this constant return is meant to suggest the divine quality of the mystery. St Ambrose in his morning hymn calls Christ, 'the true day which shines on day, the true Sun which casts everlasting splendour'. Christ is therefore the day which is splendid with the light that knows no evening, as the Greek liturgy says.[2] Christ is also the true year, whilst the world's day is the *aion*, or rather, Christ is the Lord of all the ages (αἰῶνα).[3] This is so not because he perpetually renews himself, like natural light, but because

---

[1] This does not mean a rejection of natural symbolism which, on the contrary, has great meaning for the church. But it is to be noted that the earliest fathers see in the change of the seasons not an expression of natural life, but a symbol of resurrection. Therefore on tombs in the catacombs we often find the four seasons. The same picture had a completely different meaning in ancient painting.

[2] Φῶς ἀνέσπερον.

[3] Cf I Tim. 1, 17 where it is said of God: 'to the King of ages, immortal, invisible, only God: honour and glory in age of ages.'

he is light and life without winter, darkness or decline. Christ saves spirits; he is the saints' light in heaven; in the church year on earth he gives us a mystical reflection of his own everlasting day with God.

In heaven the glorified Lord is the very content of eternal life for all the saints; on earth his mystery is the spring of the church's life. They live seeing; we walk in faith. We do not see the Lord in glory but possess him already in faith and in the mysteries which he gave to the church on leaving her. The church year is therefore the mystery of Christ.

As the uninterrupted sun Christ shines in heaven; 'that city needs neither sun nor moon, because the glory of the Lord shines upon it and the Lamb is its brilliant light'[1] so the light of Christ shines upon us through the symbols of the mysteries. Therefore St Ambrose addresses Christ: 'I find thee in thy mysteries.'[2]

The mysteries of Christ, however, have a special two-sided character of their own. In themselves they are divine, supernatural, Spiritual; yet they mirror temporal action. We live the Lord's year in this world, have here experience of his birth, growth, maturity, suffering and death. His resurrection and upraising to the Father's right hand truly take us across into the kingdom of God. But the second coming, the last entrance of Christ into the world (παρουσία) is an event in time; at that point the glorified Lord will show himself for the first and only time to the whole world; that will be the last moment of succession in time.

In any case the church year contains so much of the Lord's earthly life, that since the end of the late middle ages it has been taken as a spiritual participation and contemplation of that life.

Would this still be a mystery? It would be a moral sharing in the life and feeling of Jesus, but no mystical, oneness with Christ the Kyrios in the order of being, not the oneness which, according to his teaching and that of his apostles, is the aim and meaning of Christian life. We should not be plunged into his Spirit, into God's eternal life. If that life has its rôle in the church's year, then the year must have another meaning.

It is not that common life and consciousness with Christ are excluded; the church reads to us from the gospels for us to consider, weigh and imitate. But because she knows that our own thinking can never lead to the heart of God, that our prayer lacks wings to take it up unless it is carried by God's Spirit, she plunges all the moral meanings into this Spirit.

[1] Apoc. 21, 22   [2] *Apologia Prophetae David*, 58

Christ comes to us in two ways which are really only one. There is a Christ of history and a Christ of faith; but the two are one: it would be dangerous to regard only the one or the other. Jesus, a man living in time, could not redeem us; the Christ we see in the mysteries alone would move in a breathless air. Our redemption rests upon the fact that God has really appeared in the flesh and that this man is the Son of God and *Kyrios*, glorified at the Father's right hand. The Christ of history was born as a man, lived in Galilee and Judaea and the streets of Jerusalem, prayed and struggled on the Mount of Olives, died on Golgotha. The glorified Christ, in Spirit rose, awakened, and went up to the Father; thence he sends his own Spirit, dwells, an invisible powerful presence in the church and in every man who has faith, is baptized, and has love.

The man Jesus has risen up to a name above all names, through all of this: he was crushed in the flesh of sin, bore the form of a servant, was obedient to death; he became *Kyrios, pneuma*. He is, then, the same Lord who walked unnoticed and persecuted through the fields of Palestine and at last ended his time like a criminal on the cross; now he rules the world as King and the church is his bride. All his life, beginning in the Virgin's womb, is the great mystery of salvation, hidden from eternity in God and now revealed in the *ecclesia*. The deeds of his lowliness in that life on earth, his miserable death on Calvary appear now in a wholly different, light, God's own light; they are his acts, revealed, streaming with his light.

This life of the *Kyrios*, this great course from the Virgin's womb and the manger to the throne of his majesty on high, this mystery, is what we in the church share. The great facts of redemption are for us to celebrate and possess, not merely heartfelt considerations of our Lord's earthly life in all its details, and an imitation of it. A person without baptism could do that: a Christian and a Catholic celebrates the mystery of Christ.

And celebrate he does in a wholly concrete, immediate fashion, vast, divine. It is not thoughts of our own devising we are to think—how powerless we are before the acts of God—but thoughts to which the Spirit gives power; nor do they come in simple acts of illumination and special gifts of grace, but in the same Spirit's objective reality. The liturgical mysteries represent the saving acts of Christ to us, from incarnation to eternal rulership in living, concrete reality, yet in a manner telling of God their spiritual source: it is from the Saviour's own spring we drink. We who are not yet in glory, who still are in pain beneath the burden of sin, can go the way of redemption with the humbled Christ for company, die to sin. Christ has made his way present in the mystery, a saving way. Christ's phrase, 'I am the way'[1] is realised here in the deepest fashion. He does not merely point the way to us, he is the way; he carries us forward to the goal. His birth is now no longer an unimportant birth in Bethlehem, the idyll of the crib which so many took it for, but a serious event of poverty and lowliness, illumined, of course, with the light of divine love and greatness. The *mysterium* shows this birth as the burning appearance of God in flesh to redeem and heal the world, to unite heaven and earth. His death is now no longer the terrible, tortured dying on the horrid wood, a criminal's execution, but the sacrificial death of the god-man, the public service of the one high priest, the Son's devotedness in bringing the only sacrifice worthy of the Father, from which all life was to flow out on the sinful world: the spring of resurrection.

So the mystery reveals to us the real meaning of Christ's saving deeds in time. It takes none of the concreteness from them, but rather places them in their real, divine context, shows them to be a part of God's saving plan, hidden from eternity revealed now in time, and flowing back into eternity. 'Through the man Christ, to Christ, God.' This great theme of St Augustine takes shape in the mysteries: man is the way and God the end. History shows itself as the carrying out of God's design and its return into eternity.

When, therefore, the church year celebrates historical occurrences and developments, it does not do so for its own sake but for that of eternity hid within it. The great deed of God upon mankind, the redeeming work of Christ which wills to lead mankind out of the narrow bounds of time into the broad spaces of eternity, is its content.

Yet this content is not a gradual unfolding in the sense that the year of nature naturally develops: rather there is a single divine act which demands and finds gradual accustoming on men's part, though in itself complete. When the church year fashions and forms a kind of unfolding of the mystery of Christ, that does not mean it seeks to provide historical drama, but that it will aid man in his step by step approach to God, an approach first made in God's own revelation. It is the entire saving mystery which is before the eyes of the church and the Christian, more concretely on each occasion. We celebrate Advent, not by putting

[1] Jn. 14, 16.

ourselves back into the state of unredeemed mankind, but in the certainty of the Lord who has already appeared to us, for whom we must prepare our souls; the longing of ancient piety is our model and master. We do not celebrate Lent as if we had never been redeemed, but as having the stamp of the Cross upon us, and now only seeking to be better conformed to the death of Christ, so that the resurrection may be always more clearly shown upon us.

It is, therefore, always the glorified *Kyrios* whom we have in our spiritual vision, even when we call out, 'Thou who dost sit at the Father's right hand, have mercy upon us'. The whole church year is, therefore, a single mystery. Its high-point is mystery in the highest sense, the *sacramentum paschale*, the sacrificial mystery which is brought to us again each Sunday. There the redemption, which reaches its height in the sacrifice of the Cross and the glory of the church which goes from that resurrection, are mystically carried out and brought to the faithful. In the course of time this celebration of the paschal mystery has been extended from Septuagesima to Pentecost. Of course there is, especially in this season, a rich unfolding of the mystery for us to observe, one which in greatest part is connected with the historical acts of Jesus' life. But nonetheless it is not a sort of dramatisation of Christ's earthly life. This is clear since throughout it is the whole mystery which takes place in the mass; the mysterium is always whole.

Out of the paschal mystery, which in the first age of liturgy was the one ruling motif, there developed the epiphany, for which Advent (*adventus*: ἐπιφανεία) prepares us even today, although the Christmas feast has now been placed before it. The showing, epiphany, includes Christmas but is more than the feast of Christ's birth. Again, it is the entire redemptive mystery, seen under the view-point of the incarnation. When God takes flesh, he consecrates it. Is there, then, a proper mystery of the incarnation, as there is of Christ's death? No. We celebrate the culmination of epiphany, too, by the memorial of Christ's death: redemption was first finished upon the cross. Because the world lay in sin, it had first to be quit of this burden. Epiphany is, therefore, the entire mystery of redemption, seen from another vantage point: the Lord only became man, as the Scripture and the fathers teach us, in order to die on the cross, so to give back to the Father mankind which was dead through sin. 'When he came into the world he said, sacrifice and gifts thou wouldst not have; but a body hast thou readied for me. There was no good pleasure in thy eyes for burnt offerings.

Then I said, look, I come—thus it is written of me in the book—to do thy will.'[1]

The mystery of the church's year is one. Does not this emphasis on unity then take away the attractiveness of variety which never leaves the spirit weary but informs and stimulates it continually? No; unity does not mean uniformity. The more single an idea is, the deeper it is and the more powerfully it fills the mind: so the fullness of its conception seeks an outlet in a variety of rites. The mass is always the high-point of liturgy, because it contains the mystery of redemption in its source, the passion and resurrection of Jesus. But from the source a mighty stream of mysteries flows into the Church's ground, and on its banks the Spirit's Word forms ever new pictures in the liturgy, to clothe and express the rites. The words of Scripture and the liturgy are no mere human words, which arose in a merely human mind and pass on, like a breath of wind, without a trace. The Word of God is full of the power of God. 'As snow falls from heaven and rain as well, and returns not, but the earth drinks it down, and grows fruitful and green, so is it with my word which leaves my mouth: it comes not back to me empty. It carries out what I will, goes the way whither I send it.'[2] The Word takes part in the active power of the mysteries. 'Sacrament is also the divine writings where the Holy Spirit acts inwardly by the quickening word,' says Paschasius Radbert.[3] In the word, too, there is a divine presence. 'We would hear the gospel, the Lord present,'[4] says St Augustine, and this was the reason why the congregation stood at the reading of the gospel. 'The Abbot should read the gospel aloud while all stand in reverence,'[5] St Benedict writes. St Jerome is not afraid of putting the mystery of the Holy Scripture immediately after that of the eucharist: we eat his flesh and drink his blood not only in the mystery but in the reading of scripture.[6] In an old sermon for the Annunciation we read, 'the coming of our Lord and Saviour . . . is celebrated by the church in the whole world, and its yearly return brings it great joy; for what the world of believers once came to know when its salvation came, has hallowed the feast for the world which came after, throughout all generations. . . . Now, therefore, the miracle

---

[1]Heb. 10, 5–7; Ps. 39, 7–9.
[2]Is. 55, 10 f.
[3]*De Corpore et Sanguine Domini* 3, PL 120, 1276; cf J.L.W. 8, 207.
[4]*Tract. in Joan*, 30, 1.
[5]*Regula* Ch. 11.
[6]Cf passages in J.L.W. 8, 210 f.

of the past is put before our eyes when the godly readings tell us year by year of things past, and these are piously celebrated in yearly recurrence.'[1]

From this presence of the God-man's acts in *Logos* and *ritus* it becomes clear, too, how the church, although she always possesses the whole of the mystery of Christ, can still, on certain days when a definite aspect of it is brought into the light, sing, 'to-day': at Christmas, 'to-day Christ is born'; Epiphany, 'to-day the heavenly bridegroom is joined to the church'; Easter, 'this is the day the Lord has made'; Pentecost, 'to-day the *pneuma* appeared to the disciples in fire'. The entire holy year is an image of the eternal design of God, contains the mystery of Christ; within this circle the mystery unfolds to the Vision that cannot yet see the whole as it is in the world to come. As the entire year carries in it a divine presence, the individual day within this cycle takes up once more the saving event which once sanctified it.[2] While the visible symbols give expression, by their abiding sameness, to the mystery's oneness, the lighter, more mobile word can make present its variety and fullness. We celebrate mass each day as a whole redemptive mystery; yet, in the divine Word, it is the incarnation which is present at Christmas and Epiphany, the suffering and up-raising of Christ which is present to us at Easter. Always it is God present, not mere human reflections, which is the meaning of the mystery. How otherwise could St Benedict tell his monks, 'let us await the Pasch with the joy of the Spirit's longing.'[3] The mystery of worship is presence then, not in the bonds of time, but in the freedom of God and his Spirit.

When the man who has been knit into the church celebrates the mystical year with her, his mother, as a true mystery, all the truth it contains becomes his own; what Elizabeth said to Mary is fulfilled: 'blessed is she who has believed; for the things said to her by the Lord shall have their fulfilment.'[4]

[1] Perhaps by Proclus of Constantinople. Printed among the works of St Leo: PL 54, 580.
[2] Cf e.g. the hymn for Christmas: ' "This present day" (*hic* not *sic!* is the older reading) shows, as the cycle of the year returns, that thou hast come as the world's salvation.'
[3] Regula Ch. 49.
[4] Lk. 1, 45.

5

THE CHURCH'S SACRED DAY

As the year is an image of the life of man and of mankind and thus of sacred history, each day too, with its rising of light and life, its growth to zenith and descent to sleep, forms an image which can serve as framework and symbol of the mystery of Christ. As Christ's sacrificial death is the climax of the world's history, mass is the climax of the day. In the church's year the *Logos* explains and expands the paschal mystery; in a single day the office clothes and comments on the mass: the office is the prayer which the Church puts round about the sacrifice.

The highest acts of every religion are prayer and sacrifice. The more spiritual a religion, the higher and more spiritual its concept and vision of these things. The exterior material sacrifices of Jews and pagans had an external, ritual prayer: the more pure, deep and inward, the more spiritual this prayer, the higher the notion of sacrifice which will accompany it. The more man sought to approach God in prayer with a real submission of mind, the less that prayer was lip-service and external form; it became a real call to God from the soul's depths, or a conversation with him.[1] To the extent that this took place, the accompanying sacrifice became a full and selfless gift to God and the community. Thus prayer came more and more to correspond to its ideal, while on the other hand sacrifice, 'gift made to God', fulfilled its task of expressing the inner devotion of the will to God; the two drew near and were formed into one: sacrifice became, in a deeper sense than had been known before, the high-point of the life of prayer.

The spiritualising of the notion of sacrifice brought a danger with it. If the essence of sacrifice is the inward adherence to God, perhaps it would be better to do away with all external and exterior acts, and have only the pure devotion of the mind in prayer. This conclusion was drawn by many circles of pious pagans at the time Christianity was growing, in late antiquity, and by many Jews, too; all external, visible

[1]'Prayer is bold, a conversation with God,' Clement of Alexandria, *Stromata* VIII, 39, 6; cf also 42, 1, 49, 1.

worship was to fall away, or be confined to common prayer, which themselves could be just as well or better performed by the individual, recollected, undisturbed by the world about him. The danger came that the whole of worship would go inside man, that all religion would end as unbridled individualism and subjectivism, revolving round men rather than God.

In this as in everything else, Christianity gave its approval to all the excellence which the ages before Christ had discovered; still it remained infinitely superior to any non-Christian religion. It recognised of course that the external, material rites of pagan and Jewish ages were to be done away with in the new covenant. Now there was to be only a 'sacrifice in Spirit': an expression which is still preserved by the *oblatio rationabilis*, the λογική θυσία of the Oriental liturgy. Yet this spiritual sacrifice is equated with the sacrifice of the mass, that is, with an external, liturgical celebration carried out by priest and people in concert and bound up with the rite of bread and wine. In spite of that, there is nothing external or material mixed up in it. For behind the visible, objective action is a wholly spiritual reality: the person of Christ, the Word incarnate, who, under the veil of mystical figures, presents his loving act of devotion to the Father in dying. The community joins with his sacrifice, its self and consciousness filled with the Spirit of God, and inspired by it, and completes with him a wholly spiritual sacrifice to God. Objectivity and personal sharing are joined in a loving unity: objectivity is made spiritual and inward; subjectivity finds a firm and changeless hold on the divine action of Christ which raises a man's action to himself and first gives it power and meaning. The vine gives the sap of life to the shoots; in this strength they can bring out rich fruit.

The act of Christ in the Christian sacrifice consists in his presenting once more his act of sacrifice and redemption beneath the veil of symbols; the share of the faithful expresses itself in the co-sacrifice, especially in the prayer which surrounds the sacrifice; therefore the *eucharistia* plays so important a rôle in the mass, particularly in the Canon, a greater one than prayer otherwise had in the sacrifice of the ancients; the relationship between sacrifice and prayer in Christianity is given deep and telling expression. Both elements are intimately joined, so much so that the elements themselves have kept the name of the prayer of thanks said over them, and are called 'the eucharist'. The objective act of Christ and the concomitant act of the congregation sharing in his experience, his thanks, his praise and his sacrifice form together the Christian eucharist, the prayer of sacrifice, the high-point of Christian worship.

All about this climax, in smaller and greater circles group the other prayers, like smaller peaks on the slopes of the highest one. First of all come the prayers of the mass with the chants, and in some measure the lessons as well. Then there is the whole day office of the church, which we are to treat in this Chapter, the gold setting for the jewel of the sacrifice. Its first business, of course, is to give countenance and place to this sacrifice; but it is also lovely and valuable of itself. Another example from art will make the relationship even clearer. There are paintings which present simple landscape and atmosphere with such an intensity that some tiny figures are required to give the moving eyes a place of rest, or perhaps they serve simply to give the painting a name and make it more amenable to the public. In other pictures the action depicted so dominates the whole that the background seems to have no weight at all. Still other works have figures and background completely in harmony; the surrounding puts the figure into a proper frame, while the figures give the whole composition greater value: the line which starts up in the actors continues, so to speak, in the trees, buildings, and other natural features, and comes to rest in them; they for their part find completion in the main persons of the picture. Undoubtedly this last is a good solution of the artistic problem, and the church has constructed mass and office on this plan. The vast and monumental ideas which are hidden and silent in the sacrificial action, and which the canon seeks to express, continue in the office and are, so to speak, resolved into the spectral colours. Much that could only be hinted at in the centre shows itself in various places, and is submitted to loving contemplation. The course of salvation's advance in the old alliance, the preparations for the appearance of the Saviour, the incarnate Christ, his teaching, suffering, death and resurrection, his mystical continuance in the church, the sufferings and glory of the martyrs and other saints, the march forward of the saving work in church and individual—in brief, the mysteries of God's saving design and grace—are all depicted lovingly and presented in daily prayers, and these again find their crown and finish in the sacramental mystery of the altar; all the rich, varied lines converge upon the sacrifice and broken colours go back to a splendid shining unity.

So the office moves, as it were, about a firm pole, the presence and display in ritual of the great event which is the heart of the Christian thing: redemption through incarnation, death and resurrection. The prayer of the office shares in the sacramental value of the act of sacrifice, and is raised to the latter's objective worth. All the church's prayer and all the prayer of each man becomes the prayer of Christ. Christ's Spirit, the Holy Spirit, carries up the congregation's prayer on strong wings and gives it a divine worth which it would never have of itself. It becomes a real prayer 'in the name of Jesus', to which the Lord himself has promised sure fulfilment.[1] 'The man who abides in me as I do in him shall bear much fruit; without me you can do nothing. . . . If you remain in me and my words in you, you can ask what you will: it shall be done for you.'[2]

This truth, that the church's prayer is not, however exalted, merely the prayer of an isolated soul, but prayer with Christ, as intimate as the bride's conversation with the bridegroom, as the body's connection with its head, must be taken as a firm principle, if we would really understand the character and meaning of the office. The church prays; but in her the Spirit prays with unspeakable groaning.[3] The church makes petition, thinks and grows in consciousness, from the Spirit of Christ; it creates not merely human thoughts and feelings, or rather it brings them forth purified in the blood of Christ, glorified with the splendour of Christ. Of this prayer, too, St Paul's saying holds good: 'I live, no, no longer I, but Christ lives in me.'[4] All her words carry the mark of Christ her saviour, and are fashioned after him; all have passed through the atmosphere of his Spirit, and have a divine odour about them. All, therefore, have a meaning and a breadth which ranges high beyond every human meaning.

Upon this teaching rests a method of both practice and selection in liturgical prayer which is of very great importance, that of spiritual interpretation. The method is well-known; our Lord employed it, after his resurrection, after his exaltation to *Kyrios* and *Pneuma*. He 'interpreted the sense of scripture concerning himself'.[5] It was expanded by the apostles and fathers of the church. But it has a perhaps even more important place in the liturgy; of course biblical and liturgical allegory are often in harmony, as to method and object; their great principle is the same. But the liturgy, by selection and placing, and giving a point of view to the texts, gives new and special material to the allegory: it lends it new bloom, freshness and variety.

[1] Jn. 16, 23.   [2] Jn. 15, 5 and 7.   [3] Rom. 8, 26.
[4] Gal. 2, 20.   [5] Lk. 24, 27.

Allegory (ἀλληγορία) comes from the verb ἀλληγορεῖν (ἄλλος and ἀγορεύειν). It means to say something other than what is directly expressed; a second meaning is there beside the plain sense of the words, and must be attended to. Allegory in religion rests on the view that the divinely inspired author, or the inspirer himself, spoke in this hidden way, partly in consideration for human weakness and lack of development, partly because of the impossibility of expressing the things of God in human language; in this way more is shown to deep vision than a superficial view would indicate. The spiritual sense towers above the literal one; its high places are not open to everybody. Only gradually does the light of later events and revelations bring this sense into view; but when this happens, the words gain a royal splendour, and point to the peaks where God's thoughts are. The Old Testament in particular was the object of this allegorical interpretation. The fathers, with the light of faith to guide them, saw everywhere—in the law, the prophets, the acts of Old Testament kings and saints here more clearly, there less— the figure of Jesus, glowing in the half-darkness, until it emerges in the gospel's brightness. What the ancients gradually and wearily came to was as clear as noon-day when the world's own light shone: the keys to all mysteries were in Christ; when this unfailing instrument, the key of David, is put to the explaining of scripture, the whole beauty, depth and clarity of Christian allegory is seen for what it really is in the liturgy. Its heart is the redeeming work of Christ and everything we read and pray in these texts points to that. All of them open their deepest secrets; all become a hymn to Christ which the church sings. As the bride speaks of her lover, sometimes openly, sometimes in hidden approaches to meaning, the church sings, and the soul with her, of the bridegroom from heaven; at one time she uses the clear words of dogmatic formulae, at another mysterious images and poetry, the speech of love, which show only their depth and beauty to the initiate. The fate of mankind, the sacred history of the Old Testament as it is delivered in the lessons, gain its full meaning because the Son of God, mediator between God and man, appears as its centre, high point and end; in him the world and time find fulfilment. So Christ reveals himself in the liturgy as the Lord of all time, ruler of the earth, 'King of kings, Lord of lords',[1] as the leader of the people of God to everlasting salvation: he is God-man; only God-man could do all this.

Christ and the church: this is the content of the liturgy throughout,

[1]Apoc. 19, 16.

and so the content of the church's office—Christ, the God-man, the Saviour who showed himself to be the end and purpose with the words, 'I am the way, the truth and the life'.[1] The church, not the casual sum of Christians now alive, but the sacred communion of all who go to the Father through Christ, all who bear within themselves the Holy Spirit, and whom grace makes perfect like our Father in heaven: one sacred body, unified and enlivened by the breath of life, the *pneuma*; one supernatural dwelling house of stones, chosen for variety and beauty, and joined together, the stones dependent one upon another, make up a work of art. This church is not only content, but subject of the liturgy: it is the church which prays in the office.

This gives us the deepest ground for the 'givenness', the objectivity of liturgy we have so often spoken of before. When the bride, filled with the Holy Spirit, prays with Christ, her head and bridegroom, this is no prayer of individuals casually come together, but a prayer in the spirit of God and therefore in the spirit of truth received; it is the prayer in which the communion of all Christ's members join. That all of this aids the deepest and most personal conscious life rather than hindering it, is obvious; we shall come back to the consideration of this fact.

Considered in this way, the church not only stretches far beyond all national boundaries of one age, but from the beginning of the world to the end, from penitent Adam the just man, to the last saint at the world's end. All pray and work in the building of our liturgy. There are times when it grows in a lively fashion, springs up, when life in the Spirit of Christ and the body is so strong that it creates a forceful artistic expression for itself; the first centuries particularly were an age of this kind. There are other ages which have been less fresh, less rich; they keep the truth and goodness they have inherited, cultivate and hand them on. In no case is it 'historicism' on the church's part when she holds fast to the ancient and traditional fashion of her worship; rather, this love of what she has received comes from her very nature, from the timeless personality which we have seen, belongs to her; in a fashion she shares God's everlastingness. The church does not belong to yesterday; she need not be always producing novelties; she has treasures which never grow old. Therefore she is happy with tradition. Men, creatures of a single day, can come and go, with no joy in antiquity; the church can wait. Other generations will come to be grateful for her conservatism.

[1]Jn. 14, 6.

When, therefore, the church of our time makes her celebration one of rigid pattern this follows from her loyalty to tradition and a love for real value which rests upon her everlastingness. The deepest realism, however, rests not on a mere adherence to traditional forms, but in the mind of Christ and the church, which reaches beyond all individuals. The discipline of the church, of course, prefers to hold fast to the rites and texts which were created in Christian antiquity, and does so in the belief that those ancient times created what they did with a peculiarly high awareness of the church's mind. Realism and a sense of form here protect not merely inner reality: exterior discipline serves inward order and proceeds from it.

It is characteristic of the church that every individual group, a part of the body, and under the one head forms in its own time and place the image of the whole church; the whole church is in that place, by virtue of the small group's presence. St Cyprian writes in his *de Unitate Ecclesiae*, 'the office of bishop is one; individuals have such a share in it that each possesses the whole'.[1] There are, then, many bishops in the catholic church, yet their office has the mark of unity; their number brings no diversity into the church. So it is too, with the whole community. Where one congregation is united to its bishop, there is the church; there the church acts. Hence the ancients spoke of the 'church which is at Corinth', or just, 'the church at Corinth'.

We said earlier that the liturgy is the church's prayer: in practice this means a given community celebrating its office under the leadership of the priesthood. The community as such is therefore the subject of the liturgy; it enters this service as a community under discipline. Everyone takes his part in his own place: the bishop has one task, the priests another, the deacons another still, also the other clerics, virgins, and lay people. All together form a whole which praises God with one mouth.

From this it follows self-evidently that the office is to be celebrated in common, and, as far as the leaders of the congregation are concerned, in public. It will naturally be oral, then, audible and solemn as well.[2] A common silence like the silent worship of the Quakers is no liturgy, although Catholic worship too has periods of pause and silence.

Thus Catholic worship has strongly objective lines: they are

---

[1] *De Unitate Ecclesiae*, 4.
[2] It follows as equally obvious that the Christian must share personally in the community's worship, if he is not kept away for important reasons. Participation by artificial means such as radio is not enough.

expressed in its form. Nothing subjective or abitrary, no personal enthusiasm, momentary ecstasy or expressionism are to mark it; what it seeks are clarity beyond the limits of any single person, roots for a content that is divine and everlasting, a sober peaceful and measured expression of what belongs to it, in forms which give direction to the over-flow of thought and emotion, which put nature and passion within bonds. In this the liturgy shows herself the heiress of the ancient world for which the highest law of life and art was σοφρόσυνη, the observance of bounds; it revered order and measure as a reflection of the divine number and idea. Not lawlessness, lack of bounds, but things formed and measured, whatever their greatness and their depth, was divinity for the Greeks. The Book of Wisdom teaches that God has 'ordered all things according to measure, number and weight'.[1] Not chaos but cosmos is the work of the creating spirit. All the struggling powers are brought to their end and their harmony in him. The liturgy, too, knows how to moderate and bring to order the terrible struggles which, for example, run through the psalms.

The musical setting of the office is to be judged according to the same standard; it proceeds from the very heart of worship. The filling of men with the Holy Spirit, 'enthusiasm', must needs show itself in a song of the Spirit, as St Paul taught us; 'be filled with the Spirit, speak to one another in the Spirit's psalms, hymns and canticles, sing and chant the psalms in your hearts to the Lord'.[2] If every kind of music rises on the one hand from deep emotion, away from the triviality of daily life and mere calculating reason in the open spaces of the mind, on the other hand it possesses a deep vision of harmony and beauty in rhythm and number. The plenitude of God's power and the up-raising of the mind bring us into his freedom and order and lead to music, and music in pure, classical form. 'A lover sings,' says St Augustine.[3] The church says of love of God, 'he has set my love in order'.[4] So, too, her song is put in order: it is made an image of God's rest and of rest in God. No peace of the grave but movement, lasting flow, movement with purpose and rhythm, and, for this reason, restful. The music of the Latin Church, called Gregorian after Pope St Gregory who arranged it, is full of such peaceful movement and lively order. While there is often trouble and storm in the words, the music prepares the rainbow of peace, points to the harmony with no end. Sometimes the psalm melodies—usually

[1]Wis. 11, 20 (Vulg. 21).   [2]Eph. 5, 18 f.
[3]Sermo 256 *de Tempore*.   [4]Cant. 2, 4 (Vulgate).

those for the office—spread a sort of epic restfulness over the lyrical
excitement of what the texts give us to sing. More mobile, yet with a
steady measure, are the antiphons and hymns. Their task is to express
the mood and words proper to each of the church's feasts, but they
know better than to allow those moods a tone of excess or unrestraint.
Fullness within limits, lively action in measure are the marks of
liturgical form.

Language belongs to the very essence of liturgy. It is not the speech
of every day, not the formal language of a single people, but a ritual
language which age, tradition and history have made venerable: in the
Western Church, Latin. A special characteristic of the language is that
it transcends the national boundaries of the modern age, and gives
recognition to a culture and religion which are universal. It takes us back
into the Middle Ages, where the life of the nations was certainly vigorous, yet there was a real oneness in European culture as well, above and
beyond their boundaries. The one Latin language gave the church in
the West opportunity to display an *Imperium Romanum,* and in fact the
use of the church's language depended on the continuance of the Roman
Empire. In the Orient, where the Romans came up against a surface of
hellenistic culture, the church keeps up Greek, Syriac and Coptic. But
in these places, too, it is not a living language but an older, changeless
form used specially in worship. This worship which turns to God,
honours him and aims to lead men from all nations to him, prefers to
use precise forms exalted above the language of every day, and thereby
redolent of mystery, casting shadows of God's life. The mystery cannot
stand in the crude light of day; it must show its supernatural worth in
rare and precious vessels.[1] *Cotidiana vilescunt:* 'the things of every day
grow base', is an old and true saying. At the same time, the foreigness
of the language makes for greater peace in the liturgy. What might have
a harsh and importunate effect in one's own language becomes more
moderate, takes quieter and nobler shape in the splendour cast by
ancient and holy words. So, then, liturgical language also performs a
task which belongs to worship: it speaks to man of God, not in order to
delude him about his pain and suffering, but to enable him interiorly,
to overcome them and give him a taste of the glory of heaven, its happiness and harmony, as the sun at evening gives heat to the places of men's

---

[1] It should be noted in passing that our language, decomposed by subjectivism, is not, in any case, capable of expressing the divine, given, values of
the liturgy, without purification and a raising of tone, just as our ordinary
gestures cannot be taken into worship.

daily trouble and pain, brings them colour, clarity, and splendour.

The content of the office gives voice to the whole relationship between the Church and her members on the one hand and God on the other through the mediation of Christ; better, its content is the mystery of Christ and the church. We shall say something on this very broad subject later on.

Externally the office is made up in great part of texts from the Old and New Testaments. It is obvious that in her prayer the church should use the books which God himself has given her at the hands of inspired men. No one can speak better of all that passes between God and the church or her individual member than the Spirit of God and the man filled with God. Fundamentally the church did not simply acquire the sacred writings but bore them under the breath and guidance of the Spirit. Throughout thousands of years she has set down her experiences in them. It is no wonder that she is glad to fall back upon them in her worship; the inspired writings in the strict sense, those of which it can be said in a special sense that they are written by the Spirit of God and the church, end with the apostles. But the Spirit has not left his church; again and again he moves her to write songs of love and of wisdom; men and women sing and pray. What they have said has been both the deepest expression of their own hearts and at the same time something coming from the mind of Christ and the Christian community: it thus became everyone's possession; and as such it was taken into the cult of the church. Hymns, antiphons, lessons from the Fathers and teachers came into the liturgy along with the scripture: the bishops and other leaders of worship created, from their contemplation, the solemn prayers and prefaces: even the use of Scripture became an act of re-creation to the whole; music gave the final completion and consecration, bubbling up 'as the Holy Spirit dug in the hearts of holy men'.[1] Human things and godly things are joined in unbreakable conjunction.

This bond between God and man, between grace and nature, is, throughout, the essential mark of the Christian life of prayer. Until now we have emphasised its givenness, because the whole age of modernity, resting as it does upon man's self-rule and self-created experience has need above all to learn submission to the given, divine norm. The individualist consciousness of modern man 'emancipates' the personality and isolates it: in so doing it reduces society to atoms and clears the

[1] *Spiritu Sancto rimante in cordibus corum. Instituta Patrum* cited in Graduale Solesmes (1910) p. xiv.

way to collectivism; it sacrifices the person to the mass. The objective consciousness of community which the church possesses, submits the individual to a higher, God-given norm and gives it definite place; thereby it protects the personality, develops it and assures its status: place which belongs to it alone. The modern kind of order is a casual stone heap whose parts have no relationship to one another; they are pushed about, increased or diminished at will, and the picture they yield is one of immense confusion. The Christian thing is like an ancient temple which can be only as it is; in it every stone, every pillar, every beam and every statue has its place and displays its own beauty; together all the parts form a single work of art from which no part may be removed without injury to the whole. In this way liturgical prayer unites strong norms and respect for law with free movement and meaning for individual life. Even within the liturgy there are degrees of freedom. Just as ancient art, particularly Egyptian, Greek and ancient Christian painting and sculpture used the strictest forms for the greatest and most divine things, and then accepted freer movement as they came to human ones, yet avoided naturalism throughout, the church's prayer gives recognition to more volatile human feeling outside her solemn liturgical acts, and knows well how to express them.

It is neither possible nor necessary to depict all this in detail; some brief notes will suffice. We shall make them on the psalms, which are the heart of the office. In them no sort of religious experience is lacking; from deepest misery and sorrow, to abandonment and the full joy of oneness with God, from the feeling of oneness with the Lord's great congregation to the most intimate and personal experience of God; from the knowledge of God's dread majesty to enjoyment of his love: adoration, praise, thanks, the child's asking are all present. If, in addition, we take the allegorical interpretation regarding Christ and his church, the saving work of the new covenant, the changing lights which the festival, season or day have cast upon the psalm give us some shadowy glimpse of the inexhaustible riches of liturgical prayer. Usually the church tells us what use she is making of a psalm on a particular day and the mood she wants to express through it, by employing a particular antiphon as background or accompaniment. There are many of these refrains, or repeated verses; originally they were put in by the people after each verse or each three; now they frame the psalm, and come from it; their effect is, therefore, to make emphatic a particular theme of the psalm. Later, longer and more elaborate antiphons were created, to stand in looser connexion with the psalm, and lend it definite colour on a given day. The choral music, too, which is sung to the psalm, changes according to the musical tone of antiphon. One can see how simple and yet great are the means which the church uses here; the alleluia, for example, brings an Easter note to all the psalms it accompanies, even the serious *miserere*, and to the whole office an exalted and joyful aura.

Like the songs which David and the other God-inspired singers sang on their harps, the whole Scripture of the Old and New Testament, containing as it does an immense and inexhaustible sea of teaching, prayer, poetry and wisdom for living, is tuned into liturgy, and receives back from it a new and extraordinarily diverse life. Everyone knows how the prophecies, songs and sayings, the epistles and gospels are read, and begin to live, sparkle and send out new life. In addition the creators of the old liturgy who lived completely absorbed in the scriptures: men like Justin martyr, Origen, St Ambrose, Gregory the Great and many others. They applied these texts to the sacred mysteries of Christ and the church, and brought out gold to mint from the scriptures' rich mines. They did not proceed with the exactitude of a modern philologist, but with an artist's freedom, as ancient man loved to do; yet they did not become fantastic. Their vision went to the great things, to the whole picture. For this reason they opened up the mysteries of those inspired books. Their work is not a scientific reference work, but a free composition on God's word. Here is revealed how God's truth can become man's real possession. Cassian requires of monks,[1] that they should pray them as if they had written them. Christ is the first model of this; he prayed the words of a psalm, as he cried out to his Father in the depths of agony on the cross; so, too, the liturgy knows how to choose the right word from scripture for the right time, and to bring light from the other hemisphere into all the by-ways of this life of ours.

To inspired sources, then, are added the church's own creations, those of her saints, artists, teachers. The whole is a wonderful treasure. Different ages, peoples and ways of living, men and women, learned men, contemplatives have done their share in fashioning the garment which the liturgy has assumed to do God honour. How well the hymns, for example, give their own tone to each feast and season, so that a few words from one of them will call up before the mind's eye thoughts of the whole of it. How majestic is the Hymn for Christmas: 'Christ,

[1]Cassian, *Collat.* X, 11, 4–6.

redeemer of the world, the Father's only Son; thou wast born in ways beyond all speaking, before time ever was. . . .' Or the Hymn for Vespers of Easter, fragrant and intimate, binding together the mystery of Easter and the Eucharist, the true sacrament of Easter first food of the baptised: 'prepared for the banquet of the Lamb, clothed in white, the Red Sea past, we will sing to Christ, our Prince. His sacred body, his rose-coloured blood, his body, made ready on the Cross we taste, and live for God. We are protected from the angel of vengeance in the paschal night, set free from the hard yoke of Pharaoh. Our pasch is Christ now; he was sacrificed, as a lamb; as pure bread with no leaven his flesh was sacrificed.' A mixture of joy, love and longing marks the Hymn for Vespers of Ascension: 'Jesus, our salvation, love, our longing, God the creator, man at end of ages—how could goodness stretch to bring thee to bear our sins, suffer a terrible death, to set us free from all death. . . . Be thou our joy, as thou shalt one day be our prize. . . .' And on Pentecost the song is of the Spirit who moves the winds, full of power, like the rush of a great bird's wings yet gentle as a dove's song: 'Come, Creator Spirit, come: visit the minds which are thy own; fill with godly grace the hearts of thy own making. Thou art called the advocate, gift of the most high, living spring, tongue of fire, fire of love, oil of anointing. Thou art seven-fold in thy gifts finger of God's right hand, his promise, giver of tongues to speak. Light the flame within our spirits, pour thy love into our hearts, stiffen weak bodies with staying strength of thine. . . .'

Let us look briefly at the variety of lessons from the writings of the Fathers which form so pleasant an alternation to liturgical prayer. Each Father mirrors the light of Christianity in his own fashion; the writings of each differ in point of view, mood, content and form. There is sober exegesis, and then suddenly a burst of allegory; there is theological depth and practical wisdom, then mystical fires rise. But always it is a voice of deepest culture, and the most profound grasp of Christianity; often there is high and classical form as well.

Responding to measured variety of content are the vast and lively differences in carrying out the office, the result of which is that it is never monotonous, never tiring, but keeps the mind always fresh. The psalms rise and fall at a gentle pace; the melody is simple and pleasant, and for all its liveliness and constant exchange between the two choirs, spreads an epic peace over the whole. On the other hand the melodies are not lacking in lively variety. Each of the eight tones in which the antiphons are composed and according to which the psalms are sung has its own character: by its choice of tone, the church gives each new song its own proper colouring. The second, for example, is full of longing, the fourth more mystical, the seventh festive; the fifth full of deep emotion, the eighth strong and masculine. Still more precisely fitted to this varying content are the antiphons, which with their short, clear lines of direction, their freshness and buoyancy are miniature works of art, moments of Greek movement beside the oriental stillness of the psalms. When the mind is weary of the psalms' prayer and the burden of soul-searching they contain, the versicle brings up a shout at the end, like a blast of trumpets, breaking the monotone of the peaceful line, and passing on to something new: reading, petition, or the high points of the office, the Magnificat or Benedictus. These last in turn are sung in a specially solemn psalm tone, the eighth, for example, which recalls a royal march. The lessons have a simple tone of their own, which takes away all personal rhetoric, but leaves clear the divisions of meaning. Responsories follow the lessons; they are marked by a rich, solemn, slow-moving melody, and by the repetition of parts, as one choir answers the other. Thus they give shape to the moment of after-thought and contemplativeness which revolves deep, slow thoughts, and considers them now on one side, now on another, returning with alacrity to old sayings that can never be wrung out. The so-called long responses *responsoria prolixa* usually come in matins which have a particularly contemplative character, and join the lessons, with their stimuli to new thoughts. The short responses are usually found in Lauds and Vespers; one such may show how deep is the grasp which these forms of prayer have for the working of men's minds and prayer, and how finely they express the simple things they have to say:

℣   From the lion's mouth, Lord, deliver me
℟   From the lion's mouth, Lord, deliver me
℣   Lord, deliver me
℟   From the lion's mouth
℣   Lord, deliver me

We can see and hear in the text and melody how this prayerful cry first springs up and forms itself in the soul of an individual or a few devoted persons, and then passes over to the whole community; a second, stronger cry is added; the choir stays with its first petition; the whole comes to rest in slow stages, and ends in a repetition of the first phrase by all which at the same time means that it has been heard. The hymns run more quickly in the same direction; their charm and liveliness is Greek. The church was very long in taking them into the office; only the activity of St Ambrose brought them gradually closer to the church's seriousness. Then their light, impressionable, characteristic tone began to set the mood for the different feasts, and to give a stronger feeling to the individual days; as creations of the West they represented action as against the Oriental psalms, even more than the antiphons, of which we have already spoken.

In the last section we spoke frequently of the psychological basis for liturgical prayer and told how it became stylized in liturgical form. The structure of the office, too, both of individual hours and the day as a whole, is a psychological masterpiece. We shall give a view of the whole day office at the end of the chapter; here we want only to remark how some of the hours develop, Terce for example. After a moment for recollection, a cry of petition goes up to God, by which the leader also, so to speak, rouses the group: 'O God come to my assistance'; then the community answer, 'O Lord make speed to save me'. The *Gloria Patri* and alleluia which follow bring rest into this stormy cry, and at the same time mark the aim of the hour and its joyful character; then comes the freshness of the hymn, expressing briefly and clearly its meaning. At least one antiphon is struck up, to bring in the themes of the day or feast. The three psalms follow which make up the heart and high point of the hours: the antiphon is said. All of this brings the soul into the deep world of contemplation. But it cannot stay there forever; it grows tired, needs new stimuli; these come from the short lesson. From contemplation the soul passes at the versicle to petition, and so up to the intentions of the church, man, and the day: Lord have mercy; Our Father, then the special prayer of the day. With the verse of praise, *Benedicamus Domino* the brief, rich office closes; here was contemplation of divine truth, praise, thanks, adoration, petition: all drawn into one, every kind of prayer in its proper place.

The psychology of Vespers is even more striking. More psalms, given character and thrown up into a particular light by their antiphons, make up the contemplative element. Here too the weary mind is refreshed by a short reading from the scriptures, and then, in the Responsory, returns to the contemplative prayer we have mentioned before. The meditative response is followed by the melodic hymn, strongly connected with the day, its effect a fresh and lively one. After a versicle to lead the way, comes a particularly well-constructed antiphon for the Magnificat, which usually summarises clearly a feast's themes, and then carries its effect through the praise hymn of the Holy Virgin, enhancing its beauty. The Magnificat itself sinks deep into contemplation of the deep things of God and makes the offering of a humble mind to God's infinite love: it is the high point of the feast. When we go beyond it, it is to the *Our Father* and the prayer of the day; the latter, of course, is wholly caught up in the great mystical mood of the Magnificat. The structure of the morning and night services which belong closely together, is also quite remarkable. Three times we sing, 'O Lord open thou my lips,' 'and my heart shall declare thy praise'; dulled minds are called out to the joy of God's life. The prayerful psalm three puts the hindrances to prayer out of the way, so to speak. Then begins the invitatory, the great invitation, through which an antiphon runs, like an encouraging promise of all the feast's thinking, in the shortest possible space. In Psalm 94 the happy encouragement to be glad in God's presence stands side by side with earnest warnings, even threats, to the careless and the hard of heart. When the hymn is over, the mind is sufficiently awake and prepared. Now we come to the real purpose of night worship, contemplation. Vast, mysterious, difficult psalms pass before the soul's eye; the mysteries of God make themselves known in hard phrases. The soul wrestles with God for salvation, for knowledge of him. It joins its voice to the words Christ speaks in the psalm; it lives the life and suffering of the Lord with it; with him it hates sin and turns to the divine light; sees the miracle of God's mystical city, goes out in longing beyond the confusion and darkness of the world into God's freedom and clarity; it longs to go over out of the confusion and darkness of this world into God's freedom and clarity; it mourns loneliness and abandonment in this world, the faithlessness of men and is happy with the one true friend, God. Still, who could exhaust in words all the depths of contemplative prayer in the psalms? When the soul is weary of this pilgrimage on the high places, it goes down to the fresh waters of scripture; in the responsories it carries on its contemplation. Again a series of psalms and a refreshing group of lessons there follows. In the third nocturn come the shorter, brighter Cantica, songs from the prophets or wisdom writings; a homily from the Fathers goes with the gospel, interrupted and slowed down by responsories preparing for the appearance of Christ in whom all the difficulties of inner life find their solution. Yet before Christ himself appears in the gospel, the confident hope of the church breaks out in the majestic, powerful hymn *Te Deum*, which praises the Trinity and the Saviour, and at the end passes over to humble petition. Now the light of the world himself appears, and spreads his light over all the difficulties and confusion of church. Man's longing is fulfilled, the high-point of the office is here: the Lord speaks. So with a short word of praise and the prayer, Matins ends, and the mind gives itself to that jubilation which already sounded in the *Te Deum*: it grows stronger as Lauds progresses and reaches its far highest point in the *Benedictus*, the wonderful song of praise for the redemption in Christ. Throughout the whole of this as of every office, the church shows herself mistress of the deepest psychology, the psychology of prayer.

Before considering the psychological and artistic strength of the Day office, we should refer to a very important matter: the relationship of liturgy to nature. The polytheism of the heathen made the powers of nature divine, and submitted man to them; this 'service to the elements' often has great sensible joy, but ends in evil and in terror of the terrible power of nature which takes a man up and, after brief sport, destroys him. Pantheism makes man feel his oneness with the whole web of the cosmos; but this daemonic feeling, too, leads to the enslavement of the spiritual in man, to the tyranny of sense, and to panic before the predatory beasts which lurk in unredeemed nature. More or less pantheistic, restless and full of muddy emotion, and 'sentimental', is the feeling which the Romantics had for nature. The gnostic overestimates the evil of nature, treats her like something evil, is full of fear before her, runs from her; he is 'full of the sorrow for things'. The Christian too, knows that nature groans under sin, along with man; it longs for redemption, which will come to it when it comes to the children of God. But he also knows that nature is a work of God's; because it is, he can love it, see in it the print of God's passing. Yet he stands over it; nature is tool and image of the spiritual. The liturgy, therefore, from the very beginning, from the time when the Lord made bread and wine the elements of the mass, has given nature its part to play. The church was not afraid to take over natural symbols which the heathen had used in their worship and, by putting them into proper place, to give them their true value. By doing so she has made them holy, just as through the sacraments and sacred gestures, she made the human body; in fact the church has given to nature the first fruits of glory, the gifts of the children of God. For our theme the symbolism of light is of particular importance, connected as it is in the first place with the sun. This phenomenon in nature is much more striking to a Mediterranean than to us, because in that region its forms are so vivid and definite. The sun really stands in the heaven like a dread king, spreading terror and blessings: *sol invictus*[1] as the ancients called him, the author of the 18th psalm among them. Terrible majesty glows, burns from heaven; it wakes life and kills it, giving life and blinding the eye that is too keen. It is no surprise that first orientals and then dwellers of the Mediterranean region should have honoured the sun-king as their high God. Even the philosophers gave it honour: Plato regarded the sun as a symbol of the good which was the sun in the kingdom of spirits. But in later neo-Platonism and the heathen religions of the first Christian centuries the invincible sun god was the centre of worship; this was expressed in many prayers. The morning light above all was revered as something divine. In Northern Europe and America one is fonder of broken colours, light and dark patches, where fantasy and emotion can be lost in muddy clouds. The typical man of antiquity had a sense for clarity and truth, for the genuine and the whole; he valued above all the dawn light with its unlimited fullness, 'glorious as on the first of days, as it streamed out of the hand of God over land lying dark and still a little while before; it streams up and gives things back their colour and brightness; it awakens life and joy. The East, therefore, a symbol of God, became itself divine; men turned to it when they sought God in prayer. Evening like morning was especially a time for prayer; yet the other phases of the sun's course all had their meaning in worship too.

The church has nurtured these ideas insofar as they are true, but purified them of their limitations, of their enslavement to the elements. For her the visible sun is not the godhead; it is, as Plato has already glimpsed, a symbol of the Spirit-son, Jesus Christ the incarnate Logos, who in the life of nature as in the world beyond wakens life and spreads it, as he himself says, 'I am the light of the world'.[2] So the church has set up her office according to its changing course, and thereby given it new depth and beauty. 'Grace builds upon nature': it is fitting that man should fashion his daily life of prayer on the great image of nature, and give back its beauty, spiritualized, to the creator.

Still another point for brief consideration is the warning of Christ and the Apostles, 'pray always'. How does the church fulfil this command? In mind she is always with the Lord, as the Lord is always with her.

[1]The unconquered sun god, particularly Mithras.   [2]Jn. 8, 12.

This cannot be carried out literally, in external worship, but she nonetheless fulfils it. For in accordance with the ancient view there is a kind of earthly eternity in like, regular recurrence in time. As time renews itself in the regular movement of the years and moons, and by this continual re-birth becomes in a sense eternal, so an event becomes celebrated 'eternally' by being celebrated every month or year. The *sollemnitas*,[1] yearly feast, becomes *aeternitas*, everlastingness. The celebration of the church year, especially the sundays, rest on this principle. Always the mysteries of salvation are carried out in the same rhythm; they become eternally real, until the solemnity in heaven passes into eternal reality in every sense of the word. The exhortation to pray always has been carried out by the church's praying each day at the same appointed times. These hours (*horae*), are laid down according to the sun's course; as we have said, the sun is a symbol of Christ. Historical occurrences from the life of Jesus yield symbolic meaning, or fall in with such meanings. Thus the sun's rising is the most striking image of the Saviour rising from the dead, and in fact the hour of his rising; Sext, the time he was nailed to the cross, but according to ancient tradition the hour of his ascensions as well, the high noon of his life; None was the hour at which he died on the cross. At the third hour of day, Terce recalls the out-pouring of the Holy Spirit.

Thus prepared we can consider the course and construction of the daily office. It begins on the previous evening, with 'first vespers'. For the ancients the day did not begin at midnight, a point which can only be determined by mechanical means or a mechanical clock; it ended when the sun went down, and the new one began. The service of worship held at the hour of dusk in the evening light (vesperus, ἑσπέρα, evening) belongs in time to the day before, but leads over to the day following. Hence at least the second part, and on great feasts the whole vespers, belongs liturgically to the feast of the following day. The mind is led into the ante-chamber of the feast's circle of ideas, and receives a first taste of its content. This is especially well expressed in the first vespers of Christmas.

As soon as the sun has disappeared behind the horizon, a new day begins in the night. Out of the night day rises; this deep consideration of ancient man which only children seem to have kept until now (they often reckon in nights) is the measure for the liturgy. The construction of the day office has its firm foundation in the night service.

[1] From Oscan word *sollus* (like Latin *omnis*), and *annus*: 'event in every year'.

The night gives darkness and silence; in it we see far out into the stars, feel comfort and dread, know the smallness of man and the greatness of his spirit: night is the time of great yet single vision. For Christians it has lost the terrors which pursued unredeemed mankind, but kept its sweetness, recollection and gentle dread. So it became the proper time for prayer, for raising the mind up to God. The work of ordinary day is over, consciousness less disturbed by the outside world, the ear enjoys valued stillness, and the stars give light. A shadow of eternity rests on the night; time seems brought to a point. For this reason the Romans called the night *intempesta*, timeless. The heathen had already shown preference for night in their deeper and more moving rites; the mysteries in which they hoped to be conjoined to God were celebrated at night, with no light but flickering torches, until the moment came when the light of the mysteries flamed up and told that the God was at hand. The church also celebrates her greatest mysteries, the incarnation, the resurrection, as they occurred, in the dead of night. The greater feasts are begun with night watches, vigils. Like the Greeks with their παννυχίς, the ancient church watched the whole night through before a principal feast, with prayer, song and reading. Holiest of all was the night of Easter, in which the splendour and glory of the risen Christ came streaming out of the passion's deep darkness, and brought the sunrise in high heaven to man who sat in the shadow of death. In the night these Christians of the early church waited for Christ to return: 'this is the night which shall be celebrated with watches for the coming (adventus, παρουσία) of our God and King. Its essence is twofold; after his suffering he returned in it to life, and later he will enjoy in it the Lordship of the wide world.'[1] There is a note of mystical expectation lying on all vigils:[2]

> This is the very time
> when, as the gospel tells,
> the bridegroom shall come one day
> the Lord of everlasting heavens.
> The holy virgins run to him,
> run out as he will come
> They bear their lamps along
> and have their fill of joy.[3]

[1]Lactantius *Div. Instit. VII*, 19. Cf other passages in Franz *Die kirch. Benedictionen im Mittelater* I, 1909 p. 519 f.; Tertullian, *De Baptismo* 19.

[2]A. Löhr: 'Der eschatologische Gedanke in den Ferialhymnen': *Lit. Ztschrift.* 4. p. 11–21.*

[3]From the hymn for midnight, *Mediae noctis tempus est* (fifth century).

Monks kept such a vigil every night, and because it was not possible always to watch through the whole night they took certain hours of it. This night celebration (called Matins, because held in the early morning) is all devoted to contemplation. The mind moves contemplatively, praying, loving the infinite thoughts of God; it struggles with the spirit of God, as Jacob once fought with the angel until dawn, and finally won God's blessing and the name Israel—who wrestles with God. Thus strengthened the soul can enter into the great mystic actions of the holy mass, carry them out with understanding and worth.

The night is over, the light comes in the first brightness of morning: the stars grow faint; only the pale morning star shines on. The church begins her morning service of praise: *Laudes.* The soul comes out of its deeper contemplation, and passes on to acts of praise and thanks. It can never be content with its praise; it must call up all creatures to help it in this work. Christ is already near, the sun of justice, the church's healing. The dawn of morning which precedes him is rosy: the Ambrosian hymn speaks of it: 'dawn goes up her path; let the Son, true dawn come all in the Father, as the Father is in him'. The mind looks in longing to that 'last morning' when it will see the divine light which will never be extinguished. Then at last, the sun comes like the victorious hero Christ after his long night of pain, blazing from the tomb to blind the watchers. This is the moment for the schola to begin the hymn of praise to redemption in Christ:

> Blessed be the Lord, the God of Israel
> He has visited his people
> and wrought their redemption . . .
> Salvation from our enemies, and
> from the hand of those that hate us . . .
> passing all our days in holiness,
> and approved in his sight . . .
> Such is the merciful kindness
> which has bidden him come to
> us, like a dawning from on high,
> to give light to those who live
> in darkness, in the shadow of
> death, and to guide our feet
> in the way of peace.

The sun goes higher; light calls to work, to the burden and heat of the day. It is the first hour, Prime. Before going out to work the Christian puts on the armour of prayer—plain, simple prayer, full of thoughts for the weariness, the earnestness of work, of petitions for help against difficulties which can come from both evil spirits and men. All the 'little hours' carry this strong character of petition, particularly Prime; the depth and exuberance of the night and dawn service has not gone out, but come to rest in the heart. Now is the time for work. The sun has lost the bright freshness of early morning and gone up into the heaven.

We think about this ripening power of God's living warmth, at the third hour, Terce, as we celebrate the descent of the divine *pneuma*, the *calor verbi* and sing of it in our hymn: Holy Ghost, one with the Father and the Son. Pour thyself out into our hearts and fill them. Mouth, tongue, unconscious and conscious mind, all life's powers are to sing praise of God, let its love spring up in full fire, its glow light the neighbour.' But the psalms tell of the misery of exile, of longing for the home country, of looking out to the eternal mountains of salvation and the Lord's city, Jerusalem.

Sext is prayed at the heat of mid-day when the mid-day demon goes about to bring harm to body and soul; it begs for cooling to the heats that do harm, soothing of contrary strife, health and harmony of soul and body. All that is what it hopes for from the Lord, to whom alone it looks, as the servant to his master.

The ninth hour, None, brings relief to the heat. Rest is at hand. The petition is for a bright evening, a holy death, and eternal glory after a life of weariness. The soul sees itself already free from imprisonment happy to gather the sheaves and bind them and enjoy rest with those it loves now rest is done.

Now the sun goes west, and descends. The marvellous play of colour at evening, the glory which spreads itself over the tired earth gives men a certain sight of the other, better kingdom; evening is ready to bring sorrowful longing for peace, harmony and unity to the heart of man. The ancients thought that the kingdom of the dead and the islands of the blessed are found in the West, where the sun goes into the sea. The Christian, too, is glad to think at evening of a happy departure from this world's weariness, to the light that stays. When St Ignatius of Antioch takes up the word sunset in his epistle to the Romans, he thinks immediately of another setting, and writes, 'It is good to go down from this world and rise in God'. In this mood the church sings second vespers; after the psalms, responsories and hymns in which she has buried herself in the feast, she intones the *Magnificat*, the high song of the virgin of virgins which, so different from the strong, masculine freshness of the *Benedictus*, is deep, tender, as it were feminine. In it man thanks the Lord for the overflow of happiness he has experienced, for all the Lord, ever true to his promises, has done for him. Union with God, the great aim of all prayer and all worship finds its clearest expression in the *Magnificat* at the end of the day office. All the joy of liturgical prayer leads to oneness with God, and flows out of him again: 'And my spirit rejoiced in God my Saviour.'

Compline ends the day as a quiet night prayer with no special meaning.

If now we look back once more on the many questions with which the church's office confronted us, and the answers we gave, brief and hesitant though they were, it remains clear that the liturgy is as broad and as deep as the life of Christ and His church, the life they have in the Father. The liturgy is a hymn of love; at one time the bride praises the bridegroom, and then the order is reversed; at others it is they two who praise the Father. God's truth plays in the liturgy like sunlight in water; for liturgy is founded upon the words of Scripture and the fathers, upon an infallible, dogmatic faith. But it is in itself a stream flowing from God's great goodness; it does not merely teach, it leads to love. In it the word becomes a song of love; and where truth and goodness stand together beauty will not be lacking. In the liturgy God's truth is given form and shape, and so becomes a work of art, not through isolated aestheticism or dilettantism but of its own weight.

No other prayer can challenge with the liturgy's right, to hold God's truth, God's goodness, and God's beauty, and to send forth their splendours; no other is so near to the heart of Christ and of his whole church. In the last centuries has not the office become too much a mere duty while more intimate piety has passed over to the so-called devotions? It is our business to give back to the office its proper place, to make it once more what it is and has a right to be for us. God's honour and men's salvation cannot be separated: both proceed from the one great sacrifice. So too the office brings both glory to God and healing to men. 'The sacrifice of praise does me honour; it is the way on which I shall reveal salvation' (Ps 49).

PART II

A Miscellany of Odo Casel's Writings Collected Under Two Headings

THE texts which make up this second part of the book are taken from the literary remains of Odo Casel and have been arranged in their present form by the German Editor, who is responsible for the headings, introductory sentences and footnotes. These texts are fragments from various notes and letters; some also are notes written by other people who listened to his talks given in the abbey of Holy Cross at Herstelle. At the end of each fragment the source is given, though the names of correspondents have been omitted in the case of letters.

I

THE MEANING OF THE MYSTERY

In the context of Christian theology we ask, what is the essence of the mystery? Our point of departure remains revelation, even for our use of the special sciences in general and the history of religions in particular; our first source is Holy Scripture.

WHEN we are considering the meaning of the term *Mysterion* in scripture, it is right to say that the word seldom has a direct relationship to ritual in the text. On the other hand, of course, Anselm Stolz advised caution in saying this;[1] for the Council of Trent expressly related the text in First Corinthians, IX.1, *Dispensatores mysteriorum Dei*, to worship (Denzinger, 931), and defended the authority of the Church over the sacraments with this text. I agree that it is not necessary to take the primitive text unreservedly as referring to worship; but an interpretation like this one of the Council, has, nevertheless, great authority. Moreover, anyone who has gone more deeply into the history of the word *Mysterion* is aware that the primitive meaning of the word lies in worship, and that this deepest layer never entirely disappears, not even as the word gradually acquires an abstract meaning. I have gone into this matter thoroughly in an article,[2] and in my review of a book by von Ghellinck on the word *Sacramentum*[3] (among others) I have sketched the whole philological development. It is shown in these works that precisely within a Christian framework the word returns to its original and vivid fullness of meaning.

Moreover, when I am charged with employing the ancient language of the mysteries, the attack goes against the church itself; for whoever reads the fathers is aware that they have closely and widely employed that language for Christian things. Above all the Liturgy has made constant use of this language and has done so surely from intrinsic

---

[1] *Manuale Theologiae Dogmaticae* Fasc. VI: *De Sacramentis*, 1943 p. 9, note 10. Yet on the other hand Stolz is expressly against the abstract interpretation of the concept which Prümm gives to it: cf. p. 8, note 6.

[2] In the Miscellany *Zum Worte Sacramentum*, pp. 225–232.

[3] *Theol. Revue* 24 (1925), 41–47.

reasons: only in this way could it bring Christian ideas home to men. The church would not have used this language if there were not here an inner relationship: the forms and words of the old language of sacrifice (the scripture tells us) were used by God himself in the old testament; so, too, the terms of the language of the mysteries have been used in the new Covenant because, by means of this analogy, it was possible to give form to the unutterable truth of revelation. These are really self-evident truths which I have remarked upon more than once. When Stolz seeks to prove[1] that for the fathers the word *Mysterion* means nothing other than 'spiritual' and 'divine' he runs flat against evidence. On the contrary the word gradually acquired a specific limitation first of all to the Eucharist; and this is the case in the church's language and usage, even today. The evidence is to be found in all the Liturgies and in many patristic texts.[2]

The first task is a brief clarification of terms.

Mysterion, or more usually the plural *mysteria,* is the Greek designation for the ancient Hellenic and later Hellenistic secret cults which are unlike the cults of the Polis; they give to the worshippers of a god, who have been specially initiated and thereby joined to the god, a closer and more personal union with him; this union reaches beyond death and promises a happy existence in the next world. The divinities concerned are usually chthonic mother goddesses, related to the earth and its mysterious life. The way of the mystery passes through initiations and the mysteries proper, in which the deeds and decrees of the gods in the first age are presented in ritual and thereby made present. In this way the initiate, by carrying out the rite under the direction of the priests, takes his own share in the god's deed and attains the god's life: in this he finds salvation.

The Christian church always rejected the heathen mysteries because of the sensual rites, but even more because of the fundamental opposition of attitude between them and the revelation of God in Christ; but at the same time it has used their language in order to clarify for the faithful the essence of revelation and the religion of the next world, and especially the interior meaning of its own ritual and worship which makes present and permits participation in God's saving

[1]For example p. 16, yet with the reservation that the root meaning is for all concepts which are connected with mysterion, especially the adjective mystikos.
[2]From a letter dated 31.10.1944.

work in Christ. This is the explanation of the frequent use of the word *mysterium* or the synonym *sacramentum* and the terminology which goes with it in the Roman missal.[1]

What does St Paul understand by Mysterium?

Mysteries mean for St Paul realities beyond the comprehension of the human mind. They are not merely, as Prümm would make out in his *Der Christliche Glaube und die altheidnische Welt*, mysteries for so long as they are unknown. (The book was reviewed in J.L.W. 14, pp. 187–224.)[2] Rather, here are realities of a sphere into which man cannot break with reason alone; realities which can only be grasped in function of revelation; in other words, when God gives man the light of his understanding. It is God, then, who first gives the capacity for grasping the mystery, and not by reason, but by faith. The Christian faith is not a noesis of truth and a compliance with law, in other words something which is purely of the will and the mind of man; rather it is an exaltation of the whole of human being and existence into God's sphere. God must raise man up onto his own Spiritual plane, in order to make him capable of receiving the mystery. The best image of this attitude of faith which God gives to man transforming him, is that of the bride; she gives herself wholly to the bridegroom, and he fulfils her. This is the experience which St Paul had of the mystery in his inward union with Christ.

For St Paul the content of the mystery is, first the sacred design of salvation; it proceeds from God's own love, his *agape*, and has creation for its goal. Here is I Corinthians, 2, 1:

> For my part, brethren, when I came among you it was not to proclaim God's mystery in high flown words or words of wisdom. No, I would know nothing among you save Christ and him crucified. (*Mysterion* is the best reading: Cf. Nestle on the passage.)

The mystery of God then is Christ, the *Logos* of God who made himself visible for men's sake and for them was crucified.[3]

Mysterium means for us what it means to St Paul in his letters to the Colossians and Ephesians, the great fact that Christ is a hope of glory. The incarnation of God's Son, and his death on the cross,

[1] From a contribution for the French edition of *Das christliche Kultmysterium*, October 1943.
[2] Especially p. 215, on Prümm, Volume II (1935), p. 310.
[3] From conferences on Romans, Chapter 11, 25, from the years 1935–1942.

together with his passage into glory and exaltation which flow from it have fashioned the church, the body of Christ; it has but one life with that Son of God; he is the real life of the church through Christ. And all of this is made ours through the Lord's Word and the mysteries —the sacraments in which the God-Man continuously conveys to us his theandric life. Since the end of the high middle ages in the West, men have been minded more and more to make themselves independent, and so to move further and further away from the mystery of the God who dwells in us. It is really a question of giving once more to God the honour which is his due; of letting Christ be seen for who he is: the one from whom alone all God-life in the church flows. Hence, too, in worship there must be a return to the church's centre; the Word as well as Sacrament must regain its place. The holy communion ought not to stand merely next to the service of worship, but form its high point.[1]

Is the mystery of worship one of the three species within the genus cult; is it a species of cult?

Remember that *eidos* (εἶδος) in this context does not mean the external image; it corresponds to the Latin *species*. The genus of worship has three species, namely prayer, sacrifice and mystery, for the division is one into genus and species. But when I make this division I constantly meet the criticism that I am making the Christian mystery a derivation from the ancient ones. On the contrary I would say that it is not the content of the mysteries which we find in both, but the concept; within the genus of worship, on the other hand, all three species are to be found in Christianity, mystery among them.[2]

How does the mystery of worship differ from the mystery of Christ?

Then, one may ask, what is the difference between the mystery of Christ and the mystery of worship? According to the letters of St Paul, the first is the reality of Christ himself: God, revealed in his Son made man; the revelation of himself which reaches its climax in the sacrificial death and glory of Christ the Lord. The mystery of worship, on the other hand, is the presentation and renewal of that first mystery, in worship. By it we are given the opportunity of entering personally into the mystery of Christ. The mystery of worship, therefore, is a means whereby the Christian lives the mystery of Christ.[3]

[1] From a letter to an evangelical pastor written on 7.11.1946.
[2] From a letter dated 23.1.1936.   [3] From a letter dated 20.4.1943.

How does the mystery of worship differ from the mystery of Christ?

In St Paul the mystery of Christ as an objective reality occupies the centre of the stage; it dominates the whole of his thinking. But that does not make the mystery of worship superfluous: far from it! The one requires the other, if we are to draw near to its reality; by the mystery of worship we make entry into the first, primaeval mystery. Yet this mystery of worship only has value if life with the Lord stands behind it, if we are crucified with him to the world, and live his life. The transformation through the mystery must have its off-print in a new form of living. Even the hellenistic mysteries strove for this transformation; but they could not reach the goal, for Christ's blood had not yet flowed.[1]

They differ as the images from their type; Christ is the prototype of our salvation.

The world of imagination which lies behind the words of St Paul about participation in the saving deeds of Christ, his death and resurrection, is shot through with Platonism; death and resurrection are archetypes, in the sense of *idea exemplaris*, of the Platonic doctrine of ideas which generate their images. The images are the mysteries which conform us to the archetype. Through participation in the mysteries we enter into the image and so reach the archetype. Thus, the Mass not only represents the death of Christ and communicates to us the effects of his sacrifice; it is an active image of the Pasch of Christ, and makes us immediate members of what once took place in and upon him. It is therefore within the power of the Mass to bring us into the same temporal dimension with the saving deeds of Christ, and to place us in their immediate presence.

Lastly Christ is himself the archetype after whom all the mysteries are formed as images. This has very important practical meaning. It is not pious feelings of devotion which bind us to him, nor even our own moral efforts; it is the objective accomplishment of our salvation into which we enter through the Mystery. The Mystery is the way to the body and to the Spirit of Christ; this is the content of the formula ἐν Χριστῷ.[2]

[1] From a conference delivered on 20.11.1944.
[2] Cf above p. 55, particularly note 2. The text is from a conference on the church as the body of Christ.

The true knowledge of these relationships can properly bear the ancient name, gnosis.

Like this holiness, the *gnosis*, the sacred knowledge of Christ passes on to us.[1] St Paul and St John are witnesses to this.

> This is eternal life (life in the *aion*): that they shall know thee the one true God (Jn. 17, 3). I have made known thy name among men whom thou hast given me from the world (Jn. 17, 6). The words which you gave to me I gave to them, and they have known in truth that I came from you (Jn. 17, 8).

It is the height of knowledge that we should know the Father. The knowing is not for reason to grasp; it is contact with and possession by God, through his Son in the divine reality which is the Son himself; this is the true *gnosis* which the Lord wills to give to his own. The world which has fallen prey to the Evil one has not got it: 'just Father, the world has not known you, but I know you . . .' (Jn 17, 25). This knowledge of the Father the Son alone has, because he is begotten of the Father. He gives it to those who hold fast to him, those of whom St John says in the prologue to his gospel that they are begotten of God (v. 13). We may compare this passage with Ephesians 1, 8: 'in all wisdom and understanding he has shown us the mystery of his will.' John uses abstract language; Paul speaks most concretely in the language of the ancient mysteries. The incarnation, passion and resurrection of the Lord are the world's supreme mystery play; in them the Father gives us vision of the mystery of his will to love. Thus, in the verse before the one just mentioned, St Paul says that he will pray for the faithful, 'for the Spirit of wisdom and revelation'. He then unfolds before them in a few words the whole drama of the mystery. We are taken up into this drama and in our day by day enactment of it we receive the *gnosis*, deep knowledge, which belongs to the Son.'[2]

This gnosis *is possible only if founded in faith.*

It is faith which gazes beyond the symbols at God's higher world as we experience it in the Christian mysteries. When later ages sought to make the liturgy impressive by outward pomp, that was only a

---

[1]*Gnosis* means a deeper kind of insight, God's gift, into the reality of God himself; a vision which rests on divine illumination born of faith, fulfilled in love. Cf Odo Casel *Vom Wahren Menschenbild*, 1953, p. 189.
[2]From a conference on the church as the body of Christ, from the period 1943–46.

substitute for the faith, for the mystery which Christians no longer understood; the liturgy of the ancient period was very simple because the people's faith was lively. The utter simplicity of the mystery's symbols could speak volumes to them; it was able to make divine reality visible. Something of the like was true of the pagan mysteries. At Eleusis where everyone went, the high point of the whole was the showing of a single ear of corn; yet those who saw were convinced that in this way they entered the world of the gods.[1]

Yet faith is not in the last analysis something abstract; it becomes concrete and alive in the mysteries, which are its visible signs.

The mystery is a necessary expansion of faith; it is the mysteries which first make faith a truly living thing. Of itself faith is purely spiritual. Yet because we men are flesh and blood God has given us in addition the visible sign of the mysteries. They attest for us, in a way we can touch and see, the reality in faith. This has always been God's way with us. Christ himself became visible, and when his human form was taken away we became able to see him in the visible signs of his mysteries. Scripture itself gives us proof that God communicates himself to men by means of visible, tangible things. We have only to think of the Lord's healing of the sick; his restoration of the sick body was a sign for the healing of the soul; or the multiplication of the loaves pointed to the eucharist. Now Christ is risen it is no different: he let himself be known to his friends in visible signs; he has Thomas touch him, he eats with the disciples; they recognize him at the breaking of the bread.[2]

The mysteries will make possible man's most intimate participation in Christ.

In the liturgy, it would seem to me, the essential thing is the interior sharing of the Spirit's life with our Lord and Saviour. Of course that will lead to forms which fit it; but the forms will develop where there is right understanding to begin with, while it seems dangerous to seek first for the outward form and then to build the mind upon it. The so-called liturgical movement may perhaps too often have confined itself to communal forms; we have thought it 'liturgical' merely to

[1]From a conference on Colossians, 28.8.1947.
[2]From a conference of the period 1943–45.

get people closer to the altar. There is in all this the danger of mistaking the husk for the grain.[1]

It is an impression of mine that perhaps most of all we must encourage and promote the interior participation of the layman in the church's life. It is my hope that worship understood as a mystery which brings in its train the intense participation of all initiates will encourage this interior participation. The more interior the religious life which lay people share in the church, the more they will be able to take part in the works and the offices of the church. In this too there is a measure of preparation for the union of all Christians.[2]

This takes place first in the deeper understanding of Christ's saving gifts and a living, interior, participation in the life of the church; these were the source of the fathers' power in creating the liturgy.

The ancient Fathers still had the vision of deep places, *gnosis*. This was the source of their power to create the liturgy through which we are able to enter the primaeval saving action. The sacred liturgy is the great act, full of power, which we owe to primitive Christianity. We should be poor without these sacred symbols of our worship which have been handed on to us; without the liturgy Christ's saving deed would be for us a past thing, not one which can take hold of us and lift us into the sphere of Godhead; it is the liturgy which takes us up into the first mystery, the source of all the rest. The liturgy makes visible the truth that worship is truly God's gift. St Ambrose was right when he said, 'I find thee in thy mysteries: *te in tuis invenio sacramentis*'.[3],[4]

Liturgy, then, means the fulfilment in ritual of what the Lord did for our salvation.

 We act out the mysteries as the body of Christ; as his body we do all that the head does. In the rite we have an image of Christ's act in which we did not share while it was being fulfilled in time and place. The same thing is true of the last supper. Then Christ said, 'this act of sacrifice done once for all time on the cross is here being anticipated in image, and you are to imitate it afterwards in image'. The whole church does now what the Lord did at that moment. Yet certain men are chosen and consecrated to carry out this rite for the church.[5]

---

[1]From a letter written on 3.7.1947.   [2]From a letter written on 2.5.1947.
[3]*Apologia David* I, Chapter 12, 58.   [4]From a conference of 27.11.1944.
[5]From a conference of the period 1945–46.

To interpret and give a linguistic grasp of Christian worship many of the Fathers were glad to make use of the ancient mystery language. It is our task to show how this was done.

The West has a trained sense for clarity and lucidity which it has cultivated from Roman times and perfected to the highest degree. This *clarté latine* which deserves both its name and praise nurses a certain suspicion of the half-darkness and hazard of the mystery. Indeed, the Romans, with a healthy instinct for such matters, rejected and persecuted the hole-and-corner mysteries of the Greeks and Orientals from an early date. But in the end they fell victim as well to the foreign magic of this world, with its power to satisfy a secret longing of their own souls. It was much the same with the Greeks in their time; they brought with them from their Northern homes a sense for bright and sober geometrical patterns. But later they came to recognize that the vision of the world in the clear bright *Logos* needed completion and warmth from the mother-inspired depths of the mysteries and their cult. Even such great rational thinkers as Plato did not scorn to go to school to the priests and prophets of the mysteries—Orpheus and the Eumolpidae of Eleusis; he made use of their pictures and hints, in attenuated and deeper form, having different aims in mind, while he constructed his own world of thought. Plato, the greatest spiritual power among the Greeks, acknowledged that the Hellenes were eternal children with much to learn from the deep visions of the mysteries of the East, and from their own past. It was, then, only by its return to much of the remains of the 'Pelasgian' first age, and by the union of its own visions with the religious and mythological insights and ideas of the Orient —all brought to the final stage of maturity by its own peculiar depth of conception and scientific technique—that the Hellenic World rose to the height which made it the model of the West until our own day.

This harmonious fructifying of East and West has passed over into the Christian era. The two have often parted company both before and after the turning point of history, indeed have come into conflict, whether with the weapons of war or of the mind. But the most fruitful times have been those when there was a marriage of the masculine edge and practical bent of the West with the more mysterious, mother-like mind of the East, nursing its intuitions and seeking out the deep places. Christianity came from the East, if from the Semitic soil of Judaism, which was less mystically inclined: from a soil which indeed placed emphasis above all upon the law, piety of act and the rational will. For this was the reason of the rage which rose against the Son of God and his revelation. Hence that revelation cut itself off from its hostile native soil and went into the heathen world, united to some degree even in religion by Hellenistic culture. Paul, a Pharisee of the Pharisees, was the one above all to overcome the narrowness of the Jews; he preached grace, Χάρις, a word which the Greeks had long known; for as Pindar had sung, the Gods themselves do nothing without *Charis*. One might go so far to say that precisely the Hellenistic world, with its inclination towards mystic union with the Godhead was better prepared for some of the good things of the new ways, the revelation of Christ, than the men whose pride was in the Law. The Greeks who found faith soon learnt that what they had half-perceived in silent longing and dreamed of was made real in the new message of the Son of God made man, dying on the cross as sacrifice for the sin of the world. For this reason it was called the *mysterium* by St Paul, its greatest proclaimer: the mystery which was hidden from all ages in God, now shown forth by the solemn appearance of the Saviour (Σωτήρ). Following the apostle, the fathers of the church beginning with Ignatius the martyr speak freely of the new 'mysteries' of Christ; and as Christianity like every living religion sought in worship the presence of the salvation in which it believed, it too began to call this worship its mysteries. It was indeed the Greek Fathers, who had considered the depths of revelation with all the penetration of their Hellenic intellectual training, who were unafraid of applying the language of the mysteries to the wholly new realities and doctrines in God's revelation.

If such great men of ancient depth and penetration of mind were not afraid to draw from the half-darkness of the mysteries precious stones of understanding, and in the light of the newly given salvation allow them to display their highest brilliance surely it should not be impossible to-day to do the same. We have only to think of the great Hilary of Poitiers, who brought the fathers' teaching about the Son of God from East to West and gave it to his own people in a language rich yet full of light.

With that we come to the question of language. Just as every world of thought, every profession, every community has its own language besides the common speech it shares with others, a special language which gives expression to its inmost spiritual possession, so too the first announcers and possessors of the gospel had their own language.

It unfolded gradually in the Greek East and Latin West, and bore fruit, which languages to-day still live upon. An example is the word ἔρως (erōs) which had become worn and abused by daily use just as much as the word 'love' in modern languages; the first Christians replaced it with a word current but little used, ἀγάπη (agape); this was the term for the new, pure, selfless love which God had brought in Christ. The Latins translated it with *caritas* or *dilectio* when they did not simply leave 'agape' as it stood.

Today many words have lost so much of their former objective value, thanks to the closed circuit of the self which the Renaissance put forward, that they mean to us almost the exact opposite of what they originally meant. For this reason, like the ancient Christians, we are sometimes really forced to make use of the 'peculiar' Christian language. Take for example 'spirit' or 'mind'. In function of Idealism this word has come to mean not the divine, given, power of knowing, the wisdom which is of God and its reflection in man, but rather the self-contained 'modern' mind which imagines that it is creating the world by its own power. In order to draw attention to the wholly different meaning of ancient Christian terms it is, therefore, highly desirable sometimes to leave them, particularly New Testament terms, untranslated. Even words like Lord have fallen into such a state that a phrase like 'Jesus is *Kyrios*' loses its whole force in translation.

We may therefore be allowed, in works which would bring to light the treasures of the earliest Christian tradition, to keep the peculiar language of the church in that age, a true language of the mysteries. There is nothing to prevent the theologian from using the language of the medieval schools in order to clarify in a systematic way much of what the earlier language brings before him. Yet in any case it should be allowable to listen once more to the language which the apostles and fathers spoke, and from whose deep places all generations since them have drawn.[1]

It is proper even now to make use of this language; by doing so we spare ourselves the least loss of nuance in the mystery-tradition.

One would be right on the whole in saying that our knowledge of the ancient mysteries is poor. But that is not the point in question in these discussions; rather, it is the concept of the mystery itself which concerns

[1]From a sketch for his introduction to the French edition of this work, October 1943.

us. And here we are on surer ground; our knowledge is in fact testified to by the Christian use of the concept. As has been said more than once by me, when the fathers saw a mystery in the mass they did not do so only because of the analogy, the resemblance between the mass and the pagan mysteries. Indeed, with their aversion from those mysteries they never would have used the term for this reason alone. How dangerous it would have been continually to talk about the mass as a mystery if on the one hand there had been no analogy and yet on the other the very term had recalled to Christians the mysteries of Attis and all the rest! Would we call the mass to-day a Revue?

One seeks for a definition of the mystery which the theologians will understand. What can that mean? Is the language of Christ, the apostles and the fathers unintelligible to the theologians? The whole of tradition teaches that the mystery, the ἀνάμνησις, *commemoratio, repraesentatio* is the primaeval act of salvation. I do not deny that this can be expressed in School language too; but as a liturgist I should like to keep to the forms of the *traditio*. Some say that it is a silent source of misunderstanding for the layman. This almost amounts to an attack on the church, which has taken the word, untranslated, into Latin or has only translated it by *sacramentum*. If the church can call the act she celebrates a *mysterium* I think we may do likewise. This does not mean that we must, therefore, reject a vernacular translation; but such a translation should answer the reality which the original contains. Continual use of 'secret' or some still more meaningless word does not fulfil the purpose; it is a falsification of content; it twists and waters down the whole context of many passages.[1]

I have more than once emphasized that St Paul's idea of the 'fullness of time' in which Christ appeared implies too that the culture of the civilised world (οἰκουμένη) at that point in time had reached such a maturity as to be able to serve the growing Christian thing with a number of forms of which Christianity made use; in this way, it was able to make its message, the content of revelation, more intelligible to men. Thus it was that the mystery religions of late Antiquity were able, by reason of their analogy with Christianity, to furnish it with many forms of what was to be realised in revelation, on an infinitely higher plane of course. In concrete terms, if Christianity had appeared in the time of Periclean Athens or the Rome of Cato the culture of those ages would not have been ripe for a universal religion of revelation.

[1]From a letter 10.7.1926.

The hellenistic achievement in its Roman phase was by no means the culture of a race; it was an achievement of mind, which had grown up through the work of many races, and by that fact had something universal about it.[1]

Yet it is not as if we had need of the pagan religions after the revelation of Christ; rather, because our subjectivist ways of thought have taken us so far from the Ancient world and its concentration on being, it is worthwhile for us to feel our way back into that habit of mind in order the better gradually to learn the ways of thought in which revelation is at home.[2]

I have emphasized so often that what we are dealing with here is not a derivation but an analogy, that I do not need to repeat it again. There is simply no question of identity between the two objects: on the one side is God's revelation, and on the other, at the very best, is man's striving towards God. Naturally this striving is not altogether unattended by God; but it lacks the full purity which is Christ's. God's revelation and mythology confront one another. Yet revelation is not fulfilled in solely historical acts; it passes over into the liturgy of heaven, as Hebrews tells us; we may not overlook this fact. The Eucharist is the *anamnesis*, the memorial not only of the death but also of the resurrection and ascension of Christ. It therefore embraces things which go beyond the 'historical' realm, and reach into the immediate sphere of God himself.[3]

One says that the pagan mysteries gave only an illusion, while the Christian mysteries on the other hand give the reality. I would prefer to say that the pagan mysteries gave a reality but remained caught in the net of the cosmic forces, while the Christian mysteries, through the cross of Christ, give a sharing in the transcendent God. Even the pagan mysteries had no automatic effect; the pious worshipper had to give himself to the cosmic and divine forces. Thus, in the Christian mystery the believer must wholly offer himself to the surpassing grace of God which streams into him through Christ.[4]

We must now attempt a first view of the types of the ancient mystery.

We can distinguish three of these ancient mystery types. There is a myth, containing the story of a God's appearance on earth, which is lived out in a rite. This form is nearer to Christianity than the second,

---

[1]From a letter of 10.10.1935.
[2]From a letter of 9.2.1944.
[3]From a letter of 31.10.1944.
[4]From a letter of 3.2.1946.

M.C.W.–E

the cosmic mysteries. For at the centre of our religion is God who has appeared in time, as a man. In later times many mysteries of the first type were given a cosmic twist. Yet while these bring union with a God who has appeared on earth, the second turn on a union with the cosmos itself. At Colossus a cult of this kind was active, concerned solely with the 'elements of the world'. Between these two, there is a third which we meet in the tenth book of Apuleius: it would unite the two other types by bringing together gods and the physical elements, the στοιχεῖα which are given the form of a queen and honoured as such.[1]

Here follow some characteristic examples.

Evidence that myth is an early form of explaining the world can be found in the story of the island of Ceram. It goes something like this. The nine first families of mankind came in their wanderings from the first place they had known to the district of Western Ceram, to the place in fact which even today is venerated as a sacred dancing floor. Among these immigrants was the man Ameta. He was unmarried; but he became a father by casting his blood on a palm tree, from which the girl Hainuvele sprang up; she was a wonder worker whose kind behaviour towards men and continual good deeds towards them made her feared, and they murdered her. From her body grew all kinds of nut plants, which had been unknown to men before. Yet in penance for the murder they had committed and at the command of the goddess who ruled over the maiden, men were to perform a ritual dance in which they imitated the death of the girl; in this dance they were to pass through the door, the door of death and once more come to the goddess who had been angered and so turned away from them. The goddess herself explained the rite in these words: 'you shall see me no more; only when you die you will come to me again. But the journey to me is hard.' After saying this, the goddess disappeared from the earth and lived thereafter on the mountain of the dead. This myth which we first came to know from Frobenius' expedition some years ago is very instructive.[2] The girl first reaches her real destiny by passing through a terrible ordeal; from her death the life of the soil is born. Before her death there was a time when men neither married nor died. Ameta had no wife; he became a father by shedding his blood, and from this blood

---

[1]From a conference on Colossians, 4.11.1946.
[2]Details of this myth are given in the book by Jensen which is mentioned in the following note.

the girl took rise. We see clearly here how dying and begetting belong together; when man has become guilty of life death enters the scene and death makes begetting necessary. To reach true life, the sight of the godhead, man must now pass through the door of death. The goddess spoke at the institution of the rite: 'I will not live here. Now you must pass through the door of death and come to me. He alone shall remain a man who succeeds at this.' All men sought to do as she had said; but not all could do it. Those who failed ceased to be men; they were changed into ghosts or animals.

This myth is still acted in ritual on the island. Many people have recognized its meaning.[1] Kerenyi points out quite rightly that this myth makes better sense of the Greek myth of Demeter and Kore. Kore or Persephone too reaches her true fullness only by passing through the doors of death. In the way a Greek hymn puts it, Pluto, the god of the underworld, with the approval of Zeus takes Persephone away in order to marry her. But when Demeter, her mother, avenges the deed by causing all life on earth to cease, Hermes takes the stolen girl back on Pluto's own horses. But Persephone had taken food with her husband and eaten pomegranate seed which he gave her; she belonged to him forever and therefore she had to return to him for a third of every year. From this time onwards she spends a third of every year on earth; and it is she who makes the corn grow and gives the earth its fruitfulness.

Let us see what new light the myth of Hainuvele casts on the Eleusinian mysteries; they are of particular importance to us, since they have had a share in forming the terminology of the Christian liturgy. In what follows we are making use of an article by Walter Otto, *Über den Sinn der eleusinischen Mysterien* from the *Eranos Jahrbuch* for 1939, pp. 83–112. Although Otto is far from Christianity, he comes remarkably close to our own views about ritual, from a background of his own deep knowledge of the history of religion. Unfortunately he does not seem to have recognized that Christian worship too can throw light back on to paganism.

Otto rightly says that the worship at Eleusis gives us the best picture of the special nature of man's communion with the gods in the pre-hellenic age of Greece. It is from this age, that of the old Mediterranean culture, that the mysteries come. The Greeks who took over the

[1] Cf K. Kerenyi, Labyrinth-Studien: *Albae Vigiliae* 15, Amsterdam n.d. (1941) and A. D. Jensen, Hainuwele, 1939.

mysteries gave them a greater measure of clarity and so made them the image for later times of a unified mother and father religion.

The mysteries gave to man the hope of a blessed life with the gods in a world beyond. This hope was awakened at Eleusis; it was closely connected with the marvel of natural growth. Demeter who was worshipped there was a pre-Greek goddess of the shore people. She gave the fields their fruitfulness and above all she gave fruitfulness to men. It was she then from whom all the life of nature came. Her daughter Persephone too is a pre-Greek death goddess who lives on in the Greek Kore. Otto notices with great penetration that the ruin of vegetation does not follow immediately upon the rape of Kore, but rather when Demeter has long sought in vain for her daughter; Kore is therefore not to be identified with the seed.[1] Of course sowing and reaping have only appeared since Kore went down into the underworld, since she became a death goddess; death must be if the seed is to bear fruit. Death makes begetting necessary; through it man lives; he dies as an individual, lives on in the type. All the life of nature stands in this unbreakable bond with death.

Otto is right as well to point out the connection between this and Genesis. After man had fallen away from his first estate by sin he was made subject to death. In order to keep his life on earth he had to cultivate the fields; in order to win a degree of earthly immortality he begot children. (Cf Genesis 3, 17 ff; 4, 1 ff.)

Thus, at the bottom of the Greek and the Ceram myth there is the idea that a mythical figure must die in order that life on earth may flourish and grow.

Anyone who goes to Eleusis where Demeter wept for her daughter, to the place where she brought her and where she then introduced the culture of the fields; whoever receives the initiation here receives also the certainty that he too will be able to lead a blessed life with the gods after death. The rites of initiation were above all a παθεῖν, a passion as Aristotle called it in a classical formula (Rose, fragment 15): 'those who are made initiates are not to learn (μαθεῖν) but to suffer (παθεῖν) and so to bring about in themselves a true change (γενομένους ἐπιτηδείους)'. Yet before the *myste* reaches the vision which gives him happiness he must pass through darkness.

Plutarch gives us a fine picture of the initiation. (The fragment is preserved in Stobaeus, 407.) He likens initiation into the mysteries to

[1] Cf Otto, op. cit. 90–93.

death. 'Thus it is we say that when the soul is transformed and adorned it passes below and emerges new. It knows nothing of all this, until it is near to death. Then man undergoes a suffering such as they undergo who are caught up into Bacchus in the great mysteries. Thus it is that word is like to word and action to action: dying and being made an initiate are given a word of the same origin: τελευτᾶν, die; τελεῖοναι, be initiated; both express a perfecting. The German word *vollenden* gives the meaning of these two words quite well. Plutarch then goes on to describe the rite in the *Telesterion* of Eleusis.[1] The initiate wanders about in darkness until he finally comes into the light; then he looks with a new insight on the unclean mass of the living whom he has left behind; they 'remain in misery for their fear of death because they will not believe in the goods which surpass this world'.

No drama can have such an effect as this. The ancient mysteries could have it because behind the visible rites there was a reality;[2] only this reality could bring about such awe in men. It must have been something wholly new, which had the power to change men so. That the hope the mysteries awakened was of a life beyond, we can see for example in Heracles who went through the initiation at Eleusis before going into the underworld, so as to come well out of his journey. Euripides has him say, 'because I had seen the rites of the initiates it went well with me' (Heracles, 613). The ideal which lies behind the descent of Heracles is that of the ancient saviour, the σώτηρ; it finds fulfilment in the descent of our Saviour into hell.

It has already been indicated, says Otto, that the pre-Greek goddess of the dead, Persephone, later called Kore by the Greeks and Proserpina by the Romans, is not identical with the corn. In the study of ancient mystery religions this identification has often been made; but it does not meet the facts. That would be to reduce the old pelasgian religion to a mere vegetation cult, and to miss its true depth. To look on the myths as mere skits on the life of nature, as has been done in modern times, is to degrade them to a mere cult of natural life in mythical forms. But this sort of thing has no religious force in it; rather it would be the sort of purely functional cultus which we have been able to observe in our own day. For such a cult as this and the ideas of the world which underlie it life stops with death, and nothing remains of

---

[1] The hall of consecration, the hall of completion: in Eleusis a hall with many columns.

[2] A reality which of course remained imprisoned within the forces of the cosmos.

man's personality except the life he has in his race. Such ideas have no power to form a religion. In later times recognition was no longer given to the real tragedy in ancient life, to the abyss of pain and misery which surrounded it. Yet in fact it was just this side of ancient piety which brought the men of that day nearer to Christianity. For Christianity means that someone has really risen out of the underworld again; Christ passed through death and the abyss, rose from the dead and brought to men the life of the *aion.*

In the mysteries of Eleusis the cult does not content itself with mere veneration for the life in nature; the fundamental notion in these mysteries, that of the bond between life and death, is one we meet as well in the Greek hymn to Demeter. The end of this hymn is an introduction to the mysteries; this is a wholly new moment, and it shows us clearly how inadequate is the merely material explanation of the Eleusinian worship as a 'cult of the fields'.

Before Demeter returned with Persephone to Olympus she taught the great men of Eleusis her mysteries.

She went to the ruling kings; she showed Triptolemos, the horse-taming Diocles, the powerful Eumolpus and the ruler of the peoples, Keleos, the doing of sacred things. She taught Triptolemos Polyxeinos and Diocles the good *Orgia,* the holy matters (*mysteria*) which no one is allowed to counterfeit or to penetrate or to betray; for great reverence towards the gods holds back the tongue of man. That man is blessed who has kept all this from mortals. But the man who is not an initiate and not a participant of holy things does not have the same share or the same lot when he is gone from the earth; he remains in miserable darkness. But when the goddess had put everything aright she returned to Olympus, to the gods' assembly. . . .

Demeter showed . . . the doing of holy things and taught the good *Orgia* . . . the holy mysteries: δ[εῖξε] . . . δρημοσύνην τ' ἱερῶν καὶ ἐπέραδεν ὄργια καλά . . . σεμνά.

The initiation into the mysteries is a showing (δεικνύειν). Something is shown which is to be imitated. So too Christ himself showed at the institution of his mysteries exactly what they were to do; they were to imitate exactly what he had shown them. In the imitation, exactly that takes place which did in the first act.

What is shown is the doing of holy things (δρημοσύνη ἱερῶν). The root verb δράω is the one from which is derived the word drama: a term which unfortunately has, among us, become completely secular. Drama is in the beginning something holy; Clement of Alexandria speaks in one place of the mysteries as a δρᾶμα μυστικόν.[1] Worship consists in actions and sacred formulae; the goddess teaches both to men.

The designation of the mystery action as ὄργια points to the fact that we are concerned here with a sacred *action*; this word is connected with the normal Greek word for work, ἔργον.

Then comes mention of the discipline of the mysteries. Reverence before the gods requires that one should not counterfeit the mysteries; literally, go beyond them, and make them known to the uninitiated. Thus, seven centuries before Christ, we have evidence of a complete discipline of the secret in relation to the mysteries.

The poet then speaks a blessing: ὄλβιος, ὅς τάδ' ὤπυπεν ἐπιχθωνίων ἀνθρώπων. . . . It is the first blessing of the initiate. By initiation into the gods' mysteries men who would otherwise die and come to nothingness gain some call on eternity. We too know such blessings from the gospels.

Those who are not initiated go down after death into the kingdom of darkness; in much the same way as the ancient Greeks, the contemporary Jews imagined this as a kingdom of shadows, which they called Sheol.

After the celebration of her mysteries has been ordered the goddess returns to Olympus. So too Christ rose up to heaven once more after he had instituted his mysteries. But as they are carried out he remains present on the earth.

Perhaps this hymn was a prelude (προοίμιον) to further hymns in honour of the god.

Looking back we may pose the question once more: what does this hymn tell us about the content of the Eleusinian mysteries? The blessing upon the initiates at the end of the poem tells us that the *mystai* have the assurance of an everlasting and blessed life; they will not go down to the kingdom of the shadows. This worship can therefore by no means be exhausted in a cult of the fields; cultivation is not even mentioned in the hymn. If the hymn does promise earthly riches to the man to whom the gods are gracious the promise is not the essential thing; this is life with the gods. This is the same case with the gospel (Mt. 19, 29) where Christ promises similar things to his disciples. 'Every man who leaves home, brothers, sisters, father and mother for my sake will receive a hundred fold for it, and inherit eternal life'. Again, earthly and eternal blessings together.

[1] Cf Protreptikos II, 12, 2.

The decisive idea, which meets us over and over again, is this: just as the field cannot bear fruit except from the death of the seed, all the life of nature is immediately related to death. Even in begetting and birth from which life takes its rise, death is at work.

The way of Persephone into the underworld and her return from it do not signify the ruin and re-birth of vegetation. Sowing and reaping were given to men long after her descent there; this important fact is hidden in the poetic version of the myth in the Hymn to Demeter.

The point is that man, in order to preserve his life, must turn to the goddess of the dead; at Eleusis he finds her. Here Demeter has given him a consecration and a sight by which death is to be overcome. This thought of the overcoming of death is what brought men to Eleusis; there everlasting life was given to them. The high-point of the mystery was the point at which the symbol was given to them in which death was overcome.

The death of animal life brought man to the mysteries. Death is the condition for the rise of new life; if there were no death there could be no reproduction. This too is the deepest idea of the myth of Demeter and Persephone. Fruitfulness which man needs comes from the hand of the goddess of death.

We have a pagan sermon about Eleusis; its author is Aristeides who was born in 129 after Christ, in Mysia, and so is a contemporary of St Polycarp.[1] The speaker had called on the gods of healing because he was ill and also visited Eleusis. He praises the city in this way:

'Who among the Greeks or the barbarians is so foolish and so slow of mind that he does not hold Eleusis to be a temple common to all mankind; of all places man holds divine the one most full of awe and joy. (φρικωδέστατον) (the fathers sometimes use the expression φρικτὰ μυστήρια; the word is derived from φρίσσειν to shudder. This is the essence of religion: after the first fear comes the height of joy.[2]) 'What other places have been so celebrated in the stories of the poets; where have the sacred deeds (δρώμενα) greater power to bring men to awe; where are things given men to see (ὁρώμενα) in greater competition with those done here? All that belongs to the vision which many generations of blessed men and women have seen in unutterable images is put into the shade here; what the poets and the tellers of great deeds

---

[1] Aristeides 19, 421, Turchi's Fragments. Cf note 40.
[2] Cf Quasten *Mysterium Tremendum* in *Vom Christlichen Mysterium* Patmos, 1951.

and the writers say is that Kore, the daughter of Demeter was for a long time invisible; that Demeter in seeking her went over land and sea, and for a long time could not find her. Then she came to Eleusis and gave the place its name. Eleusis means *adventus*, arrival ἐλεύσαμαι = veniam = I shall come. Then she found her daughter and instituted the mysteries.'

Roman writers too give Eleusis the highest praise. Cicero for example writes in his *De Legibus*, II, 14:

> It is my opinion that Athens has brought much that is noble and even divine into the life of men; but of all this, nothing more so than those mysteries by which we are trained out of undiscipline to human ways. They are called *initia*, initiations; but we have come to know them as *principia vitae*: the springs of life. *Through them we have not only received the way and manner of a joyful life, but also have learnt to die with a better hope.*

As the text expresses it, Cicero is conscious that both lives, that of this world and of the next belong inseparably together. The Christian hears the same theme in the communion of the eleventh Sunday after Pentecost: '*Honora Dominum de tua substantia et de primitiis frugum tuarum; et implebuntur horrea tua saturitate et vino torcularia redundabunt.*' Bread and wine have the meaning of life's highest joy; at the same time they are symbols of a higher life after death. The song in this communion is a harvest song of life in the Spirit.

We have another blessing of the *Mystes* from Pindar, which Clement of Alexandria has preserved for us:[1] 'Blessed is he who, after he has seen these things, passes under the earth. He knows the end of life; he knows as well the first beginning which is the gift of Zeus (new life); the man who has seen the mysteries knows new life'.

This blessing is a real liturgical song to be sung in a service just as we Christians sing benedictions in the celebration of the Mystery. The communion of the feast of All Saints comes to mind: 'Blessed are the clean of heart. . . .' Scripture contains a number of such blessings; Psalm one begins with a blessing. The genre is one which has its origin in cult.

A similar blessing is found in a fragment of Sophocles preserved for us in Plutarch: 'O thrice blessed among mortals who, after having seen

[1]Fragment 137a (Schroeder) in Clement of Alexandria, *Stromata*, III, 3, 17, 2 (Staehlin pp. 203, 16–18).

these rites, pass under to the kingdom of Hades; for him alone is it *moira* that he shall live; for the others all is evil there.'[1]

This too is a formula from cult, employed in poetry. In Apuleius we have also the formula, *beatus et ter beatus*.[2] (It is a very ancient usage in cult to repeat a formula three times, sometimes in a higher tone each time.)

No play can have had such effect upon men as the mysteries of Eleusis; this was possible only because the onlooker was certain that these mysteries were no spectacle in the modern sense but experience and reality. The truth which was revealed in Eleusis must have been something wholly new, something beyond proof which could be experienced only in the mystery; it was something which turned to another world.

We have a single piece of evidence about the highpoint of the action, which is found in Hippolytus of Rome, *Elenchos*, V, 8, 39, in his discourse on the mysteries of Attis: ' . . . the Phrygians know it as a green ear which has been plucked; and after them, the Athenians when they are initiated at Eleusis and show to the onlookers the great and marvellous, the most perfect mystery for their sight: an ear plucked in silence.' (It would be possible, by moving the comma after μυστήριον or σιωπή, to translate as above, or as 'the mystery of silence, a plucked ear'. Still, content and probability lean very much towards the 'mystery' being presented as 'an ear plucked in silence'.)

This vision, the sight of an ear of grain, is what gave countless men such happiness. That might seem at first thought something remarkable. But for us Christians too at the high point of our mystery celebration we are shown a piece of bread and a cup with wine. In the ancient mysteries they needed only to see the ear; in this vision was salvation for the initiate. To it came educated men from all over the world; we have only to think of Sophocles and Plato. At the moment of seeing the ear they received the highest of all visions and felt that they were finally saved.

All of this gives us some idea of the simplicity of ancient and at the same time early Christian liturgy. All its strength lies in faith; and faith does not need external help, like that which grew up in the late Middle Ages.

---

[1] Fragment 753 (Nauck) in Turchi, *Fontes Historiae Mysteriorum* (1923), No. 52.
[2] In the Metamorphoses XI, 16.

In the attempts to interpret the mysteries of Eleusis it is again and again forgotten that what is involved is not something which reason can explain, but a mystery; the mysteries give men the capacity to live in anticipation what in fact lies only in the world beyond. This is so too in the participation required in the celebration of the Christian mystery: in the daily mystery, in which the memorial of the death and resurrection of Christ is carried out, we exercise ourselves in dying and rising, in order one day the more surely to be able to die and rise in truth. The food of this sacrament is called *Viaticum*, accompaniment for the journey, when it is given to a man for nourishment in the hour of death. It is to be his food for a journey into the next world.

What Hippolytus of Rome tells us about what the initiates were given to see, 'the great and wonderful, the all-perfect mystery, an ear plucked in silence' is not open to doubt, says W. F. Otto. That it should have been an ear is in keeping with the tradition that Demeter taught men the cultivation of the fields, in particular the cultivation of cereal crops. The ear was the gift of the goddess which was passed on from Eleusis to the rest of the world.

Yet the showing of the ear must have had a still deeper meaning as well; the sight of an ear of corn, taken just as that, can call up no happiness in man, but rather awaken only sadness and resignation; for nature lives again after it has died for a time; but man, once dead, does not return. Throughout the whole of ancient civilization a breath of sorrow and complaint passes at this, man's fate. It was the Christians who first took the exchange of dying and coming once more to life as a comfort and a proof of their hope for resurrection.[1]

Deubner in his book *Attische Feste* (1932, p. 86) has rightly understood that what is at stake here is no mere ceremony of nature. But his notion that it was the custom to leave an ear standing in the field at harvest in order to have it as a symbol of assurance for the new growing life for the celebration of the mystery in October, in other words at a time when the corn was no longer growing, would be a kind of forgery. We do not make progress with this kind of interpretation.

There can be no doubt that something took place on the level of wonder. It is a custom, known of from many sources, to show in religious cult plants which have had some kind of wonderful growth. This can be observed today in Africa. It may have been something

---

[1] Cf Clement of Rome, *Epistle to the Corinthians* I, 24 and 26; also Minucius Felix, *Octavius* XXXIV, 11.

of this sort which was done with the ear. The ear which has grown by some marvellous means is a revelation of the risen goddess; it is the appearance of Persephone herself after her descent into the kingdom of the dead. The *Mystai* are brought by means of it into the realm of the marvellous, into the presence of the goddess. This was the certainty of the *mystes* born of what he saw and bringing him joy. Isocrates, the fifth century orator, tells us in his *Panegyric* (4, 28) that our ancestors had once done great services to the goddess as she wandered through the land in search of her daughter, services 'of which only the initiated may hear'. The goddess was well disposed towards men; she made them gifts: 'fruits and the rites which awaken in those who participate joyful hopes for all eternity'. This is a most important indication of what the mystery of the ear revealed to the *mystai*: the exaltation of the life of this world through cultivation of the fields and the hope of a life to come. The main object of the Eleusinian celebration was therefore sadness at the loss of Proserpina and the passage of this sorrow into joy at the re-appearance of the goddess. Clement of Alexandria tells us about the content of the night part of the celebration in the *Protrepticus* II par 12: 'A mystic drama was made for Demeter and Kore; Eleusis shows the wandering, the rape and the mourning for her by the light of torches.'

The real object of the pagan mystery celebrations was the fulfilment of the longing to overcome death; we find this as well in the spring festival of Attis and Cybele which was observed at Rome and turned sadness into the highest joy. Here is the *Fasti* of Philocalus, a calendar of feasts for the year 354:

Idibus Mart.	Canna Sacra	
XI Kal April	Arbor intrat	22 March
IX Kal April	Sanguem	24 March
VIII Kal April	Hilaria	25 March
VII Kal April	Requietio	26 March
VI Kal April	Lavatio	27 March

In the grove of the mother of the gods a pine tree was cut down which represented Attis. It was garlanded, and on the 22nd brought solemnly into the city; there the dead god was mourned. On the twenty-fourth this mourning came to its high point, the day of blood, when the priests of Attis, the Galli, wounded themselves in wild dancing and let their blood flow on the altar. After a night celebration, the twenty-fifth turned the sorrow of the past into great joy as the god came to life once more. On the twenty-seventh of March the image of the goddess was bathed with solemn ceremonies and on the twenty-eighth there was a special rite as well.

We gain some idea of what these ceremonies meant to a contemporary from a remark of the Neo-Platonist Damascius who wrote in the fifth century. In his life of Isidore he says:[1]

> At that time he went to sleep at Hierapolis and in his dream he thought that he became Attis. The feast of the mother of the gods, the Hilaria as they call it, was ended which reveals our salvation from Hades.

He had then made the pilgrimage to Hierapolis and here entered a sacred sleep in the temple, in order to receive a revelation; and the mother of the gods who has Attis in her care celebrated an Easter with him, now her initiate; this feast meant for him salvation from everlasting death. We Christians could not give a finer description of Easter: we are set free from everlasting death because Christ has gone down into the lower world and overcome death. The words, 'he thought in a dream that he was Attis' show that the initiate becomes identified with the god. This is the aim of all mystery celebrations; thus, in this story, we hear the longing to overcome death which is fulfilled in Christ.

The celebration of the mysteries took place at the point in spring when day and night were equal; the emperor Julian tells what the meaning of this timing was in his fifth Oration to the mother of the gods:

> witness for this is found in the time at which it takes place. The sacred tree is cut down on the day upon which the sun reaches the height of likeness between day and night; then the trumpets blare, but on the third day the sacred and unutterable harvest of the god *gallos* is cut. These follow the Hilaria and the feasts.[2]

At the time of the Emperor Julian, Salustius writes in his book, *On the Gods and the Cosmos*, Chapter 4, concerning the myth of Attis:

> Because then the myth is so closely related to the cosmos we celebrate a feast in imitation of the cosmos. First of all, because we have fallen from heaven and live with the nymphs in lowliness, we keep our-

[1]Photius, *Bibliotheca* 242, (Bekker); Cf J.L.W. 14 (1938), p. 63, note 114.
[2]Cf J.L.W. 14, 63, note 115.

selves from bread and all other coarse and stained foods (for both are
opposed to the soul). Then comes the felling of the tree and the fast in
which also we are cut off from the march in the kingdom of becoming.
Then we are fed with milk so that we may be reborn; then comes the
feast of joy and garlands and as it were a return to the gods. Even the
time at which the rites take place give witness of that; for this is spring,
at about the point when the day and the night are equal, when becoming
ceases in its becoming and the day becomes longer than the night,
which is fitting for the soul which is journeying upwards.[1]

The Christian Easter has therefore been set on the course not of
the Jewish pasch but of the pagan Spring festivals; it is always in
accord with the first full moon of the Spring. A special place in Christian
worship is also given to the 25th of March; it was not only the high-
point of the Roman, pagan Spring festival, as we have already seen,
but in parts of Gaul it was a fixed date for Easter as well. The prayers
for the feast of the Annunciation which mention all the saving acts of
Christ indicate this even today. (Cf the postcommunion for the mass
of the 25th of March in the Roman Missal.)[2]

In the ceremonies which we have described the content was cosmic
mysteries: the *mystai* were made one with their cosmic deities and came
to have a share in the life of those gods. But by his mysteries the
Christian is made one with God who stands over and above the world.
The understanding of those other mysteries however has its meaning
for us because they do make clear what is man's end: union with God.

As we have already seen, worship is inseparably bound up with the
myths of the first age; so too the information which is available about
these myths is most important to us because it brings us to the *eidos*
of worship. In Christianity, too, man will first be a real man and so
a real Christian when in the celebration of the mystery he takes part
in what Christ has done.

According to the myth of Ceram men on their way to the goddess
Satene are marked with the sign of death; hence the ritual. Maro dance
means initiation into death. The cosmic mysteries remain bound up
with death; the Christian mysteries on the other hand lead man the
way across death into new life in which there is no dying any longer.
Myth and cult belong inseparably together, in the Christian religion

[1]Ibid, note 116.
[2]Cf also Ämiliana Löhr, *Der 25 März—ein österliches Datum* in *Vom heiligen
Pascha*. Patmos, 1950, pp. 81–89.

as well as any other. Yet the consciousness of this connexion has been greatly lost in modern Christianity. What is lacking is the bond at the level of being itself, which is not to be won by ascesis and teaching alone. The very power to live as a Christian is what the mystery gives; in the mystery the Christian comes to a share in the life of Christ. It is all important that he should be placed into the great design, the *oikonomia*, of Christ; all the rest is a development from this bond at the level of being.

On the island of Ceram the ceremonies which accompanied, or better still carried forward and promoted the whole of life were in fact repetitions of the mythical events of a first age: thus the event of the present was brought into contact with the mythical first deed. This means that life is being returned to its proper place; it is being re-placed in the order of the world's course, set into the primaeval act in which the gods themselves take part. What took place then is made presence in the rite for the worshippers; the rite returns to the first age and binds men to it.

These myths however are no literary descriptions; what is revealed in them is a vision of the world whose reality, present to them in the rites, commands men to-day. Only by and through the rites can we grasp the true meaning of those primaeval events; the rites are necessary for life itself.

This last idea is most important for the Christian. At the centre of his life stands the liturgy; he is conscious that his life hangs on its celebration; it can never become for him mere tiresome routine. This is so because the life of every day draws its meaning from it, is continually stimulated by the presence of the primaeval fact.

The primitive man lives in this vision. So, then, for him the chance happenings of every day are not chance at all; he sees in everything its connexion to the primaeval age which is made present in his ritual. This is the reason for the happiness which primitive men have; modern man who has lost this consciousness sees everything which happens to him as mere chance. The separation from God's world makes him miserable by delivering him up to this apparent chance; it drives him at last to doubt and even to crime. At the end of it all there is nothing but the hero's downfall. Hence it is all the more important that the Christian should understand what worship means.

Karl Kerenyi and C. G. Jung collaborated on a book, *Einführung in das Wesen der Mythologie* (fourth edition, 1951), which enquires into the relationship of mythology and the origin of things. They conclude that the myth was first lived; to-day we look at the myth most often as a work of literature and so miss the essence of the thing. What the myth is in the life of Ceram to-day it once was in the lives of the ancient Greeks, Romans and Teutons.

The lesson which all of this has for us Christians is this: we must live our own sacred history. For example when the church on Septuagesima Sunday begins her reading of the book of Genesis, she brings the primaeval fact to life: creation, the Fall and all the rest. When a whole community celebrates the reading of these lessons solemnly, that makes not a 'reading' in the usual sense like the reading we do for curiosity about news. No, with the reading of The Scripture we return to the first age; we place ourselves into the primaeval act which is made present; from it we learn to understand what our own very being is, at the beginning of which there is creation and sin. This reading is live and takes possession of us.

At the beginning of this lesson stands the all-important words: *in principio*; in the first beginning, in the first ground of our being. It means that we return to this first ground, to God. We do not go back, as the philosopher does, to the first principle in science, but rather to the first real principle of being. In doing so we do not seek science as he does; science, Virgil tells us, seeks *rerum cognoscere causas*. Only when science comes to its limits does it give testimony to God's working there; the life of the liturgy for its part goes straight to God. Man cannot understand him as the ultimate cause but only in contemplation give him recognition. The writings of the New Testament begin too, in the gospel of St John, with this same decisive phrase: ἐν ἀρχῇ: in the beginning was the Logos. It too takes us back to the heart of our being, to God's new creation, the saving deed. Continually, the Holy Scripture shows us this beginning which none of us can comprehend, although we may contemplate it in faith and the deep knowledge which flows from faith: *Gnosis*.

The difference between a scientific and a contemplative way of looking at religious life and the life in the mystery can be well illustrated in the doctrine of the sacraments. In the view of some theologians Christ placed the grace which he had earned by his sacrifice in the sacraments; when the sacrament is performed those who perform it receive the grace it contains. The sacrament is the cause of grace. In the mystery conception it is the primaeval saving act which is made present; from it flows immediately to men the life and the grace of God.[1] The myth is lived out in worship; the rite is living myth. It seeks in the past a model which will give to it the meaning of its present action; the Christian sacraments make this clear enough.[2] A child is born and baptized; it is passed into the water, the Trinity is invoked upon it and it is brought out from the waters in the name of the Trinity. As Christ died, so man dies too by being buried in the dark womb of the waters. As Christ rose again so man rises from the water in the name of the Trinity, to a new life. By this rite in which man is plunged into the primaeval saving act his life which in itself was a small and petty thing gains a vast dimension: man becomes a second Christ.

Still more strongly do we perceive the power of the primaeval saving act made present, in the Eucharist; by the transformation and the consumption of the bread and wine man is filled with the power of Christ. He returns to that primaeval force with which God gave life to the world in the death and resurrection of Christ. Man's action in the rite is made one with God's action. In doing so, man seeks for examples in ancient times to give meaning to what he does. Hence, in the Canon of the Roman Mass, we find as types of the present sacrifice the sacrifice of Abel, Abraham and Melchisedech. Behind all these types there is Christ, the highest archetype. In the sacrifice of the mass we do the deed of Christ; we place our being in the most intimate relationship with the act of the God-man. Thus our act takes on a truly divine dimension.

All these examples show that the myth is no mere tale; rather it is a reality which is lived.[3] In this perception the Christian must read Sacred Scripture. It is not merely biblical history; in any case it is not its ultimate meaning, to be past history. No more are myths literary inventions; they are the expression of a greater reality which continually

[1] This is of course only in relative contrast to what has been said before; the sacraments are only instrumental causes of grace. They act, according to the classical teaching of St Thomas in the power of the passion of Christ, so that through the sacraments the primal saving act is made actively present. Cf *Summa Theologiae* III, 65, 5; also Polycarp Wegenaer, *Heilsgegenwart*, Aschendorff, 1958.

[2] The detailed exposition of the myth and its live form in the rite should give a very clear picture of what is involved in the type: a sacred action of the past becomes present, to effect the salvation of the worshippers. Yet at the same time Casel's foremost intention should not be overlooked: through such analogies, he is seeking to make intelligible the formal structure of Christian worship; and the foundation of Christian sacraments and worship is not some kind of myth but a real, historical fact.

[3] Cf Malinowski, *Myth in Primitive Psychology*, London, 1926.

influences and moves the life of man. They give man at once moral understanding and directions how to fashion his life in keeping with that understanding.

The living reality of the myths is what we experience in worship. By the solemn reading the deed of the first age is made immediate presence; so then the readings in the mass are in a sense a *sacramentum*. As we read in the Matins of Septuagesima how God fashioned the world and man, this act becomes once more a Spiritual presence in our midst. Of course we know that man has crossed God's plan by sin. Adam took on guilt; we who by our sin share in his sinful life can have no example or help from him. Our way must be the way of penance to the Pasch where the second Adam, Christ, makes his appearance. He is our type; his life is the life we must learn to lead. Baptism used to take place in the night of the Pasch so that man might bind himself as closely as possible to the primaeval act, the act of Christ, and thus bring to realization the plan which God had from all eternity. This is the vision to which Lent gives witness: by penance we must turn from the first Adam to the second; we must die and rise with the second Adam who gives to man the fullness of life, the life of the *aion*.

There is to be found in Herodotus (I, 131) an example of how the ancient peoples thought a recitation of the primaeval act necessary in connexion with sacrifice. He tells us that the Persians offered to the heaven which they call Zeus, as well as to the sun, the stars and the powers of nature; they make these sacrifices on the high places.

He then goes on to say that there is always a priest present at the sacrifice to sing a tale of the gods; without him, the Persians will not have sacrifice performed. Some of these sacrificial chants are very old, going back two millenia before Christ. They tell in solemn manner of how the gods and the world came to be; it is through chant of this kind, depicting the first age, that the sacrifice gets its value, indeed its very meaning; the hymn makes contact with the primaeval act; only in such contact can the sacrifice perform its aim, which is to bind man back to God and reconcile them.

There was originally a cosmogony in the Canon of the Mass: a praise of creation. It was a solemn hymn in praise of creation and redemption; so it too brought us back to the beginning. Man is unable to speak of these things in God's presence in his everyday language; it is worship which makes him a poet.

The finest example, however, which we have today of this plunge to first beginnings is found in the liturgy of Easter Eve. Although the church has already read the recital of creation at the beginning of Septuagesima she repeats it as she begins this night. The whole of the work of salvation—creation and redemption—become, rightly understood, presence in this night.

These things of God can yield to us only the beginnings of knowledge; the *mythos* gives us no proof; it leads us to contemplation. But the first beginnings of what is from God is deeper than all that belongs to human reason. By its being placed in contact with the origins which do not perish the life of man, which can perish, receives a meaning which abides.

Indeed, Christ himself tells us in the gospel that we must go back to the first age in order to find a lasting meaning for our life (Mt 19, 3–12). The Pharisees ask him whether a man may leave his wife for any cause at all. His answer is, 'Have you not read that the creator of the world made man and woman *in the beginning?*' Christ does not explain what he thinks; he does not ask these learned men what their studies about the matter have led them to believe. He says, 'have you not read . . . ?' He places his reliance on the primaeval act which had for its content God's idea; this is what decides the matter. As we saw was the case with the myths, he gives no proof here; religion goes the way Christ showed to it, the way back to the primaeval fact. The Pharisees come along with casuistry: 'why then did Moses command that one might draw up a bill of divorce and send one's wife away?' At this for the second time Christ reminds them of the first ideal form: 'in the beginning it was not so'. Moses as a lawgiver had to take account of human weakness which was not prepared to answer the challenge of God's ideal in living. This ideal was that man and woman should be one flesh. God said this through Adam when Adam looked at his wife . . . 'for this reason a man shall leave father and mother and hold fast to his wife and the two shall be one flesh'. In the gospel Christ says, 'God spoke'; Genesis assigns the words to Adam; Adam then spoke them as medium for God. Everyone who leaves his wife commits adultery because he offends against the ideal form of God.

Man has, in fact, as time has passed, watered down and corrupted by his sin and weakness the first idea which God expressed in his creating work.

Christ came to restore the beginning, the ἀρχή. Christianity, in contrast to the myth has then a second ἀρχή; the other had only one, which was ever more being corrupted and lost by men. The ancient world conceived this in the image of the dying world; the first age was that of paradise, the golden age. Then came the silver, the age of bronze and finally the iron age. Still, even in this course of ruin there remained the hope that the golden age might return: Virgil in Eclogue IV is looking for a child who will bring back once more the age of Saturn, in other words, the first age. This hope did find fulfilment in the mystery of Christ's birth when the virgin's son, the *puer* in all the meaning of that word, brought back the new kingdom. From this vision of the work of salvation we are first able to grasp what is meant by the ἀνακεφαλαίωσις, the 'recapitulation' of the universe in Christ its head, as St Paul tells us the case is, in Ephesians 1, 10: Christ brings back the primaeval age; creation regains its largest estate (κεφαλή). In Christ's religion the marvellous grace of God is revealed which gives us back a second first estate; this is, by faith and the mystery, made present. We do not need to long for the paradise that was lost.

The idea of the recapitulatio (ἀνακεφαλαίοσις) meant a great deal to the Fathers; Christ restored the beginning; the primaeval thought which God had thought was brought back to its place by Christ and the church; the prayer after the second prophecy for Easter Eve in the old Rite expresses the notion in this way: let the whole world know and see how what was cast down is made upstanding; what was grown old is made new; and through him from whom they took their Origin all things shall return to their wholeness: Jesus Christ thy Son. *Totusque mundus experiatur et videat deiecta erigi, inveterata renovari et per ipsum redire omnia in integrum a quo sumpsere principium: Dominum nostrum Iesum Christum filium tuum.* In the night of Easter even more than in the night of the Nativity we come to know the return to our Origin. What has gone to ruin through the sin of man is now restored through Christ in accordance with God's first design, his idea.

Worship is the means which brings back the Origin; in it the new Beginning is made present for the Christian. What he experiences in his worship is not only an after-effect of the saving act; the saving act itself takes on presence. The object of all Christian worship is this saving act of Christ; the deeds of the first fathers which we read of in connexion with it are types, signs, prophecy. Take for example the story of Noah. His name is a saviour's name; it means the comforter. 'One shall give us comfort in the toilsome work of our hands in the fields which the Lord has cursed', says Lamech when his son is born (Genesis 5, 30). After the flood Noah becomes the second father of the human race; the father of the chosen race of God is Abraham. His story too points clearly forward to Christ. Naturally the actions of these first fathers are not without the influence of human weakness and sin; yet, even though God's first idea may seem weak in them for this reason they keep their significance as types. At God's command Abraham offered his son, a type of Christ. He was allowed by God's same will to spare him and sacrifice an animal in his stead. But God did not spare his own son; he sacrificed him in death. The deeds of those fathers and the cult of the Old Testament are a shadow; the body which casts it is Christ. In the night of Easter we read the prophecies of Abraham's sacrifice; in that same night we find them fulfilled in the sacrifice of Christ.

At this point we may return for a moment to consider Malinowski's studies (Note 1 on p. 125) on the myth and primitive psychology. He holds that in a primitive society the myths are living primaeval form. He gives the example of the rites of Ceram which we discussed at length previously. But the myths turn lifeless when they are no longer believed. So then for the Greeks who no longer believe, the myths fall to the state of mere literary materials; they are reduced to purely human level, indeed deprived of all value. This fact is the key to our understanding of what the church fathers thought about the myths; it is the corrupt form in which they find the myths which they reject; this is what they have to battle against. Yet they do not overlook the fact that there was an original content of religious ideas of a fundamental kind in both the myths and the mysteries of the pagans. They not only recognize this, but in part they even take over the language of that world for use in Christian worship. Clement of Alexandria (*Stromata* VI 4, 2) speaks of the relation which the mysteries have to the Origins of things.

The constitutive essence then of myth is a living reality, not literary invention. The worshippers believe that these events were in the beginning and influence the fates of men to-day. The myth tells of a higher, abiding reality which man must come to know, in order to possess his own existence and from it form his own conduct.

Thus the Christian must live his life in a continuous relationship to Christ; he must seek his exemplar in the gospels and, in everything which happens, ask what he is to make of it in the light of Christ.

Christ is the form by which we are to be fashioned; each of us lives his life, each of us is a second Christ.

Yet in considering what the myths mean Malinowski does not allow any such symbolic meaning to them. If we start from the modern concept of symbol this will be well enough; but in the ancient meaning of symbol as possessing and seeing reality in it, the myth does indeed have such a symbolic value; it possesses something of the primaeval order of the cosmos.

Malinowski does conclude that the myth is not explanatory or aitiological; the myth does not give a cause, an αἰτία. What it does do is by recital to restore a primaeval perfection. Now this consideration is a decisive one for Christians in evaluating the liturgy: the word which is spoken in it brings back the primaeval perfection of reality; not merely the sacrament but the word. Indeed even better than the rite, which remains the same throughout, the word sets out the various phases of the saving work. For example at Epiphany it is the glory of Christ which is put more before our sight and in Lent his sacrifice. The word belongs to worship.

The myth does not then explain but give out a precedent for events. The events of the present are to be seen in the light of this precedent; something is so now because it was so in the first age. Malinowski does not come this far; he does not say what the myth is; it is Kerenyi who concludes that the myth casts its light on the events of the present, and in this light they receive their first significance. The myth tells us how to interpret in the present what would otherwise be a perplexing matter. Take for example again the fourth eclogue of Virgil: the birth of a child is symbol for the entry of a new age.

This means that the Christian must look at everything in Christ's light; the signs in the passing events which would threaten to bring so many people into doubt can only be rightly understood in connexion with the saving design of Christ; this design begins with sin and ends with redemption. In this sense clarity and light flow from every true myth onto what is and what is to be for us. The myth casts its light not on a cause but on the primaeval state of things; what we can grasp by strict reason lies below this; in contemplation and contemplation alone we can learn of the beginning which is so far above us.

For ancient philosophers the beginning, the ἀρχή or first thing— water for example or fire—was not a cause but a primaeval *state* from which all the rest arose, yet did not perish in so doing. This was how they explained the fashioning of the world. The attempts to explain these things in a scientific manner have not reached their aim; for the Christian it is accepted that everything must be traced to God as the creation recital in Genesis traces it. This recital does not however intend a scientific explanation of the world; it shows God as the creator of all. In the first place the earth was a chaos; the Spirit of God moved over the deeps; God uttered his first decree; then light came into the chaos. God made the cosmos, the ordered universe, by the *Logos*. For the Christian, therefore, God's own depths are the primaeval beginning, the ἀρχή, from which the cosmos proceeds.

As the primaeval state is unique, so are the data of the myth. They are fixed in the timeless past and they are themselves changeless. The first note of myth is return to the origins and the first age: thus Kerenyi explains how the ancient peoples came to the myth as they sought to explain the world. From this we are to understand what God's revelation is: a creation from the first beginning. In the revelation through Christ God has spoken in clear language without human addition. The Word itself, the *Logos* has expressed itself. 'In the Beginning was the Word (*Logos*) and the Word was with God and the Word was God (Jn. 1, 1). The question about the first roots of being is therefore a question about the first state of being; Kerenyi says, 'the question which seems to be "why" is really "whence".' All study is therefore a search for the origin and when we give reasons we can, at the deepest level only, be permitting the mind to fall back on what is most fundamental; as one can try to do with the German word *Abgrund*: the foundation with no foundation; which yet upholds us.

Most important of all is that we are taken back to the first age; when the individual realizes the myth and acts in accordance with it, he himself steps into the background. Christ shows us this in the gospel passages just mentioned: in them he points to God, the primaeval idea. So also the real teller of the myths goes right back beyond the first age which is the subject of his story; the story counts rather than his personality, as Kerenyi puts it.

In his book Kerenyi goes on to speak of the birth of the divine child. This child in the myths is God himself; he is the symbol of a new age: the *pater futuri saeculi*. He brings back the lost age of the past and makes of it a gift to men in more precious form than ever. God's new rule is established; hence, the prophet calls the child *Deus Fortis*. The birth of a child is a sign for the deed God does. Other events in nature

—the rising of the Sun for example—are signs of the appearance of God. The whole of nature has its deepest meaning by pointing to what belongs to God himself.

Then come the ceremonies of ritual: they are the translation of a myth into action, in Kerenyi's words. This is a most important thesis for us, and we should not forget it in the celebration of our Christian liturgy. In this liturgy the death of Christ is portrayed in image, as when a man is plunged under the water and thus killed 'in figure'. Here is the presentation of the first act of our salvation, and not merely in words but in gesture too. Still more strongly is this expressed in the mass; the bread is Christ's body, the wine is his blood; they lie separated upon the altar and are consecrated by the formula. The first great fact, that all the reality of heaven plays in earthly things, is presented here in ritual: the separate forms are an image of the God-Man, offered, for only in death are body and blood separated: the Lord lies as one dead upon the altar.[1]

But the ancient vegetation cults have their importance for us too; upon them the later mysteries are constructed. Examples of such cults are Osiris, in Egypt; Adonis of the Phoenicians, something very much like it in Assyria which we have come to know from texts and pictures found there. However strange it may seem, these cults can help us to understand our own mystery. In those ancient mysteries the initiate went through death and resurrection into a new life; how lively this idea was in the ancient Orient we may see from a text of the prophet Osee which the church reads on Good Friday, and again in the third nocturn of the old Matins of Easter and finally in the little lesson of the hours for the whole of Eastertide. It is the first verse of the sixth chapter:

> Come, let us return to the Lord. For he has broken us, and he will heal us too. He has smitten us and he will bind us up once more. After two days he will give us life again; on the third, he will raise us up and we shall live before his face.

Here is a most important text; it contains the whole of the Paschal mystery. We notice that not only is the people to be healed after a terrible blow has befallen it, but that after two days it is to rise. 'After two days he will give back our life; on the third, he will raise us up and we shall live in sight of him.' Death strikes at the joy of resurrection.

[1] From conferences 1944–45.

vegetation cult

What we have here are the deeper ideas of the vegetation cult, expressed within the religion of Jahwe; in Christ, God made man, it is fulfilled literally. For two days he was hammered for our sins; on the third he rose from the dead. The mourning for his death during the *triduum sacrum* is transformed at the Pasch into the joy of resurrection; this joy moves onward through the whole Pentecostal season. Looked at from the vantage point of the old vegetation cults, we gain a whole new perspective for this passage in Osee; we see in it a real mystery text. After two days of sorrow and mourning the pagans were wont to celebrate in those rites the return of life; again and again in the vegetation cults we meet the theme of mourning at death which then turns to joy at new life. We should notice that in these rites it was originally only the god who acted; gradually then the idea arose that the believer acted along with the god and became the god. Thus for example in the Egyptian cult of Osiris the mystes becomes an Osiris. In Christianity we know the highest fulfilment of this idea; the Christian is another Christ. The text which we mentioned from Osee is especially apt to be brought into contact with the oriental cults which the Jews knew from the peoples living about them; for example the Syrian cult of Adonis. Christ himself went to Tyre and Sidon; there is the meeting between him and a woman from that region recorded in Mt. 15, 21. Nor is it without significance that just on the border of Syria and Phoenicia he asked the disciples, 'whom do men think the Son of Man is?' (Mt. 16, 13). The Jews were in fact less well prepared for the idea of a son of god than the Phoenicians whose god had a son as well.

In a text from Herculaneum which has been handed down with similar texts from Philodemus it says among other things: 'most often Adonis is made out to be a dying god and the cities which honour him mourn for him in each year'[1].

Origen writes in his commentary on Ezechiel (8, 14) 'they mourn for Tammuz'; this is a celebration of the death and resurrection of Adonis:

> The god whom the Hellenes call Adonis is called Tammuz among the Hebrews and the Syrians. As the name would imply we saw the women sitting before the door of the god's house, that great door which looks to the North. According to a heathen custom of theirs, those who are outside the doors of the honour to the god bewailed Tammuz. It

[1]Philodemus: Cf Baudissin *Adonis und Esmun* 1911, p. 134, n. 3, and Gomperz *Herkulanische Studien II*, (1866) 16, 14.

is known too that each year they carry out certain rites; first, they mourn him for dead, and afterwards they rejoice at his rising from the dead.[1]

The oldest literary documents about the feast of Adonis describe it only as a feast of sorrow; there are only a very few, vague indications of a resurrection and return of the god to be found in the older reports.

Yet we do have a description from the age after Constantine which treats the feast as one of both mourning and resurrection. It is from Macrobius, a conservative pagan, the leader of certain aristocratic circles at Rome in the fourth century, circles which had not accepted Christianity and remained fast to the old paganism. He writes in his *Saturnalia* (I, 21, 10): 'after the presentation of sorrow in the rite is past (*simulatio luctus*) the act of joy is celebrated (*laetitiae exordium*).' Because the festival of Adonis' death took place yearly the *exordium laetitiae* must mean the return of the god to life. The same thing is to be found in Lucian, *De Dea Syria*, 6.

> And I saw in Byblos a great shrine of the Aphrodite of Byblos in which they also carry out the Orgia of Adonis. For they say that the downfall of Adonis was brought about in their land by the wild boar. In memory of his suffering (μνήμη τοῦ πάθεος, *memoriam passionis*) they strike themselves each year and mourn. (This means a mourning with musical form, a lament). They carry out the mysteries (ὄργια) and they carry out great mourning feasts throughout the land. But when they have struck themselves enough (meaning when they have exhausted their feeling of sorrow) and have wept enough they sacrifice to Adonis; first a sacrifice of the dead, as to one who is dead; then, on the next day, they recite the myth that he is alive, and they send him up into the air.

The meaning of the last phrase is not quite clear. Perhaps this sending up into the air means a praise of the god; but perhaps also it is a delicate hint of the resurrection.[2] According to this text we must take it that the mourning lasted for two days and on the third the resurrection was celebrated. It would seem quite likely that behind the text of Osee there is some ancient usage of a mystery festival which also consisted of a two days' mourning for the dead god and a third day upon which this was transformed into joy and gladness at the resurrection and new life of the god.

[1] M.G. 13, col. 797 ff.
[2] Cf J.L.W. 14, p. 63 f, note 117 and 118.

There is another parallel from the cult of Attis; we have it in the work of Firmicus Maternus, *De Errore Profanarum Religionum* (22, 1):

> We shall mention still another example (*symbolum*) so that the crime of this corrupt way of thinking may be laid bare. We shall have to tell of the whole rite (*ordo*) so that we may show clearly how the law of God's saving design was corrupted through the devil's evil imitation. On an appointed night an image is laid upon a bier with its face upwards; it is mourned with a hymn set to music. Then when they are weary of their false lament a light is brought in and a priest anoints the necks of all who have mourned. When he has anointed them, the priest whispers with a quiet voice: 'have comfort, mystai, for the god is saved; for us too sorrow shall be turned to healing'.[1]

There is a mystery image which was found at Rome on the Janiculum, not far from the grave of St Pancratius; it comes from what would seem to be a similar oriental cult. It too shows a dead god not on a bier but resting in a grave. The mystery is the buried god; that Jahwe, the God of the Old Testament could lie in a grave is unthinkable. For the Greeks as well who thought of their gods on Olympus radiant with beauty and power, health and freshness, a god in a grave was equally inconceivable. But the mystery religions do know such a god, who bears the deepest fate of man, even death; who bears it to the end and so overcomes it and gives the initiate the hope that he too may overcome and win a share in the everlasting life of god. 'Take courage, *mystai*, for the god is saved; for us too sorrow shall be turned to saving'. Here is a mysterious foreshadowing of what Christianity has brought; for we too give honour to a buried god. In order that he might share in human fate to its bitterest end, death, the immortal Son of God became a mortal man and by death, the tomb and the overcoming of that tomb in his resurrection fulfilled in an infinitely higher way what the pagan religions foreshadowed; he has taken the fear of death from us all who must undergo it; he has given us the faith and hope that we may share in his resurrection. In him we have the full reality of the oriental symbol: Θαρρεῖτε μύσται τοῦ θεοῦ σεσωσμένου· ἔσται γὰρ ἡμῶν ἐκ πόνων σωτηρία.

What Firmicus Maternus says in introducing the phrase about corruption and the aping of divine things makes it clear that he is trying to show how the ideas which lie behind these pagan mystery cults are in themselves God's ideas; ideas of the design for salvation,

[1] Cf J.L.W. 14, p. 62, note III.

the *Oikonomia* which the devil has abused and perverted. It is he who brought what was divine down to the level of the purely natural, who has put cosmic forces and powers in the place of the personal God so as to hinder men from finding the true God and the real mystery. This comes still clearer in the further discourse which follows (c. 22 ff):

> Why do you exhort these miserable men to rejoice; what is it which drives these deluded men to gladness? What hope do you promise them, in their sickness of belief? What is it you rouse in them by a false promise? Everyone knows that your god is dead; and his life comes no more. There is no oracle from a god which predicts his own rising and claims to be believed, once dead. He has given no proofs beforehand that he will work such a thing. (After mentioning the prophets of the Old Testament who did prophecy the death of Christ, Firmicus goes on . . .) He has given no examples that he would do this. What you bury is the mere image of an idol; that is all for which you mourn; that is all you bring out of the grave again. And then, when you have done this, you would rejoice! O miserable men. It is you who set your god free; it is you who arrange the feet of that block of stone; you who place this unfeeling stone upright again. Oh, that your god would show gratitude to you; oh that he would give to you some return with a like gift; give you a share in himself; may you die as he dies, live as he lives. Who could fail to despise this anointing when he has seen through its emptiness, this deed of nothingness? The devil too has his *Christi* now, his anointed ones; and because he is the antichrist he brings together miserable men in a criminal company, to the shame of his own name.

Firmicus lived in a time when the mystery cults were still a live danger for Christianity; therefore he had particularly to emphasize their negative side, while at the same time making clear that their last fulfilment and infinite transfiguration was present already in Christ. Today the danger is not this; we can and ought to emphasize the positive side of the mysteries. Firmicus goes on in c. 23:

'There is another anointing which God has given over to his only Son.' (given–*tradidit*. Firmicus chooses mystery terms like *unguentum* and *tradere* in order to show that Christianity is their fulfilment.) 'This the Son gives out to the believers by the power of his godhead and majesty. The anointing of Christ is prepared in an immortal form.' (gives = *largitur*; is prepared = *conficitur*).

And in c. 24:

> Who then sets your god free? Whom does he reward for the favour

done to him? Learn, learn what you do not know; see what you do not see: Christ the Son of God has in reality taken all this upon himself in order to free the human race from the chains of death, to give men back to the Father, to bring them to healing and reconciliation with the Father by the destruction of sin; to show the fruit of the promised resurrection by his own example. He closed the doors of hell and cast down the violence of the law and its harshness after he had trampled on death. For three entire days (meaning the *sacrum triduum*) the whole crowd of his elect was being called together (the meaning of the *descensus ad inferos*); now the evil of death was no longer to have power over them.

When, as we have said, those very men who had offered unholy things to the Man of Error were able in some way to cut themselves free, how much the more ought we now to show our zeal for the order of things which truth has brought.

What Firmicus says here, most likely of Attis, is true also of Adonis. He too was mourned as a dead god; indeed in his cult the mourning was the main element, as we have already seen. Yet for all of that even the most ancient cult hymns from Assyria which speak of a resurrection of the dead god point to the fact that this is a resurrection of Adonis.

In his commentary on Ezechiel (8, 14) St Jerome has this to say: 'the heathen explain the death and resurrection of Adonis most subtly; they make joy and sorrow his companions. The one is for the seed which dies in the earth, the other at the harvest in which the dead seeds come once more to life.'[1]

There is also the *scholion* to Theocritus which says: 'Adonis means the grain which has been sowed.'[2] The cult of Adonis, then, has the two characteristics which these texts reveal; it is concerned with nature and its fading powers, and this is the source of the sorrow that life must disappear; it is secondly concerned with the resurrection and new life of nature: hence the joy that this life comes each year once more to blossoming and power, while man, once dead, rises no more.

Now Adonis, the youthful figure, a god who is always shown us as a youth is mourned because he is killed in the flower of his life; and he is always shown us as the son of a god. This is of the greatest importance. In Phoenicia there was a trinity: a father god called Hadad,

[1] M.L. 25, col. 82 ff.
[2] A corresponding text is found in Pauly-Wissowa I, 385 ff, Scholion to Theocritus XVII, 2. Cf also Theocritus 15 and Bion, *Epitaph on Adonis*: Wilamowitz' edition of the *Bucolici Graeci* pp. 48 ff and 122 ff. Also J.L.W. 14, p. 64, note 120.

a female power with the name Atargatis, and the god-son. This meant that those pagans were in some way prepared for the Christian message of the Trinity; and as we have said, it was not without importance that it was just in the border district of Syria, at Caesarea Philippi, that Jesus asked, 'whom do men say that the Son of man is?' To this question Peter replied, 'thou art the Christ, the Son of the living God'.[1]

There are of course texts too which are simply cult formulae. One of these is found in Clement of Alexandria, a Christian who was not held to silence, in his *Protrepticus*, chapter 12. He tells us that at one point in the ceremony of their induction the initiates at Eleusis had to speak a certain formula. Clement calls this action a drama; the whole of it does have the form of a mystery play. 'Demeter and Kore were made into a mystical drama; Eleusis shows their wanderings, the rape, the mourning, by the light of torches.' This drama is not one in the literary sense; it is a mystery drama. The great theme is the central theme of all mysteries: how do I escape death and find the life which comes after it? Here the representation of the theme is made by the movement of Kore; she is seized by the ruler of the world below, sought by her mother Demeter, and finally, after a long time, found again. All of this was carried out in the drama of Eleusis, but in a manner in which the initiates not only portrayed but also lived as their own what they mimed. Thus then they acted out the wandering of the mother; a priestess came in Demeter's place and sought the daughter; they mourned the lost daughter as she was mourned in the cult of Adonis. The light of torches too is an indication of the light which shone when the mother and daughter were together once more. At the end of his description Clement gives a form which was really used in the cult. This formula he calls a σύνθημα, which means the same as Eleusis' own σύμβολον. Here it is: 'I fasted, I drank the *kykeon*; I took from the casket; with that I did what was required. I set it down in the *Kalythos* and from the *Kalythos* into the casket.'

This formula gives us some picture of the first part of the mysteries; it depicts what the *mystes* does at his induction, which went before the final revelation. First he fasts. His fast is broken by the taking of a mixed drink, a kind of meal which was very ancient, dating from before the time of bread and baking. Clement explains how the fast was broken in this way by saying that this is what the goddess Demeter herself had done. And it was after she had done so that courage came to her to

[1] From conferences for 1945 and 1946.

go and seek her daughter. This note shows us the relationship of myth and *mysterium*: the myth tells what it was that the gods first did; the cult, the mystery is an imitation of it. The initiates carry out what the gods did in the first age; and by so doing they experience what the gods experienced.

A great deal has been written about the several actions which the formula of Eleusis describes; but we are to-day still not in a position to explain them. In any case the formula does imply that at a given point and place the initiate uttered this *symbolum*, in order to be admitted to further stages in the mystery.

We have a Latin document on the *symbolum* as well. This is from Arnobius, *Adversus nationes* V, 26. He speaks of the '*Symbola*, to which, when you are asked in receiving the initiation, you make reply: I fasted, I drank from the *kykeon*, I took from the casket and placed in the *kalythos*; I took it up once more and put it back in the casket.'

This *redditio symboli* is clearly a kind of responsory; the *mystes* is asked questions and gives answers. We have something like it in Firmicus Maternus; he tells us that the initiates were asked questions and gave replies, *responsa*. The formula of Arnobius agrees with the one from Clement. We cannot explain all the details; but if we attend to what there is in Firmicus Maternus we may be allowed to conclude that in Eleusis as well the *mystai* spoke the formula in order to be initiated to a higher stage of the ceremony. It was then clearly the end point of a lower part of the ceremony and the beginning of a higher one; its purpose is to furnish the *mystes* with credentials, a necessary set of credentials for that higher stage.

There are however *symbola* which consist not only in words but in objects: tiny images of the god and the like, which the *mystai* were allowed to show only to one another. Evidence of this is found in the *Apologia* of Apuleius, chapter 53. Martin Dibelius mentions it in his book, *Die Isisweihe bei Apuleius und verwandte Initiationsriten*. (Transactions of the Heidelberg Academy, art. 4, 1917, p. 16 ff). It is well known that the heathen initiates were bound to strict silence and secrecy about the *symbola* of their cult. This indeed once got Apuleius into considerable difficulty; he was accused of witchcraft and the vow of secrecy made his defence very difficult. His enemies said that he was keeping in his house certain objects and using them to harm others. In fact he did have some secret objects; but they were not for witchcraft but the mysteries. How could he prove it to his enemies? He could not show them the things; this would have been a terrible impiety. He kept silence and called on the knowledge of his hearers, one or other of whom might himself be an initiate. Let them give testimony as to what are the things he is keeping.

I have taken part in many initiations into mystical worship in Greece. From the priests of these rites I have many signs (*signa*) and things for recollection (*monumenta*) and I keep them with great reverence. I am saying nothing which is unknown. You initiates of father Liber who are present—you know what it is that you keep in secret at home, and what you give reverence to in silence, when no profane person is present.

Later Apuleius raises the matter once more and turns to the members of his own cult. He wanted first to prove that there are such objects; things which belong to the initiates to keep. Now he raises the second question: what are these things? He can give no direct answer. Thus all he does is to say:

If anyone is there who has the same mysteries, let him give a sign (*signum dato*); he can show that they are things which do no harm.

We can see from all this that *signa* can also be signs, movements with the hand or something of that kind, which members of the same mystery could give to one another; some such fellow initiate was asked to come to the help of Apuleius in his danger and give witness that these things were not the tools of magic, but objects which did no harm, yet which he might not talk about.[1]

Nonetheless, for us today the pagan mysteries are only a road to the understanding of the Christian mysteries; the latter are entirely independent in themselves.

Hence, the essence of the mystery comes to be that one sees things of the spirit, Spiritual things, through the visible elements; that through our ear the *Pneuma* reaches to us. The principle in the ancient mysteries is the same. The initiate experiences, sees, hears things objectively; yet behind this there is a purely spiritual vision. For this reason the ancient mysteries can help us to understand and more deeply to live our own mystery and its celebration. What it contains is not merely rites; it is not

[1]From conferences for 1947 on Colossians.

a mere educational exercise; it is not a series of pictures for simple folk which mature men need no longer. In these things which meet the senses, the reality of God touches us. The mysteries are objective actions, yet so experienced that behind them the initiate sees, in faith, the presence of God.[1]

The Christian mystery is the memorial of Christ's saving act through worship in rite and word.

The mystery is no mere recalling of Christ and his saving deed; it is a memorial in worship. The church does what the Lord did, and thereby makes his act present. Christ himself is present and acts through the church, his *ecclesia*, while she acts with him. Both carry out the action.

The word belongs to such an action in worship; both word and action are a part of the memorial. And the word in the liturgy is also filled with the divine presence. God reveals himself to us in the liturgy; the word takes its part in the sacramental event. This is true of the words of the Old and New Testament when the church makes use of them in her liturgy. We may not stand still in the historical dimension when we are listening to the writings of the Old Testament; it makes clear to us what God is doing in Christ through his church. Indeed, often without these writings we should not recognize the full depth and the riches of Christ's mystery. The Epistle to the Hebrews tells us (10; 1) that the law was a foreshadowing. Experience tells us that the shadow image will show all the basic lines of its object; in the shadow image we see all that essentially belongs, because what is not essential is not there; hence the shadow will often give a better picture of the essential form than the object itself. Thus is the way with the Old and the New Testaments; the writings of the old will often show more clearly what is essential. Think for example of the texts for the first mass of Christmas. The New Testament, in the gospel of St Luke, tells of the birth of a child. That is the human part par excellence, the earthly message. Only the strange appearance of the angel points out that something more is involved. Yet the Old Testament texts tell us that here is the son of God in this child. In the introit the psalmist comes forward and speaks with Christ's own voice: 'The Lord said unto me, thou art my Son, this day have I begotten thee' (Ps. 2, 7). In the gradual the Father speaks in the psalmist's words to his son: 'in the splendour

[1]Ibid.

M.C.W.–F

of the sanctuary and before the day star I begot thee from my own bosom' (Ps. 109, 3).

It is the same on Epiphany. The gospel tells of the wise men and their visit from the East; the story is bare and simple. The prophet Micah is quoted (5, 2) as saying: 'Thou, Bethlehem in the land of Judah art by no means the least among the cities of Judah; for out of thee shall come the prince who shall lead Israel, my people.'

Thus, the prophecy gives to the simple history a divine and eternal meaning; it shows that in this child the real king of God's people has appeared. This is the message of the Introit and Gradual as well which are also taken from the Old Testament. But the burden lies with the epistle.[1]

The Christian mystery is a remembrance charged with such reality that it makes the saving action present.

The mystery of worship makes present among us the saving act of Christ in word and rites. God is presence; he has no past and no future; he is the everlasting point in which all hold together. All goes forth from him, all comes back to him. Hence with him there is only one Today. When we say now, the now is gone before we have uttered it; it is already past: so fleeting is the moment and the today which belong to earth. But with God the 'Today' is an abiding presence. Of course we cannot grasp that; we can only begin to understand it, and feel reverence for it. A real Christian is glad that he cannot reach the depths of God's being by his reason; he is filled with a holy wonder, the terror before God of which the Old Testament speaks so often, a fear which is not a servile fear.

God has made it possible for us, even in this life, to enter into the divine present and the everlasting Today; this possibility is through the sole door of the mystery of worship. There, for us too, there is neither past nor future, only present. What is past in history, the death of Christ for example, and what is in the future of history, his parousia, are present in the mystery.

The Christian lives two lives in this world. By his body which will die, he is bound to the earth; with his Spirit he lives in the places beyond. The mystery of worship makes it possible for him to come away from this world and enter the world which is God's, the world of the divine presence. By the mysteries God takes us into his own life

[1]From conferences for 1943–45.

and so, even while on earth, we stand already in God's everlasting Today and take part in the 'action of the *aion's* life'.[1] It is for this share in the action of eternal life which the secret of the second Sunday after Pentecost asks: 'may the sacrifice which we dedicate to thy name make us pure, and from day to day bring us over into the action of everlasting life'. The action of everlasting life is one which takes place in heaven. In the mystery we share in this action; we are taken up into it.

What that action really is we can only know in shadow. Just as God is eternal rest he is also eternal action; for God is life, life proper; and where life is, it will be active. Life streams out of its own accord. The Father gives the whole of his life to the Son; in *agape* the Son gives himself back to the Father. The Father and the Son breathe forth the Holy Spirit to one another; this exchange of life is the work of eternity and the act of eternal life within the Trinity. It is into this life and work that we are taken by the mystery. For God's love, his *agape*, willed to give itself to created beings too; from this love he created the world and men; in his Son he redeemed it; through his Son made man, streams the Spirit ceaselessly on men and on the whole creation; through the Son it then streams back again to him, the Father. Each one of us who joins in the deed of Christ stands already in the midst of the action of eternal life; his action too is God's, and is of heaven.

Thus is the feast which we shall one day celebrate in heaven; in the liturgy we anticipate this feast. Yet for all of that we are not, as we celebrate the mystery, already at the moment of this heavenly reality. The Christian's life is a feast; he is always at divine service, because the Son is always before the Father. The outward feast passes, the inward one remains. Among the Jews and pagans, in contrast, there were always special days on which the liturgy was to be performed, and certain places where it was proper to sacrifice; worship was tied to place and time. So, if anyone wanted to do God honour he went to the temple; only there was God to be found. For us men the present is only an instant; and this instant is turned beyond recall to past. We stand in time, a ceaseless flow. We cannot stand still. This was the condition of worship too, before Christ took it out of time. Before that moment, it was bound to time, to the course of sun and moon, to the growth of the earth's fruits. It was bound to time and nature; so it came that

[1]This means participation through and in faith; in the veil of the faith we stand in God's 'now' by the fact that God draws us into his action and life, and its abiding present.

nature was revered as a god and, at the end, the powers of nature in their complexity were revered as gods too. But in Christianity all that is changed. Christ our Lord entered eternity through death; he is no longer bound to the mesh of time. So, then, Christian worship is no longer bound to time but to eternity; it does not have to keep days and hours; it is always in the new age, the *aion*. When we worship we step out of time. Of course for us as well there are appointed festivals: as men who still live in time we must pay it our due. Yet what we now celebrate is not nature but rather what nature serves as symbol to. As the long nights fade and the day comes once more to dominate we celebrate the birth of the true light, Christ. When in nature the new life is coming once more to birth we celebrate the pasch, the new creation in Christ. We celebrate feasts in the Spirit which are connected with signs in nature; yet these are signs of things of heaven. In the Spirit we are in heaven; in the body we are in time still. Hence the Christian is always at a feast, for Christ is always before the Father; the Christian offers adoration to the Father through the Son.[1]

The controversy between the author and Hahn, a protestant theologian, gives occasion for attempting a broader interpretation of how the saving act is made present.

The force which has broken in upon history through the saving act of Christ is the Spirit, the *pneuma*; it is the true founding power of the new age. Sometimes called also the *dynamis* of God, this power places us within the reach of Christ's action and gives us a share in it. What do *dynamis* and *pneuma* mean in St Paul?

Dynamis is the being of God; it is the power and the strength of God, doing what he wills, creating and acting on what he has created. It reveals itself in every sacred act of his, above all in the break-through of Christ of which Ephesians 1, 19 speaks: his pasch. This act itself has the stamp of God's own act; it is then of God, something abiding, everlasting. The Lord, crucified and risen, the doer of this deed, is above all else God's *dynamis* in person. We read in I Cor. 1, 24:

> We preach Christ crucified, to the Jews a stumbling block, to the gentiles foolishness, but to those who are called, Jews and pagans alike, the power of God, the wisdom of God.

Christ, then, is the *dynamis* of God in person; in his resurrection

[1] From conferences for 1943-45.

he was made free for our sakes; now he acts in time. This power takes hold of men in the first instance through the proclamation of the gospel; it is by the preaching of the saving act of Christ that the power of his resurrection creates faith in men. (Cf also 1 Cor. 2, 5; Eph. 1, 19.) Hence faith is called faith in the power of the resurrection. (Col. 2, 12). The power which Christ gives to those who belong to him lifts them up over time and space, places them in a personal relationship to his act and knits them into the new age. (Cf II Cor. 4, 7; 12, 9.)

But at the same time the power of God is the Spirit, the *pneuma*. Often Scripture uses the two terms as synonyms. For example 1 Cor. 6, 14: 'God awakened the Lord and will awake us too through his power (*dynamis*)'. And Romans 8, 11.

> If the Spirit of him who awakened Jesus from the dead dwells in you, then will he who awakened Christ from the dead awaken your mortal bodies also through the Spirit of his which dwells in you.

Or II Cor. 4, 13–14.

> Because we have the one Spirit of faith . . . we know that he who awakened Jesus from the dead shall awaken us with Jesus and give us station with him.

The Spirit is therefore the power of God which has been made free in the resurrection; it is to be understood from that source, the action of Christ.

The new age, the new *aion*, is the kingdom of that Spirit, the Spirit of God; God's life and being are Spirit (cf Jn. 4, 24); the Lord is the Spirit (II Cor. 3, 17). On the other hand the Spirit, the *pneuma* is a function, the gift of the Lord. In this sense we can talk of the Spirit of the Lord (πνεῦμα τοῦ κυρίου); the Spirit is under the government of the Lord.

This Spirit is the real eschatological gift, for in the last days, the ἔσχατα, it will be given to all, and as a permanent possession. In this way the Christian becomes one Spirit with Christ (cf 1 Cor. 6).

We gain a share in the *pneuma* through the sacraments. (Cf 1 Cor. 12, 13).

> We are all baptised in one Spirit into one body . . . and all have drunk one Spirit too.

Communion brings a strengthening of the Spirit which the Christian has received in baptism.

The Spirit which is thus given in the sacraments is the Spirit which awakened Christ from the dead; it is the seal which attests that we belong to the new age. For this reason it is called the pledge, the bridal gift, the portion which gives a right to the whole.

Life in the Spirit is no more completed than Christ's great action. It requires continual effort. The Spirit within us is not merely a force; it keeps its personal character throughout. It remains a person at work, who urges us ever on to work. In the Spirit we are dead men who die over and over again.

The fact of the in-dwelling of the Spirit in Christians is expressed in St Paul's writings by the phrases 'in Christ', 'with Christ'. Both these formulae describe the same fact; but the 'with' expresses rather that we have entered into the life of Christ, while the other phrases, 'in Christ' and 'in the Spirit' underline more the state which is thereby reached. We must die again and again with Christ in order to remain always in Christ.

Yet in spite of the emphasis on the Spirit who dwells within us, we may not regard the Spirit only in this way; it remains an absolute, independent of us, outside of and above us, although in us, leading its own life.

In the Spirit the Christian has constant part in the resurrection of Christ; in the Spirit he is taken into the resurrection in a real though hidden manner, he is compelled to die with Christ the death which he died. He remains one Spirit with Christ, or one body with him. In the Spirit is the fulfilment of what the ancient monks asked, and what is the meaning of monastic life to the present day: that we should die and rise daily with Christ. Christian religion is the religion which rests on the mystery of the cross; the spirit is the raising of the barrier which time lays down; it brings those who belong to it, the *pneumatikoi*, into the eternal Christ, the *Christus aeternus*, it makes them eternal, like him.

We should mention that Professor Hahn, in spite of all the things he rightly says about the *pneuma*, nonetheless holds the erroneous view that the *pneuma* is a situation, an atmosphere in which we find ourselves, a sort of fluid aether, and not a substance.[1] We cannot accept this view as Catholics. The Spirit which is given us is truly an entity, though of course not a base and material one; it is a sharing in the essence of God, and God is subsistent being, not situation. This is shown from Romans 5, 5: 'the love (*agape*) of God is poured out in our hearts

[1] *Das Mitsterben und Mitauferstehen mit Christus bei Paulus* (1937).

through the holy Spirit (*pneuma*) which is given to us'. And II Cor. 3, 17: 'the Lord is Spirit (*pneuma*).' The risen Christ, in his humanity too, was taken up into the being of God; so, too, man by baptism has a share in the death of Christ, and through it in the being of God; and this is Spirit.[1]

There are a number of passages from both Scripture and liturgy which prove that Christ is God in his very being. We shall only understand them when we realize that δόξα must be understood in its full sense as God's being. Thus Phil. 2, 11: Jesus Christ is Lord in glory (*doxa*) = in the being of God. Christ was awakened from the dead through the *doxa* = glory = being of the Father (Romans 6, 4). And in the 'Gloria' of the Roman mass, '*tu solus altissimus Jesu Christe . . . in gloria Dei patris . . .*'; or the 'Te Deum': '*Qui sedes ad dexteram Dei in gloria Patris.*'

It is Romans 6, 3 which explains how the baptized Christian enters the field of Christ's power. The author declares that baptism works as a symbol: 'we are baptized into the death of Christ'; he goes on to say that this is a burial. Yet as Christ did not remain in death but was awakened by the *doxa*, the glory, of the Father so also the baptized Christian does not remain in death but comes alive in God: 'he is awakened and lives now for God in Jesus Christ'. What is implied is a union with Christ at the level of being.[2] Death, which passes, is a

---

[1]Casel's exposition is based on Scripture, which does in fact use the one word *pneuma* where we, in our search for clarity, use differing terms today. God is *pneuma*: spiritual substance (Jn. 4, 24). But the comforter whom the Lord calls the Spirit of truth and whom the Father will send (Jn. 15, 26) is a divine Person, one in substance with the Father and the Son, but differing from them in hypostasis.

For the different meanings of *pneuma* in Scripture see Victor Warnach, *Agape*, pp. 215–218. (English translation to appear with Darton, Longman and Todd.) Also Neunheuser, *Gnade, Geistesgaben, Hl Geist* in *Liturgie und Mönchtum*, 20, 1957, pp. 34–47.

[2][The original German 'substantiell' created certain problems, having regard to the ambiguity of the word in modern philosophy. What Casel meant was 'of the order of being and of essence, not external or "moral".' The translator believes that the problem does not reflect in the translation, for linguistic reasons. In English 'substantially' would suggest nothing, or at best something connected with physics or finance. But the reader should be aware that one of the most important theses of Casel is, that our union with Christ is a higher reality than that which subjectivist philosophers and the many theologians who consciously or unconsciously follow them assign to the mind and to its acts. For the modern, the mind and its causal acts are *less* real than what is 'out there'. For the classical tradition of Plato and Aristotle the mind is *more* real, and nothing as and when it is known is 'out there'. Casel was deeply conscious of this without stating it in philosophical form. But a fuller understanding of these problems is much aided by a comprehension of St Thomas' mature gnosiology, in which the human mind *is* the known and is activated by the known; *fieri*

situation from which the baptized goes over into the estate of life. Of course this estate is not finally secure in this age; it can cease again. Therefore the Christian must enact over and over the death of Christ in the supper, so as to strengthen the life of the risen Christ within him. This is what the meal means: (1 Cor. 11, 26): 'As often as you eat this bread and drink of this cup you announce the death of the Lord until he come.' In heaven where this life stands secure for ever the Christian has no more need to celebrate the mystery of Christ's death.

When the Christian has passed through the mystical death, he has won the life of the Spirit, his sharing in the being of the Spirit. This means that the life of God in its essence dwells in him. He is then made holy in a radical manner: this the Protestant cannot grasp, for he believes that man remains always in sin. This holiness is given by God, it is not a holiness of works. Man must hold fast to it and cultivate it. This takes place through good works which give witness that the life of God is there.

The fact that the Spirit is a being is clear and plain in the Fathers. One example is found in the *Apostolic Constitutions*, 3, 17: 'It is then baptism which is given in the death of Jesus. Water stands in the place of burial, oil for the holy Spirit, the signing for the cross, the myrrh for the firmness of the confession which is made. The father is named as the author and sender; the Spirit is named because he is taken as a witness. The immersion is going to death with Christ; coming up again is a rising with him. The Father is God, who is above all, Christ is the only begotten Son . . . the Lord of the glory (*kyrios*, *doxa*); the Holy Spirit is the paraclete who had been sent by Christ, taught by him to proclaim him.'

Hahn says that the means by which Christians make present the saving act of Christ are preaching, baptism and the Lord's supper; we would say gospel, baptism and the eucharist.

These rites too have their place in history; yet they are not exhausted

---

aliud inquantum aliud; and this is the very highest kind of being, not a bad photograph of 'reality out there'. In this gnosiology as for Casel there is no question of identity in essence or fusion of persons, but of participation, a scriptural doctrine in itself (cf II Peter 1, 4) which is clarified by the supreme intimacy of intellectual acts, as understood by St Thomas. Cf also John of St Thomas, *Cursus Theologicus, De Donis Spiritus Sancti*. These remarks do not conclude that St Thomas is in harmony with Casel; but that Casel is deeply conversant with the conceptual world of Scripture and Tradition, which is the world of St Thomas, too. *Trans.*]

in their historical acts, and in these visible actions a secret event is concluded: from that come all three mysteries.[1]

In preaching, and even more in the Word proclaimed within the liturgy in the gospel, the saving action of Christ is made present in Spirit. Christ's way through time is fulfilled in the word proclaimed; preaching is that side of the action of Christ which is turned toward us. In it and the faith which it conveys, man, in a real but hidden manner, enters into communion with the dying and rising Christ. In every word of the gospel we touch the living God.

Baptism, then, places man in a communion of death and resurrection with Christ, and gives him a real sharing in the fate of Christ. Christ is the subject who acts; we enter into his action; baptism is the arm by which this action reaches out for man; thrusting aside time and space, it makes him contemporary with Christ (Hahn's phrase). Baptism and the action of Christ are not next to one another; the one unique action is made available to us in the other; Christ does not as it were, die a second time. By baptism, man is made a partaker in the new age, and so is given certainty that he will be taken up in the *Parousia*, which is yet to come.[2]

The particular manner in which the sacraments operate, by which the saving act of the God and saviour who dies on the cross is made available to us, can only be finally understood and explained through insight into the meaning of pneuma: *that the Lord is glorified and acting now; that he is Lord in* pneuma.

Of course the sacraments are means by which we are made conformable to Christ who was incarnate and suffered (*Christus incarnatus et passus*). Baptism is in the first place a sharing in the Lord's death. Yet, on the other hand, it was in his glory that the Lord could first fill the sacraments with his Spiritual power. He did institute the Eucharist before he suffered, but only fulfilled it after he had done so. We may not then shut out the Lord in Spirit, the fulfilled Christ, from the sacramental realm. It is right to say that we pass by baptism into the sphere of being which belongs to the Spirit; yet it is also true that the

[1]Of course they are mysteries in different but analogous senses, for the manner in which God's Word and the two sacraments bring the saving act of Christ to us is quite different.

[2]From conferences on Galatians, 1942. The completion of these ideas will be found in *Das Christliche Opfermysterium*, to appear with Pustet. Cf also the review of Hahn's book in A.L.W. 1, 1950, pp. 315–323.

sacraments come to an end with our final entry into the life of heaven; the sacraments are meaningful only for our life on earth; they have a being which will pass away, while the life in the Spirit is eternal.[1]

There follows a short note on the meanings of pneuma.

Pneuma means first the air in movement; then the power of life in nature and particularly in the animal and human body. It is employed in the religious language of the Greeks for the life power of daemonic or divine beings. In connexion with this last use it comes to mean the share in the life of God which is given by incorporation into Christ, which first takes place in baptism. God himself is *pneuma*; within the Trinity it is the life which the Father and the Son share, and which goes forth from them as the third person of the Trinity, the Holy Spirit. The man Jesus Christ is Spirit as God, and after his resurrection as man also: this means he shares in the life of God. The risen Christ gives this life to the faithful; this life is *pneuma*, a share in the life of the Trinity. The corresponding Latin word is *Spiritus*.[2]

A series of smaller essays takes still further the question of how the saving act is present.

It is clear that the historical basis of the mystery of worship lies in the incarnation and sufferings of our Lord at a definite time and place. It is precisely the greatness of this mystery that it is not a myth, but an historic reality stands behind it. Yet the mystery does not stop at such an event; the true value of saving events is their meaning for religious life. It is just at Easter that we once more make the mystery our own; as the Lord once passed through his death in time to everlasting life with the Father, he takes us over with him. The cross of Christ is of course a part of history; but at the same time it is the end of history because it sets us free from this world and takes us to the eternity of God.[3]

The deepest descent is already the passage, the *transitus*, to the way up. In death resurrection is contained; we can never be too clear about that.[4]

One may be too much concerned about the glorified Lord in heaven, or even about his presence in the Blessed Sacrament; however one must

[1]From a letter dated 9.2.1944.
[2]From notes for a foreword to the French edition of this book, October, 1943.
[3]Letter dated 3.4.1939.
[4]From a retreat given in 1935.

distinguish between these two as to what is present *vi sacramenti* and what *per concomitantiam*. Against this, we must distinguish very strictly the presence of the saving act of Christ in the mystery of worship. It is just the extraordinary greatness of the liturgy we celebrate that through it we have with us the work of Christ: his sacrifice, as the canon expresses it, embracing the passion, resurrection and ascension, with the incarnation which must of course precede the rest. This saving work of Christ is sacramentally present to us in the *mysterium*; and because its full content is inexhaustible we are given a whole series of individual moments to contemplate in the course of the church's year. The express teaching of tradition is that the death of Christ is made present in the mystery.[1] But it is not enough that the risen Lord should bear the sign of his death about him; we have in any case to speak very cautiously in this line. For example when an old soldier comes along with his campaign ribbons, that does not make present the battles which entitle him to wear the ribbons. Yet when the Apostle Paul tells us, 'announce the death of the Lord until he come', that does mean that the Lord, once dead, is present among us.[2]

It is now—and we may be thankful for the fact—a different situation from what we met earlier: there are Thomist theologians, Diekamp for example, who teach expressly that the passion of Christ is made sacramentally present in the mass. If it were not, the mass could in no way be regarded as a true sacrifice; and that is a dogmatic datum. Fifty years ago the real presence of our Lord in the eucharist was so emphasized that everything else came second to it. It was then high time that the character of the mass as sacrifice received more emphasis; and this was most intimately connected with the presence of the suffering and blood of Christ under the bread and wine. Of course it is correct that the glorified Lord is present in the Eucharist. But if you read the decree of the Council of Trent (Denzinger, 876) it is quite clear that, by the power of the word, in other words in the power of the sacramental element as such, the body of Christ is present under the species of bread and the blood of Christ under the species of wine; further, the soul and godhead of Christ are present under both species and his body and blood under each 'by virtue of that natural connection and concomitance through which the parts of Christ the Lord who has risen

[1]This means that the sacrificial act of Christ, completed in his death and blood on the cross becomes sacramentally present in the mystery of the Eucharist.
[2]From a letter dated 24.3.1942.

from the dead never to die again are bound together; while the godhead is present in virtue of the marvellous hypostatic union'. In the next paragraph of Denzinger the same thing is said with even greater clarity. Compare these data with paragraph 430 on transubstantiation. What is all-important for the sacrament is what happens in the power of the sacramental word, not what is there by concomitance: in other words, the presence of the body and blood of Christ by which Christ clearly gives a symbol of his death and sets it out sacramentally. It is this, the making present of the sacrificial death of Christ which Scripture and all the ancient fathers and liturgists hold to be the meaning of the mass. Yet because his saving work reaches its high point in the sacrifice the entire work is set out present in the mass. If we look to the Roman Catechism, II, 4, we are taught that in the eucharist the true body of Christ is present, and indeed that very body which was born of the virgin and now sits at God's right hand. Yet that says nothing against the doctrine of the *mysterium*; it accepts this truth, while emphasizing that the Lord who rules in heaven gives us his body and blood as the body and blood of one offering himself in a sacrificial death. We can say too that the same body which hung on the cross is that which now rules at God's right hand; yet these are two entirely different modes of appearance for the one body. Thus, for example, when we say that the Lord hung on the cross in the fashion of a slave we do not thereby deny that this is the same body which is glorious in heaven now. Hence, the Lord must appear in the mass as sacrificed and not as glorified although in heaven he is such. It is Christ's great goodness and piety towards us that, although he lives in glory in heaven, still he brings his sacrificial death before us over and over in the mass, in a sacramental manner. One knows of course the passage from Gregory the Great where all this is said with great clarity. It is cited in the J.L.W. 6, p. 73f.[1]

It is quite proper not to be content with the making present of the death on the cross as such. The death of our Lord on the cross was indeed only a way across, if indeed the necessary way, to his glory; we cannot then separate his death from his resurrection. In Pinsk I miss something of the mystery of the cross. He emphasizes rather too much the transformation of the world by the sacrament. No, the world is by no means consecrated; it stands in great part under the power of Satan. Just for that reason we must make our way up to God through

[1] From a letter dated 23.4.1943.

the cross, to the place where Christ sits at the Father's right hand, now
that he has overcome the power of this world by his death on the cross.
The whole world of the stars, the powers of this world—all are subject
to the *Kyrios*, the Lord, as Colossians so wonderfully expresses
it.[1]

There is only one Christ and he is *Kyrios*: our sovereign Lord who
sits at the Father's right hand. Yet this same ruler for love of us became
a slave and took upon himself the death of the cross. Through it,
through his passion, he came to resurrection and everlasting glory.
Now he is slave no longer but *Kyrios* (cf Phil. 2, 11). We too must
make this journey in his steps through passion to resurrection; to this
end the mystery has been given us. So Christ must appear in the
mystery first of all as the one killed and sacrificed; it is the wonder of
the mystery that, as Gregory the Great says, although he is in glory
and dies no more, in the mystery he suffers for us once more. (*In suo
mysterio pro nobis iterum patitur*) (J.L.W. 6, 173).

This passage from Gregory seems to me so clear that I do not see
what I can add to it. Of course when we try to penetrate these things
in a philosophical way and understand them we can find ourselves in
difficulty. But our holy faith is revelation and not human philosophy.[2]

It is important again and again to distinguish and to remove misunderstandings

Even if, in theory, the application of grace was enough, we should
have nonetheless to say that God has in fact done otherwise. As our
Lord said before he left the disciples, he wanted to be always with his
church, and not as it were to send a love gift from afar every now and
again. From God's point of view, the mystery means that he is always
alive, working and dwelling in his church; for man it means that he is
'in Christ'.

Sacramenta efficiunt quod significant: that the sacraments do what
they symbolize may not be taken as later scholastics took it, only as an
effect of grace. In the old vocabulary *efficere* means make real.[3] Thus
what the maxim does mean is that the sacraments do not merely point

[1]From a letter dated 29.7.1947.
[2]From a letter dated 2.12.1942.
[3]Cf Casel's article on the Roman *orationes* in J.L.W. 11 (1933), pp. 35–45.
He brings evidence here that *effectus* does not mean effect but the inner reality
of what is symbolized in the outward act; modification of this view may be
appropriate, however.

to the saving action, but contain it: *continent quod figurant.*[1] Unless Christ's death is made present we can make no sense at all of Romans 6.[2] In the eucharist the passion of Christ is present, as even opponents of the mystery are beginning to admit; but the passion can in no way be taken out of the context of the whole saving action, for the pain as such did not redeem us. In ancient Christian language the *passio* was conceived as *pascha*, and contained his glorification as a normal concomitant.[3]

The making present of the saving act in mystery takes place in a sacramental manner; the saving work then receives, in addition to its natural mode of being, a new, sacramental mode of being. This does not imply any change in the work; it remains what it was, yet in this new manner is made present to us, so that we enter into it and can make it our own. It is therefore complete nonsense to imagine that the mystery doctrine is that at Christmas Christ comes on the altar as a tiny child. What is meant is that the whole *oikonomia*, the whole design of salvation from the incarnation to the *parousia* which has not yet appeared in point of time, does take on a sacramental presence and therefore can be the subject of our co-participation in the most vivid way. In this way the Lord with his work is continually present in his church giving to it his life and healing.[4]

The presence of the saving act, looked at as fundamental communion with Christ, implies that we are his contemporaries; indeed, that we have already entered God's eternal 'now'.

When we go with Christ in his way he becomes contemporary with us. He is neither past nor to come but present to us; he is always with us. And not only his person but also his saving act belongs to this present. There can be no deeper communion of living than that we should share the essential life and action of another.

[1] Cf St Thomas S.T. III, 62, 1, ad 1. One cannot deny that the scholastic axiom taken by Aquinas as general teaching is pressed hard by Casel. If we come to accept a more historical view of its meaning, we may nonetheless recognize in it an echo of the older conception of 'the image filled with the reality of its prototype: the image which does really contain the reality which it symbolizes' (Casel, *Glaube, Gnosis und Mysterium*, J.L.W. 15, 1941, p. 233). This work is worth consulting for these matters, particularly pp. 232–233.

[2] Cf the discussion between Schnackenburg, Stommel and others: Warnach, *Die Tauflehre des Römerbriefes*, A.L.W. V/2, 1959, pp. 274–332.

[3] What we are concerned with is a sacramental presence of the sacrificial death of Christ in which he gave himself on Calvary and died, yet overcame death and rose again, 'entering the holy of holies once and for all, for all of us' (Heb. 9, 12; cf also 10, 12 and 6, 20).

[4] From a letter dated 2.11.1935.

Above all it is the death and resurrection of Christ in which we have this immediate share. 'Do you not know that we who were baptized in Christ were baptized into his death . . .' (Rom. 6, 3). And the deep words of Galatians 2, 19: 'I am crucified with Christ' (Χριστῷ συνεσταύρωμαι). Here the master and the pupil are put wholly into the same point of time; both hang together on the same cross. They have become contemporaries in every detail. Yet from that it follows that Christ, although he is in glory with the Father, hangs on a cross for the church, and not merely *has* hung there; that by the same necessity the resurrection is present just through the hanging, for Christ is ruler from the cross as well; his cross and resurrection are two aspects of the same thing. St Paul says, 'carrying about always with us the killing of Jesus in our body, so that the life of Jesus may be revealed also in our body. For, alive, we are given up to death for Jesus' sake, in order that the life of Jesus may be shown in our members subject to death'. (2 Cor. 4, 10) 'One dies for all, so all died; and he died for all so that the living should no longer live for themselves but for him who died for them and was awakened once more' (2 Cor. 5, 14). 'He was crucified from weakness but he lives by the power of God. In him we too are weak but we shall live with him in the power of God . . .' (2 Cor. 13, 4). 'Far be it from me to glory save in the cross of our Lord Jesus Christ through whom the world is crucified to me, and I to the world' (Gal. 6, 14).

By his share in the cross and resurrection of Christ, St Paul has come out of the world and entered into the kingdom of God. What Christ did by dying and rising was not an historical event like any other; it was saving action, saving history. As such it burst the bonds of time and of history. Christ dies to leave the world of sin and open the new age of divine order. At the moment of his death upon the cross and the fall of Satan's power the age of sin, the age which is bound up in time, is broken, and the new age, the age to come, the kingdom of God's goodness has arrived. The death and the resurrection of Christ are, then, the turning point in the history of the world. The flesh and sin, bond-service and transition, all subject to the law of time and space, death and the Devil, are now no longer; it is God's abiding kingdom which has come, with justice, holiness and life which is to be for ever. Of course the world which we see is not yet gone; but its compelling power is over all the same, although it goes on apparently even more under Satanic power, doing ever more harm.

The Christian too lives on in his lower nature in this world; he is under its threat, persecuted, killed. But within he is the victor now; he is risen, everlasting, already he sits at the throne of Christ the Lord.

Yet the condition for all of this is that we really take a share in the death and resurrection of Christ; to this end Christ gives us a means to become his contemporaries; gives us the means to die and to live again with him: 'I live, not I, but Christ lives in me. Yet so far as I do live in the flesh, I live in faith towards the Son of God who loved me and sacrificed himself for me. I do not bring the grace of God to nothing' (Gal. 2, 20). This is the consequence too of being crucified with Christ: Χριστῷ συνεσταύρωμαι.

'In the Spirit (*pneuma*)' is the same for St Paul as 'in Christ': to have a share in the death and resurrection of Jesus. Anyone who is in the Spirit is in the body of Christ too; he has part in all the body does, in the way to being crucified, but in the resurrection also. In a truly wonderful way crucifixion and resurrection both in process and fulfilment form a pattern and a oneness.[1]

The presence of the saving act, looked at as fundamental communion with Christ, implies that we are his contemporaries; indeed, that we have already entered God's eternal 'now'.

We read in Romans 11, 30–31:

> For just as you were once disobedient to God but now have found mercy because of their disobedience, so they were disobedient that you might obtain mercy; and so now they shall obtain mercy for themselves.

There is deep significance when St Paul says in this passage that Israel will find mercy *now*. The word has troubled many interpreters, because in fact the Jews are not yet converted; for this reason they have replaced the 'now' by 'later' or simply dropped it altogether. What they have done here is to take the passage as talking about history and not in its mystical meaning, which is St Paul's. He is looking into the deep places of God's mystery; he is a prophet here, and sees what God sees: the one eternal 'now'. More than that: St Paul lives his life in the thought of the *Parousia*, the coming; it is a mystical presence always to him, although it is yet to be in history. The 'now' of this passage shows the depths of the Apostle's thought, depths which are God's own.

[1]From a retreat given in 1938.

However we interpret the manner of this presence, it will imply that the Lord is always with us (Mt 28, 20).

That Christ sits at the right hand of God does not mean that he is king elsewhere, and that only on the last day will he show his power to the world. Jesus is nonetheless the *Kyrios*, always at work in the community of those who belong to him; he is *Kyrios*. We know how important this was for the early church, this presence of the Lord after his ascension; it filled the apostles with the Spirit, showed them what they were to do, and all the rest. At Paul's call to grace he heard, 'I am Jesus whom thou persecutest'; Jesus 'the Lord' calls to Ananias as well, and he answers, 'Lord, I am here'. And the Lord again commands him to get up and go into the street which is called straight . . . (Acts, 9, 10–11). It is the Lord who sets Peter free; who speaks to Paul. Everywhere we see the Lord, the *Kyrios*, at work among his own. This is the case in their worship as well; he is present. Their highest form of worship is called the Lord's supper: κυριακὸν δεῖπνον, *cena Domini*. In it the death and rising of Jesus are proclaimed till he come, his body and blood are received; he is present among those who celebrate the rite. 'If we live, it is for the Lord; whether we live or die, it is still to the Lord' (Rom. 14, 8). In a most personal fashion Jesus is present among his own, working for them; he is the true leader of the church; all the rest do what they do through him and under him.[1]

His presence is not only presence of his person but of his action, of his saving act.

We must now examine more closely how the saving action of Christ becomes present for us in the mystery. There are some people who have to feel everything, others who have to imagine everything, others who have to think about things or make conscious acts of virtue. But the essential thing is that some action of Christ's takes place. The subjective aspect is not the one which governs; indeed, in some circumstances it can be a positive hindrance for a real sharing in the celebration with the Lord. The *Sursum corda* carries a warning; we are to leave aside what is still in us of the world; we are to open the way for the Lord who comes. It is not our feelings and our acts which count, but what God is doing. This is the important thing: that God acts upon us in Christ; of ourselves we cannot make ourselves holy. There are a great

[1] From conferences on Romans, 1935–42.

number of religions (and over half the human race hold to them) which demand of man every kind of exercise, and labour and concentration. But the Christian faith is a wholly different thing; its centre is the deed of Christ. Christ has redeemed us, not we ourselves; and he must always be at work accomplishing and fulfilling our redemption. It would mean nothing if he sat on a throne while we got up points of doctrine. Christ performed once a great action; he took flesh, went down into the depths of sin and by his dying conquered sin. Then he went up, back to the Father and now sits at his right hand. This saving work is the all important thing for our redemption. All the rest comes second. For at the centre of our religion is the God-Man whom we are to follow. Christ is the prince of Salvation, as Hebrews says (2, 10) who goes in the van of the army. I am to live as he lived before me. Now this does not mean in the first instance imitation in moral matters; it means that I am to realize his saving action; it is an imitation at the level of being itself. The act of Christ and my act become one in this. But in order that this may take place, it is also necessary that the saving work of Jesus should become present; Christ must die if I am to die with him; he must rise if I too am to rise.

It is in the liturgy of the church that Christ presents his saving work to us once again. The work is fulfilled in a fully objective manner, even without us. It is the very saving work which the Father accomplished, offering the Son in his great love, bringing his Son back to him. This saving action is what is made present to us in the mystery of worship. Because it is made present we can be joined to Christ in all reality, we can do along with him what he does. The condition is that we give ourselves to him, that we renounce ourselves; this is the way into the action of Christ.

As we do take part in this accomplishment of the saving work of Christ we are set free from the self; we learn more and more that it is God's action not our own which is important. We do indeed share; but the real actor here is God.[1]

This act of his must take effect in us by our becoming co-actors.

The mystery was formed for man; it is to bring about in him an inward change. Hence it is not enough to hear mass to do God honour; that is not what the mystery means. God has given it to us much more so that something will really take place, and by this event fashion in,

[1] From conferences for the years 1943–45.

us a new manhood which is of heaven; we are to have part in Christ and his life forever.

To bring about this change we must do all that Christ did. Just as the body follows in its way the movements of the head, we, the members of Christ must follow his movements; in the mystery we are to be players, actors with him.

There is something for us to learn in the drama of the ancient world. Their plays were, for the most part, sacred; the spectators did not look on, but took part; in a way they participated. At the centre of the theatre was a god in some masked form; the play turned about him, and somehow everyone was made a part of it.

The play was a common work of the god and men; both shared in the festival. For those ancient peoples the festivals meant that the world they could not see came down into this; they wanted its presence so that they might enter into it. In the *Laws* Plato writes, (VII 653, C.D.) 'the gods looked with pity on the race of men, born to weariness as it was; so they gave it the different festivals as times of recreation from this labour, and the Muses with Apollo their head and Dionysus, to keep them company at these times. Thus by the formation they received they were to receive fresh substance, and the formation came from their being with the gods at the height of the festivals'.

For the ancients, then, the play is a sacred thing. Men carry out its actions in a way all can see; but the real actors are the gods who dwell at the feast. They are the ones through whom men fulfil the action which they do. For this reason what the play represents is made real in the deepest fashion.

In a still higher and deeper sense all this is true of the Christian sacrifice and mystery. It is a holy drama in which men fulfil an action while Christ, unseen, carries to perfection his work of salvation. He is a comrade of our feast, but the vital centre of it; what we do he does in reality. We act with him as body with its soul; our action is one. By baptism we become the members of Christ, we become one Christ with the Son made man; in this way his act can become our act as well. In the sacred mystery he acts with his body, gathered from all the world, the *ecclesia*.

To be co-actors, co-workers in the mystery we must be of the body of Christ. It was for this reason that in the ancient church only the baptized were allowed to be present at the holy sacrifice. The *cate-chumens*, who were not yet his members were allowed to come to the readings and the prayers; but before the mystery proper began, they were sent away.[1]

But acting with Christ is only possible if we are members of his body.

We wish to examine here what it means to celebrate the sacred mystery with Christ as one body with him. We know that he is God's son made man; that he has gone before us through death into the new life of heaven; that he is already there. All of his actions are actions in heaven; all of his actions are the actions of God and in the new life. If anyone would act with Christ, he must be bound to Christ. This was the deepest reason for the exclusion of which we have already spoken, of unbaptized and sinners from the mystery in the early church. We say today that you must be in a state of grace in order to receive holy communion. This is what we learnt in the catechism. Yet with the meal of the sacrifice, communion, belongs the sacrifice itself. If we are really to make the sacrifice we must be in a state of grace as well. It would in fact be more right and proper to say that anyone who is to be co-offerer in the mass must be a live member of Christ's body. For the celebration of mass is an affair of the entire body, head and members. We cannot separate the two; a body without its head is a corpse.

All parts of the body have their corresponding organ in the head; there all the forces of life join, and from there everything in the organism is controlled. From the head comes command, and the body carries it out. So also, in the church everything comes from Christ, the head; without Christ there is no mystery, no celebration. Proof of this contemporaneity of the mystery in heaven and on earth is the beginning of the *Gloria* in the Roman rite; it sings of the Lord as present. He is there; he acts with the body. Christ celebrates and we with him; without him we can do nothing.

The church then celebrates the mystery in commission from Christ. Yet this does not mean merely that it carries out a command of his. Rather, what it does it does in the power which he gives to it. He is principal actor; from him flow all the springs of action. And this means too that we cannot have devotion on our own showing, however much we wish to. Members of Christ must deny their own private roads. Christ is the way. In Ephesians 5, 23, St Paul says, 'the man is the head of the woman, as Christ is of the Church'; and in 1 Cor. 11, 5 he

[1]Ibid.

writes, 'the woman is to cover her head', a sign that her decision rests no longer with her but with her husband.

The piety of the mystery is not an easy thing; it means giving up oneself. Only one who does this can act with Christ; only when I sacrifice myself can Christ lead and mature me. This sacrifice of self is the condition for the oneness of all his members too, for that oneness which is necessary yet a source of happiness. In it, all that is done in the body becomes the act of all the members, even though we do not realise it. All comes from the head, and every member moves the better the less it has to consider the movement which it is making. In the sacred mysteries I die as a member of Christ. Christ dies, I die only with him. Action with Christ is the ground for humility. It is man's way to think that he must do everything himself.[1]

The way of the Christian mysteries is to everlasting happiness in the closest union with Christ.

What was done in the first age, in the *arche*, every generation must repeat; this is the aim of worship. The meaning of all ritual and of the mystery ritual in particular is that by it man passes through death to blessedness. Men of different ages have gone their ways to this goal. Philosophy sought for it with reason, mysticism with intuition, contemplation or self-appointed asceticism. None could reach the goal, because none built on more than human foundations. The only way is the way God makes, the way of the mysteries. The ancient world gave recognition to this truth in its primitive gnosis, and in its mysteries sought to make that knowledge real. Christ brought perfection. The way of the ancient Christian mysteries is the way of Christ: the way of the saving acts by which God made a road through the dark place of death.[2]

In the rite and celebration which conveys the presence of Christ, word and sacrament are joined in harmony.

We must again free ourselves from the one-sided emphasis on the Word, and the solitary rule of the Sacrament. The two must be joined in mystery: in the ritual presence of Christ, who is both Word and man. The Word must once more become *Logos*, the sacrament become mystery; for in Christ both are one. I can only outline what this means,

[1]Ibid.
[2]From a conference given on 18.12.1944.

but the rest will follow. As soon as we understand clearly what this means, the question, sacrament or sermon, is answered. Of course the sermon is necessary; without it the church cannot begin to exist. St Paul says that faith comes by hearing. But once the church has been formed it stands not so much in need of the teaching word as the active mystery; this is where it lives the fullness of its life. Of course, too, one part of the mystery is the proclamation of the gospel; this is teaching, but praise is another part as well, and the crown of all is in the saving act of Christ made present, the eucharist. The supper was not the only part of the rite in ancient times, it was the crown. We see this clearly in Justin Martyr whose date is about 150 after Christ. Even at an earlier period, when the eucharist was still joined to the *agape*, all the rest was only preparation for the eucharist.[1]

Indeed, the word alone gives a presence to salvation; it forms an important part of the ritual celebration.

In Isaias 52, 7 we read:

> How lovely on the mountains are the feet of those who bring tidings of peace, of those who tell of good to come, of salvation; here is the one who says to Sion, 'your God is king'. Listen! The sentries are glad now, for with their own eyes they see the king returning to Sion. The Lord has shown his holy arm for all the peoples to see. All the ends of the earth look upon the salvation of our God.

This passage reveals the deepest meaning and power of the proclamation in ritual of the good news God has made known: the joyful message announces the moment of Messiah and his salvation in a new age, in which God will rule. The time is not a future time, but now; with the very proclamation of the world it begins, for the word which God puts into the mouth of his herald fashions this salvation. By the proclamation of the word salvation is present.[2] The sentries who hear the message, see the Lord's return before their very eyes, all the ends of the earth see the salvation of God. The vital word, the *euangelion*,

---

[1] From a letter to a Protestant dated 13.3.1939.

[2] Again on stylistic grounds the translator has made necessary a slight change in this note. *Pneumatisch* means in and of the Spirit; and Spirit does not suggest idealism to any but very old 'Greats men'. The presence in and of the Spirit is a presence of the Word of God received in faith. By this the saving act of Christ is made accessible to us, and salvation thereby offered to us as believers; it is developed in the sacramental actions and will be completed in the life to come. Cf Warnach, *Wort und Sacrament* in *Liturgie und Mönchtum* 20 (1957), pp. 68–90.

which brings about this healing is the news: Your God is king. The Hebrew verb is a perfect tense, and means a state arising from a completed action, in other words a reality already begun. It is best to translate this with the present tense and not, surely, with the future, as the Septuagint and Vulgate do. 'God will be king' does not express at all a realization already begun.

In the liturgy we proclaim this news from day to day; and our gospel tell us, after the Lord has brought his saving work to fulfilment, of God's rule is at its last stage of perfection. Our phrase, '*Dominus regnavit*', is the message of the last age of man; it tells us, the Lord, the *Kyrios*, is present and reigns. In liturgy and mystery he has already reached the goal, but the revelation of this awaits the parousia.

St Paul calls the service he gives the gospel a sacrificial service: he celebrates to make the heathen holy, a sacrifice to God. This is a wonderful image for the action of our rites, for the action of the gospel, making a parallel between the words of the eucharist and the sacred work which the gospel accomplishes; the latter is shown to be like the transformation of the sacred elements.

> 'So that I may celebrate Jesus Christ among the heathen; making service of the gospel of God, that the offering of the heathen may be acceptable, made holy in the Spirit' (Rom. 15, 16).[1]

Further emphasis is given to the power of the word in the liturgy.

The church has kept in her liturgy what the ancients believed: that the word has power of doing. Indeed, it is in the liturgy that this view of primitive and ancient man finds its deepest and finest fulfilment. When we pray holy words, the saving reality of which they tell becomes a presence among us. This is true of all the words which the church uses in her mysteries; but the highest stage is found in the eucharist, where the priest speaks not human words, but the words of Christ himself. The words of the office are filled with this reality of the Spirit, when we say them as we ought. St Benedict expresses this with great beauty in the nineteenth chapter of the Rule:

'Everywhere, we are taught by faith, is the presence of God; but we should believe this is so, above all when we are at divine service.' God becomes present when we pray the holy words; but if we are to know this presence we must speak them from an inward fullness. To God's

---

[1] From conferences on Romans from the period 1935–42. Cf the articles on εὐαγγελίζεσθαι and εὐαγγέλιον in Kittel, II, p. 706 ff.

Word, independent in itself, must come man's own devotion. To pray thus is to have a kind of consecrating power. Through the words which we say God carries out his saving action, and we come into his presence.[1]

We can realise what Χάρις (*charis*) meant to the Greeks from Pindar; he tells us that his poems were an answer to the *charis* of the gods. By his song he made immortal the deed which had come forth from *charis*, and where the song would be heard, the deed would be present once more.[2]

From this vantage point we are able to make a serious study of the relationship between the sacrificial mystery and the divine office.

The matter of the mystery presence in the office is too important for us to be able to brush it aside in a few sentences. In any case it is wrong, to start from the negative end, to make a towering difference between the mass and the office. Late scholasticism sees almost nothing else in the mass except the real presence of the body of Christ as an effect of transubstantiation; in the face of this presence, which it often conceives in much too materialistic a fashion, it makes too little of the presence of Christ's saving action in the word. For the ancient church there was only one saving action of Christ, which was the ground of the entire liturgy, word and sacrament alike, although differently in each, and so in different measure, too.[3] Christ is not divided; he is always the one and the same Christ, present to us in word and sacrament. This is of the greatest importance for personal piety.[4] You are right to say this. One has only to think of Chapter 19 of the Rule.

We are also able to cast some new light on the nature of the church's blessings.

Then there is the question, what about blessings and consecrations? Of course we cannot put a blessing of animals on the same level with

---

[1] From a conference given on 5.3.1945.

[2] From a conference given on 8.5.1944. What is said must be taken with some reserve. The bard's song gave the deed of the hero a certain permanence, a new presence, and was thus a distant analogy to the Eucharist in which the hymn of praise (eucharistia) culminating in the words of institution make present the sacrificial act of Christ. More on this in *Das Christliche Opfermysterium*.

[3] One must of course lay emphasis on the last sentence. The special manner of Christ's presence in the celebration of the office is not to be overlooked; yet it is not open to question that the presence in the Sacrament proper is greater, more active, more powerful, more intense, and that in the Eucharist both sacrifice and meal, it reaches its high-point.

[4] From a letter dated 9.12.1944.

the church's great mysteries; but even in these lowly forms, of human devising, something of the power of Christ's saving deed flows into the world. Many of the newer blessings, that of an aeroplane for example, are not mysteries at all but merely prayers for those who are to use the machine. But it is another matter with the burial service; in the ancient East it is called a mystery.[1] The death of a Christian filled with the Spirit is surely not the mere disposal of a corpse; it belongs to the consecration of a Christian who is to be fashioned in the likeness of Christ, in both body and soul.[2]

[1] Cf for example Jugie's book *Theologia Orientalium*, III, 1930, p. 20.
[2] From a letter dated 20.3.1948.

2

THE CHURCH'S COMMON LIFE IN MYSTERY

We can only properly evaluate the presence of the mystery of Christ in the sacramental actions of worship, in other words in the mystery of worship, if we first understand that these actions belong to the church. The church, or, to use the more significant expression of scripture and the fathers, the ecclesia, is the body of Christ; Christ himself is her head.[1] It was founded first in the choosing of the apostles and disciples and particularly of Peter; it comes from the Lord's side.[2] On Whit Sunday, after the Lord had been glorified and the Holy Spirit sent, it came into the sight of men when the apostles first proclaimed the saving message and began to administer the sacraments. The ecclesia is founded upon the mysteries of Christ; its oneness is that of a communion of the mystery; it is itself a mirabile sacramentum, a wonderful mystery.

Deus, respice propitius ad totius ecclesiae tuae mirabile sacramentum: God, look graciously on the wonderful mystery of thy church.

This is the prayer of the liturgy in the holy night of Easter;[3] in this night the Church knows herself to be a mystery. In this night the mystery of the Pasch brings the church to birth as the bride Christ has redeemed and the mother of those who believe in him, brings her to birth from the blood and the Spirit of Christ. The church is herself the great mystery of the New Alliance; she is formed after the image of Christ whom St Paul calls the mystery. In Colossians, 1, 27 St Paul says, 'the mystery which was hidden before ages and generations is now revealed to those to whom God willed to give knowledge of the glory and the riches of this mystery which Christ is in you, the hope of glory'

[1] Cf Heinrich Schlier, *Die Kirche nach dem Brief an die Epheser* and Warnach, *Die Kirche im Epheserbrief.* Both appeared in a supplement to *Catholica,* 1949. The first work also appeared in *Die Zeit der Kirche* 1956, 159–186. Schmaus's treatment of the church in his *Dogmatik,* III (1958) is also of great interest.

[2] For this exegesis of John 19, 34, see Methodius of Philippi supra, pp. 23–4 and J.L.W. 6 (1927), p. 144 ff. This understanding of the text was common among the fathers and older exegetes; it is coming back now.

[3] In the prayer after the second lesson in the old rite.

(an ancient reading). He says that the faithful 'are instructed . . . to knowledge of the mystery of God, Christ' (Col. 1, 26 f; 2, 2). Christ is the mystery in his person, for in him the everlasting godhead has made itself visible. Through him the church too is mystery, for in it Christ's grace and God's glory are revealed in this world. *The Teaching of the Twelve Apostles* is perhaps saying just this with its phrase, the 'world mystery of the church'. (11, 11).

Yet in Scripture we read over and over again that the action of the church, her liturgical rites, are mysteries. In the Holy Night of Easter she prays at the blessing of the baptismal water, from which the neophytes are to emerge later on, through the power of God's Spirit:

> *Omnipotens sempiterne Deus, adesto magnae pietatis tuae mysteriis, adesto sacramentis: et ad recreandos novos populos, quos tibi fons baptismatis parturit, spiritum adoptionis emitte; ut quod nostrae humilitatis gerendum est ministerio, virtutis tuae impleatur effectu.*

'Almighty, eternal God, be present to the mysteries of thy goodness to us; be present to thy sacraments; send down the Spirit of adoption for the creation of new peoples which the font of baptism brings to birth for thee; thus, may that to which our lowliness is minister be truly filled with the presence of thy power.'

What this would tell us is that the mystery of worship has its ground in the power of the Holy Spirit, in the power of God which is present: that the act of the church contains and develops a divine action. The young of the church grow up in this mystery; the church herself has the roots of oneness with Christ and her members have the roots of their oneness with one another, in the mystery. We can therefore rightly say that the church is a mystery. In this sense we are to understand the ancient phrase that the church is a *communio sanctorum*; as many explain it, it is a communion of holy things, the sacraments; it is a communion of the mystery. Often enough, for example, the church calls the eucharist simply, '*participatio sancti mysterii*' (postcommunion for the twelfth Sunday after Pentecost; see also the Postcommunion for the Second Sunday in Advent). In other places it is called a *communio sacramenti* (Postcommunion for the ninth Sunday after Pentecost.) Both these phrases refer to the sharing in the mystery which is given ritual celebration in the church, and so is realized.

Everyone who uses a Roman Missal knows how the church is always speaking of her own action, and particularly of the sacraments and the eucharist, her sacrifice, and its sacrificial meal, as mystery. In the main prayers, for the Sundays of Advent alone we find this over and over again. The postcommunion of the second Sunday reads, 'filled with the Spirit's food, Lord, we humbly ask that, by our sharing in this mystery you may teach us to despise the things of earth and love those of heaven'. In the secret for the third Sunday it says:

'May the sacrifice of our worship (*devotionis hostia*) be offered continually and thereby both the order of the mystery which you have laid down brought to perfection, and your healing come to us in wonderful manner'. The eucharist is, then, the proper fulfilment of the mystery of worship which the Lord has instituted; it bears the divine reality which stands behind the mystery. In the mass for Ember Friday in Advent the community pray at the Secret, in other words before the offering, 'make us pure by the sacred mysteries'. After the communion they pray again in thanksgiving, 'may the tasting (*libatio* means both offering and the meal) of this holy sacrament renew us (*restauret*); may it cause us, purged from decay, to pass into the fellowship of the mystery (*in mysterii salutaris faciat nos transire consortium*)'. On Ember Saturday the church prays after communion, 'may the all-holy mysteries which you have given as the rock of our reparation be a means of healing for present and future.' On the fourth Sunday we meet the idea in the postcommunion that the frequent celebration of the mystery may increase the intensity of our salvation. On the vigil of Christmas the church tells us that we are 'fed and given to drink by the heavenly mystery'. In the mass for midnight she praises God for the light he has made to shine in this night, and asks 'that we may have pleasure in the joys of him, whose mysteries of light we have come to know on earth'. In the postcommunion of this mass the thought comes up once more that in the mysteries and by them we celebrate the birth of our Lord Jesus Christ again and again: *mysteriis frequentare*. The secret of the second mass of Christmas asks 'that the oblation may be in keeping with the mysteries of today's birth'. The missal offers a broad picture of the mystery and its theology in the church.

Yet in these texts we see (and it is a fact to be taken into account) that the word *mysterium* does not appear alone; like a king, it has its court in attendance. Where the church must speak of the deep things of the eucharist, she takes up the whole vocabulary of the mysteries. We cannot go into all the details of this, but the prayers which we have just quoted will give some idea of what it is. They speak of an 'order of the mystery' which Christ has 'instituted'. This order consists, of course, in rites which can be repeated. Yet behind the rites there is an invisible, divine reality; at Christmas the birth of a divine child, the bringer of salvation has a new, mysterious presence. It is from this, and not from the memory or the activity of a long past historical event that healing comes to us; nor is this healing one for the body but the higher part of man which will remain after he dies. This part of him will live on in the new world through the power of the mysteries. . . . Yet still again this healing is not confined to the future; already now, the Christian takes his share in the things of heaven. The mysteries are purification, renewal of youthfulness, eating and drinking. They are also illumination, light falling from a higher light. Perhaps the deepest expression of what they mean is participation fellowship, *participatio* or *consortium*, fellowship: now this idea comes not merely from the mysteries of the ancient world but even more from its religious philosophy and mysticism. Plato tells us how earthly things have a share in the divine ideas; they are not merely set in motion, moved by them; they have an ontological share in them. The fathers of the church know that κοινωνία, the communion, goes beyond sharing; it gives entire oneness with the divine.[1]

These few texts of the missal are saturated with the language of the mysteries, a language which emerges not merely from the classical world but from wherever the deepest matters of religion are spoken about. Why, then, does the church employ it?

There are a number of answers we might give to this question. The first idea is that it is nothing but the sort of magic formula used by a magician; yet it is not a particularly truthful or dignified conception of the church that she is a magician. And in any case it is well known that the Roman liturgy, for all its depth and refinement, is sober and clear, while the church has always rejected magician's nonsense and will always do so.

Not much better is the idea, often heard, that the church wished to adapt herself to the religious language of the time. Of course St Paul wanted to be all things to all men; but what this means is not weakminded conformism, but rather a movement towards meeting the religious needs of different groups of men and nations, adapting themselves freely to what suits them. There is proof of this in the choice the New Testament makes of old materials.

[1]Chrysostom, Homily 24, 2 on 1 Corinthians; see bottom of page 197.

Still others say that the church has taken over these expressions in merely external ways, as empty shells, entirely bereft of their ancient content. We must of course grant that the church has in no wise taken over the ancient mystery language with the whole of its content; the church lives from God's revelation, and this is given to men from above. It cannot therefore simply accept human words and concepts as they are. But there is linguistic evidence that, for example, the New Testament makes a selective use of mystery language, leaving out many words, or taking them in a weakened sense.[1]

It is therefore all the more significant that the church should really have picked out some few words and used them, if much else has been added to them in the course of time from mysticism and ritual. Moreover, surely the church takes nothing to itself as mere empty shells; is it possible to take over words which have no content? The ancients took it that every word is necessarily the form of an idea and inseparable from it. Indeed, the connection of essence and name is so sacred for ancient man that he never loses sight of it, whatever colours of secondary meaning the word may in time have acquired. The word is always striving to regain its first place; its bent is towards the renewal of its original freshness. It is simply not possible then to take over a word as a mere sound, a 'thought-indicator', of certain concepts. Moreover, such a course would not correspond to the real manner in which revelation is made to us. When God reveals, he wants to communicate something to us; but anyone who seeks to communicate must use the language of the person to whom he is addressing himself. If I want to tell something to a Chinese and cannot speak his language I must use words and signs which he will understand. So, too, when God speaks to us, he must use our language; and this is indeed what he has always done, as both Old and New Testament show. We might, in this connection, even point to the incarnation itself; it is the first revelation of all. In it, God did not come down to us in the fullness of his inapproachable light; he appeared in our own fashion, took flesh from one of us, the Virgin, whom his Spirit had made fruitful. The Spirit of God and human flesh are joined in the revelation which is Christ. In an analogous way, in the revelation of the *Logos*, man's speech and God's Spirit are joined. In the same way that human nature was not abolished or emptied but filled, so too human language is not emptied, reduced to a mere shell but upraised in the Spirit, 'filled with divine

[1] Cf A.L.W. 1 (1950), 29 ff and note 7 to p. 29.

content'. 'I am come not to destroy but to fulfil', is true here too.

This phrase which Jesus uttered in the context of the law of the Old Testament is true as well of the whole course of human history. God let the nations go their several ways; but his providence brought even the pagan world to Christ, although along different ways, ways which it was often hard to recognize. Some of the fathers speak of Greek philosophy as a first schooling for Christ; they could not say that of idolatry. Yet that is not to deny that pagan worship also had seeds of truth within it. Indeed, the philosophy which the fathers so praised contained expressions and hints, particularly in Plato, which were taken from the mysteries.

Christ is God's acceptance of all creation; his refusal is reserved for evil, for what has turned from him; all that is positive he takes up. It cannot be right, then, to talk of the taking over of empty forms; rather what has taken place is acceptance, completion, the implementing and perfecting, the glorification and upraising of human form. There is a true analogy between nature and grace in that both are from God. Grace presupposes nature, perfects it, gives to it the last wholeness which God designed for it. When the sun's rays fall on a diamond they bring out all that rested in it before as a mere possibility.

When therefore we look at things from God's point of view, we see that he has formed everything after the Word, the *Logos*, from all eternity; he has shed his light on creation both matter and spirit and made it all after his image. Therefore, throughout the whole of nature there is a divine analogy, growing weaker as the order of things descends, yet giving to the whole form and beauty, a true participation in the beauty of God himself. We who stand here below, whose minds are dark with sin, see at first only the shadows which at once give and hide meaning. Yet the shadows too speak of the body which casts them; they give us a point of rest in our search for God. Of ourselves, however, we would never learn the full truth; the insubstantial shadows would lead us to many errors. Because of this God for his endless love's sake, gave us the light of revelation; in its brightness we can see the outlines of the figures, clear and pure. Thus, created things are made symbols: they become so luminous that we see in and through them what is eternal. So, even now, they are not superfluous. The manhood of the Lord after his resurrection is only recognizable in the Spirit's light, and for that reason it is our lasting way to the Father; so also until the plenitude of the new age the things of creation are symbols of the divine for us. St Paul says rather mysteriously that in the eucharist we proclaim the death of the Lord until he come. When he comes he will himself be the first symbol; until then we live in shadow images and darkness.

It would be right to say that all of this is particularly vital for us today. We live in an age which, after a long period of devotion to abstract intellectualism with its excessive evaluation of reasoning, is beginning once more to think in symbols, to make use of the ways in which divine truth has taken form in nature, art, and culture. For us it is doubly necessary to bring to memory those periods of history when symbolic thinking was in full flower. This is the peculiar worth of the history of religions, for it teaches us to understand and use the power and primitive strength of symbolic thinking, in contrast to the over-refinement of 'modern' methods. The first age of the Christian church had no need for this, for it lived in the midst of the mysteries and looked at everything as symbol of the divine. When we regard the ancient liturgy, the writings of the apostles and the fathers, we realize that for them everything is symbolical of Christ, and Christ is 'symbol' of the Father: *'qui videt me, videt et patrem*: who hath seen me hath seen the Father' (Jn. 14, 9).

Today we have to learn these things over again; we have to learn to think simply, in the most ancient way, and thus to become once more seers of the whole.

It is of greatest importance for us to come to know the rites of the mysteries in their essence and whole design. This brings us back to what we said earlier: why does the church use the language of the mysteries in her liturgical services? What does she mean to convey in this way?

The only possible answer follows from what we have now seen; the church wishes to lead us through the analogy to the essence of what she is doing. She wishes to speak the language we can understand best.

But for us today the difficulty is that the language of the mysteries in the natural order of things is lost to us. Modern thinking is very far from it, terribly different from it. The wholly temporal dimension of thought since the Renaissance has no way open to thinking in the mystery's terms. It is at this point that the history of religions appears, a providential moment. This science has emerged from the relativism common to modern science generally, and so, quite rightly attracts at first instance the mistrust of the church and her theologians; in practice and often in theory it has denied revelation. Yet at the same time in this study there was and is the longing for active religious life-forms. Religious life, 'piety' has become so refined, so individualist, that it has really created a hunger for vital, ritual, piety. For these reasons it is a real necessity that theologians should pursue this field and make the fruits of their studies as well known as possible among Christians.[1]

The church as communion of the mystery is, nonetheless, the church we know in this world with its hierarchic structure; it gathers about the one altar of Christ to celebrate the Eucharist, with the one bishop and his priests. Particular witness to this source of unity is found in St Ignatius of Antioch.

The centre of the economy of salvation is the *Logos* made flesh.

His sufferings and his resurrection are the facts which form this design; Ignatius martyr begs the Ephesians to pray that he may be able to make this known. His is a deep thought: the man of the Spirit, too, stands in need of prayer; he does not live isolated, but in a vast unity, the unity of all believers with their bishop. Everything points towards this unity; everything reaches its term in it. The sign of this unity is in the one bread:

> . . . so that you may give obedience to the bishop and the college of elders in unbroken unity of mind, breaking one bread which is the medicine of immortality, the remedy against death, which gives us life in Jesus Christ forever (as Ephesians 20).

Our first thought is for the eucharist, and it is possibly what is meant. Yet the breaking of the bread and the communion are the expression, through rites, of the one being, the one entity, which the faithful are among themselves and with Christ. We need not see in the 'one bread' the eucharist alone; the bishop gives his faithful the true bread of God through the Word, when he teaches them; and what gives us nourishment in both the eucharist and in the bishop's word is the one, everlasting Word of God, communicating himself to those who believe in both word and sacrament. If anyone does not eat the bread which the bishop breaks in the eucharist or in teaching, he does not taste God's true bread, and he is not in the unity.

In his letter to the Magnesians, Ignatius again commends oneness with the bishop, telling how it is the foundation of the whole church:

> . . . have a care that you do everything in God's harmony; this

[1] Mss of Casel, undated, from the period 1939–40.

M.C.W.—G

means that the bishop takes the leader's part, in God's stead; the elders have the place of the apostles, and the deacons, whom I dearly love, carry out the work of Jesus Christ who was with the Father before all ages and appeared at the last.

. . . Just as the Lord did nothing without the Father with whom he is one, nothing in his own person or through the apostles, so you do nothing without the bishops and the apostles . . . one prayer, one petition, one mind, one hope in charity in the joy without darkness: Jesus Christ. There is none better than he. You are to go, then, as to one temple of God, to one altar, to the one Jesus Christ who has come forth from the one Father, to whom he shall return (Mag. 6 f).

It could scarcely be put more beautifully: the bishop stands in Christ's place and makes the church, God's assembly, what it is. It is of no matter whether the bishop be young or experienced and mature. He is chosen by God, and he is filled with the power of God the Father; in a special way he is the expression of the Father's image. It follows then, that where the bishop is absent, God is absent, too. At this point we must recall, 'who hears you, hears me, and who despises you despises me; and who despises me despises him that sent me'. (Lk. 10, 16). As the bishop is the imprint of the Father, so the elders (*presbyteroi*) are the figure of the apostles and the deacons of Jesus the man, the Father's first servant. Ignatius sees before him the whole design: through the bishop and the elders the faithful have their communion with God. Or, as Ignatius says in his picture language, they are the coins which carry the imprint of God the Father through Jesus Christ, by dying with him in his passion. (Mag. 5.)

To bring the unity Christians have in the Spirit vividly before his readers, St Ignatius takes up images from the pagan rites. In them, the unity of the god with his worshippers was already symbolized by the altar. Ignatius starts from this; but he points out that for Christians it is not the stone altar which of itself makes unity, but the true altar in heaven, Jesus Christ.

Ignatius martyr speaks too of the oneness of the bishop with the church in his letter to the Trallians (c. 2 ff.):

. . . when you submit yourselves to the bishop as to Christ, you are not living by a human pattern, but by the pattern of Jesus Christ who died for us; in this way you escape death, believers in his death. It is necessary then that you should, as indeed you do, do nothing without the bishop. Submit yourself also to the elders as to the apostles of Jesus, who is our hope, in whom we are grounded when we live thus. And those who are the deacons, the servants of the mysteries of Jesus must in every way please all men; for they do not serve for food and drink; they are servants of the church of God. They must avoid complaints like fire.

Equally, you are to have all reverence for the deacons, as for Jesus Christ himself, and for the bishop as the type of the Father, and for the elders as God's council and the band of the apostles. The church is absent where they are absent. I am sure that you conduct yourselves in this way; and I have received the image of the love you have for one another: in your bishop I have it here with me . . .

In the sixth chapter of the same letter Ignatius tells the people that they are to avoid heretics, and he goes on in chapter seven:

keep away from such as these; you will succeed in this if you avoid arrogance and are not cut off from the God of Jesus Christ, or from the bishop, or the commands of the apostles. If you are within the altar's circuit you are pure; if not, you are not pure. This means that if you do anything without the bishop, the presbyters, and the deacons, you are not clean in conscience.

And in a further chapter he repeats himself:

the chains which I bear gladly for Jesus' sake—in deepest longing that I may come to God—my chains give you warning: stand fast in your union and in your common prayer; it is right for each of you, but especially for the presbyters to give solace to the bishop, in honour of the Father and Jesus Christ and the apostles.

From this text it follows that obedience to the bishop is a thing of the Spirit; by this obedience the believer lives no more in and for himself but in Jesus and with him in the Father's presence. This obedience makes for unity, while human obedience divides. If I obey the bishop and die through this obedience to my nature I imitate him who died for us on the cross; then I am one with the bishop, and through him with Christ and the Father. For only the dead are truly one, united in the higher life which is God's own. They alone are Christ's members.

We might be surprised at first that Ignatius makes much here of the fact that the deacons are not servants in matters of food and drink, but of the church of God. The apostles had instituted deacons just for the care of these matters. Yet Ignatius is right. Within the church such service is no mere material one; it is a holy work, a work in and of the Spirit. Thus, it is taken for granted that the deacons ought to extend their work to matters of the Spirit alone; to preaching, as we are told of Stephen in Acts 7, 1 ff.[1]

St Ignatius martyr has such a deep grasp of the hierarchy's true nature that it is almost a mystique of the bishop. Ignatius sees him as the great mediator between God and the church. God gives his Spirit and the church answers with her love, her *agape*. The living waters of the Spirit come down, the love rises back again; they meet in the person of the bishop. God gives his Spirit to the church through the bishop, and the church returns thanks to God through the bishop, in love.

What Ignatius calls *pneuma* and *agape*, Spirit and love, are fundamentally one; both are the one divine life which comes from him and streams back to him in the end. They are distinct in form, and the bishop stands as minister of life from above; this is his mystical place in the church: he is the great image of its oneness. Hence, Ignatius can sum up his teaching in the phrase, 'love unity' (Phil 7, 2): love the bishop, do nothing without him.

In his letter to the Philadelphians, Ignatius tells us more about the meaning of the bishop; at the very beginning he writes,

> Ignatius who is also called the God-bearer, to the church of God the Father and the Lord Jesus Christ which is at Philadelphia in Asia; grace and mercy have been given you, and you are firmly planted in the harmony of God, with unshakable joy in the passion of our sovereign Lord, perfected in the resurrection in all mercifulness. I greet you in Christ's blood. It is my abiding joy, a joy of the age to come, above all when you are in oneness with your bishop and his elders and the deacons, who have been introduced by the counsel of Jesus Christ; and this same Jesus has made its firmness rest in his will, through his holy Spirit . . .
>
> Children of light and truth, flee from schism and every evil doctrine. The sheep go after the shepherd; for there are many wolves with likely appearance, who would invite confidence and with evil delight, take prisoner men who are God's pilgrims. Yet they will find no place in your unity.
>
> Have a care then for the one eucharist; for there is one flesh of our Lord Jesus Christ and there is one chalice and union in his blood; there is one altar as there is one bishop, together with the college of elders and the deacons, all slaves like me. In the same way, when you do anything you will do it as God would have it done.

[1] From a conference given on 26.11.1945.

Ignatius is never weary of saying that the bishop is no mere man; that he does not owe his appointment to men, but to God himself, even when God's choice of him has been made through men. His power is from above; God fills the man he chooses with his own power, and this man has the dignity of God, is set up above the rest of men. God's love has consecrated him, set him apart and anointed him with the holy Spirit; Christ the Lord in glory has made this man his vice-regent. Thus, through the bishop the Trinity works on the community which lives in unity with him: the Father from whom all life and mercy come, Jesus who gave his blood for them, and the holy Spirit who is their rock and strength. Through the bishop alone and through those who have authority from him unity is made real and true. The presbyters and deacons are a part of the bishop; they are his hand and eye, his instruments. Just as God gave us Christ in the flesh, he gives us these leaders now. They are the visible presence of himself; their word is his, and to despise their word is to despise him and to deprive oneself of his grace.

The matter at stake is not, then, merely constitutional, but one of religious truth. We must look upon the bishop's authority and that of his helpers in a mystical way. Here is this vision at its deepest and most beautiful in St Ignatius, almost poetically expressed:

> do nothing without the bishop; keep your flesh as the Temple of God. Love unity, fly from schism; be imitators of Jesus as he is an imitator of the Father (7, 2).

The flesh is the community; it is in truth the flesh of Christ, his body. The head of this body is the bishop and from him flows all life. Through this oneness with the visible head the whole body keeps its union with Christ, the unseen head, and through him with the Father. This is still so even though the bishop does not speak, even though he lacks the charism of eloquence (Phil. 1, 1). He has always one *charism*: he shows in her person what his consecration has made him: image of the Father and vicar of Christ. His very silence has more to tell us than the empty voice of others. His greatness lies in union with God and his commandments; he is to them like the harp to its strings.

If we remain in unity with the bishop we shall not go astray; he comes and goes to God; he is on the right way; he stands on the way to the cross, the passion of Christ, and so to God. He is a true θεοδρόμος, God's runner. Here Ignatius is making allusion to an ancient custom: that of the herald who went ahead of a royal person and the magnates to announce their coming. The same image is to be found in scripture; there, John the baptist is the great herald in the kingdom of God, who runs on before the Lord and make his way ready.

The unity we have in the bishop is most deeply expressed in the eucharist. At this point Ignatius is speaking of the ritual eucharist rather than 'thanksgiving', for he adds, 'one chalice for the unity of his blood'. This eucharist in the ritual is the symbolic expression of the sacrifice in Spirit which the whole church is continually bringing to the Father in Jesus Christ. There is only one eucharist, that which the bishop celebrates. It portrays the great unity in which the church stands as it offers itself to the Father with Christ. We are not to grasp only the façade of the eucharist, but the reality behind it, oneness with the crucified Lord.

This view of the bishop in the Spirit's perspective is everywhere in the letters of St Ignatius. In the letter to the Smyrnaeans he writes,

> All of you, follow the bishop, as Jesus does the Father, and the college of presbyters as the apostles; have reverence for the deacons as for God's command. No one is to do anything in worship without the bishop; only that eucharist is valid which is performed under him or by one whom he appoints. Where the bishop is, there the community too, as where Jesus Christ is, there is the Catholic church. It is unlawful to baptise or hold the agape without the bishop; what he has examined and found right is pleasing to God; thus is all to be firm and secure.[1]

The church's character as a mystery communion is based upon its place in sacred history. This is explained from the writings of Irenaeus of Lyons.

St Irenaeus tells us that the place where all the *charis* of God will be found is the church:[2]

> We have shown that the message of the church is perfect and remains always the same; that it possesses the message of the prophets, apostles and all disciples. It goes through the beginning, the centre and the end of the whole design of salvation, its continual bent is towards the saving of men; yet only in faith may men receive it. We keep this faith which the church has given us. By God's Spirit the church remains ever young, just as a precious stuff preserves the vessel which

---

[1] From a conference given on 17.12.1945.
[2] Grace, graciousness, particularly the loving-kindness of God made visible in Christ. For example the Greek text of the epistle for the first mass of Christmas: ἐπεφάνη γὰρ ἡ χάρις τοῦ θεοῦ ἡ σωτήριος . . .

contains it; for this gift is given to the church that it may be breathed upon the whole.

Faith then is the Father's gift to the whole church through the Son; she breathes it upon her children.

> For in her is founded our community with Christ, the holy Spirit, the bridal gift of changeless life, the fixed point of our faith; to her the one is given who shall lead us upwards. Where the church is, there too is God's Spirit, and where the Spirit is, there is the church and all grace (*charis*). But the Spirit is reality; whoever has no share in the Spirit will lack the nourishment of the mother of life; he will not drink of the pure spring which flows from the body of Christ (*Adv. Haereses* III, 24, 1).

The church is the vessel in which faith, God's gift through Christ, stays forever fresh, under the breath of the Holy Spirit. This Spirit is the ageless life of God. It preserves faith; and faith preserves the vessel which it fills, the church. Through the Spirit it is the place where all God's graciousness and beauty, his *charis* is to be found. Like a fine odour this *charis* rises from the vessel and gives life to all who are in the church; yet those who have no part in the church have no part either in the *charis* or the *pneuma* of God. Such a person cuts himself off from the life which comes from the cross. For *charis* and *pneuma* are a sharing in the cross of Christ; they are communion with Christ.[1]

The priesthood of the church has two members: priests by office and the so-called general priesthood of the faithful. Its sacrifice and service in the Spirit are depicted with reference to I Peter 4–10.

In this, the Spirit's house, the church built upon Christ, Christians themselves are priests, who bring their sacrifice in the Spirit. Everyone who truly belongs to the household makes this sacrifice.

> draw near to him, the living rock, the stone whom men rejected, yet whom God chose and honoured. You yourselves, like living stones, should pray that you may be built up into a house of the Spirit, an holy priesthood, to offer sacrifices in the Spirit acceptable, through Jesus Christ, to the Father. It is for this reason that scripture says, 'look, in Sion I am raising a corner stone, selected, precious, and the man who puts his trust in it shall not be disappointed'. You, then, the believers, have honour; but for those who are incredulous, 'the stone

---

[1]From a conference given on 2.7.1945.

which the builders rejected has become the corner stone, a rock of contention and a stumbling block'. They have come against it because they do not believe the Word; yet he is the one for whose sake they are given being. But as for you, you are a race elect, a royal priesthood, a holy people, a people purchased, who are to make known the praises of him who called you out of darkness into his dread light; you, who were once no people are now the people of God; once without mercy, you know it now (I Peter 2, 4–10).

In pagan and in Jewish religion only the priest could make sacrifice. But with the coming of Christ the old priesthood is gone; there is now only one priest and one sacrifice. This is the passion and the resurrection of Christ; *passio et resurrectio,* in all their meaning. The priest who makes this offering can only be the Lord himself and his bride the church to whom he has entrusted it. Yet we now call those men priests to whom the re-presentation of the sacrifice in Christ's place has been entrusted. Their special authority lies in the consecration, and so carries out the condition upon which the sacrifice is made present.[1] Yet the sacrifice is offered by the whole church; by every man who joins himself to her. Hence in the Christian age, every man is a priest. St Peter proclaims this general priesthood of the faithful, so often forgotten in our time.[2] This is what he is thinking of when he says, 'offer spiritual sacrifices': he means the gift each of us makes of himself in the Spirit. This gift is a pre-condition and a consequence of the Eucharist. The life of Christian virtue would be impossible without the sacrifice of Christ, and on the other hand it is the crown of this very sacrifice. Only through Jesus is the sacrifice made acceptable; without him we have no entry to the Father. The church is fully aware of this, and so begs that her gifts may be made *acceptabilis*; the Roman canon keeps this term in the *Quam oblationem.*

The passage from St Peter's Epistle which we have just quoted is read in the Roman Church on Saturday after Easter, for its connection with the baptised. It is thoroughly fitting to the time; now the initiate begins to explain the mass and its rites to the young neophyte. Until now they were the guests of the community; at Milan they might not bring any gifts themselves for eight days after their baptism; they

---

[1]Just by this fact they are the first who as Christ's instruments, celebrate the mass, bring the sacrifice. It is only then that the faithful can and should take a share in this sacrifice through their general priesthood. Cf *Mediator Dei.*
[2]Cf also *Mediator Dei.*

received at the sacrifice what others had offered for them. From Low Sunday on they began to bring their own anaphora.

The words *regale sacerdotium, gens sancta,* are taken from Exodus 19, 6. There, too, the expression is a prophetic one, for the priesthood of Aaron's house was not royal. It was only when Christ the high priest came, and after his obedient death the whole world was laid at his feet for him to rule that this marvellous idea was fulfilled; Psalm 109 tells us this; every Sunday we sing this psalm, making the day a little Easter. With its head, the priest-king, the whole body is exalted to like dignity; hence, Peter can speak simply of the whole people as a holy nation, *gens sancta.* With this high title they must now become heralds of the might of God, the *virtutes Dei.*[1]

A matter of particular importance to the church is the concept of tradition or paradosis; *by it, in virtue of the apostolic succession the church is one with the apostles and through them with Christ. This is different from the oneness of the altar.*

At the beginning of the fifteenth chapter of the First Epistle to the Corinthians we are given an insight into the ancient Christian idea of tradition: what was revealed immediately by God is handed on by tradition. For only revelation taken most realistically, as what our fathers, the apostles saw and experienced can be the foundation of our faith, not philosophical speculation. From the apostles onward there is a continual succession in the Spirit, as from Father to Son, of knowledge of the facts of revelation. In the most real fashion each begets the Spirit in the next.[2]

There is a broad discussion of the concept of tradition, in connection with a book on the subject.[3] Der Ursprung des Katholischen Traditions-prinzips (1931) by J. Ranft.

A penetrating study of *traditio* has been made by Ranft; his work takes in not only the reigning idea among the Jews, but the complex and more variable concept of *traditio* among the Greeks. First of all among the people who observed the mysteries the concept of *traditio* or παράδσοις played a great part. In this last context it means the secret delivery of a hidden salvation to the initiate, his initiation and incorporation into the circle of the elect, in the way characteristic of late

---

[1]From a conference on I Peter.
[2]From a conference on I Corinthians delivered in 1931.
[3]Cf A.L.W. I, 1950, p. 39 ff.

Greek and oriental mystery religions. *Traditio* and *paradosis* thus become a word for the initiation into the mysteries. It is not a scientific *traditio*, but a religious one, which is passed on in ritual; for the initiates it is given in the form of a revelation, an experience of the certainty of sacred things and sacred hopes. The age-old revelation passes, through this tradition, on to later generations, and is handed down through an act of consecration.

The same principle is present in Christianity. The Christian does not fashion himself a doctrine by means of his own reason, he takes up the teaching of the church which, in virtue of the apostolic succession, gives us the unfalsified teaching of Christ, brought down through the apostles and the bishops. Thus, the teaching of the church is a *traditio*, a mystery in the fullest sense. We receive the Christian doctrine of salvation not by our own reflection but by this sacred *traditio*, going back in unbroken succession to Christ himself. It is of great importance now to realize what a place this tradition had in the ancient church, for the apostles and the fathers. The *consensus patrum*, the agreement of all the fathers in a matter of faith is a criterion of dogmatic correctness. This is an attribute which the later authors do not have; the teaching of the apostles and the fathers always has first place.[1]

This means, then, that when in the mysteries the teacher and leader, the mystagogue, gives his disciples the things necessary for worship, this is itself a *traditio*; the high point is not a lecture, but a vision; Apuleius tells us this in his story of the experiences of Lucius (Metamorphoses 1; XI, 21, 23). Of course there is oral instruction first; but the end of the matter is contemplative sight, in which the learner, the initiate, enters into immediate contact with the god. This is the way for Christians. In the person of the bishop the believer hears Christ himself speak; and the instruction in word passes over into the seeing which God gives; at the highest point, the reality behind the mystery, the *effectus* for which the Roman missal so often prays, is fulfilled.[2] We Christians come close to Christ, we touch him in all intimacy. Ranft rightly says that from this intimate contact a deep knowledge, *gnosis*, arises.

Ranft would therefore define *paradosis* as the initiation of a disciple into a religious world by the use of a complete, secret rite. By this initiation the candidate becomes witness to the secret revelations of the

---

[1] To the extent to which they are witnesses to the teaching of the apostles.
[2] Casel on the Roman Orations J.L.W. 11 (1933), pp. 35–45.

cult god and shares in a new, higher life and as well as a new teaching and mysteries which he may now practice. This tradition, in both content and form is for both giver and recipient a sacred legacy to be kept in all good faith; the *mystes* believes that it is not from men but God, and hence not within the power of men's fancy. This is the reason for the obligation of silence towards the uninitiate. The whole character of these acts requires that they should be made by word of mouth and not by writing, and that any communication of these things to outsiders and uninitiates will be looked upon as profanation and subject to punishment.

We may now look at some of the texts which will give us a picture of *traditio* in the New Testament.

In 1 Thessalonians 2, 13 St Paul says, 'hence we never leave off thanking God because you, having once received the Word of God in hearing (λόγον ἀκοῆς παραλαβόντες) not as if it were a word from men, but for what it really is: the Word of God which acts in you who believe'.

St Paul gives thanks that the faithful have taken up the λόγος ἀκοῆς, the Word which came through hearing. In the mystery circles it is characteristic that the initiate should hear, and the leader speak. What the bishop hands on is God's teaching, not his own. He is only the channel not the spring; he may only teach what comes from God. This of course does not rule out that he will turn God's teaching to personal experience and give it a new life rising from his own being, and in this form pass it on. But the two moments must be bound up one with the other: the historical and objective with the subjective and Spiritual. Our text gives a fine picture of the enthusiastic element in *paradosis*, tradition. The *Logos*, the word which the faithful take up is not of man, although men are the instruments of handing it on; it is God's Word which acts upon the faithful. It is first God at work in them who gives the capacity to take up this Word and let it fashion them intimately. Ranft is right to notice the plain relationship here to the Greek mysteries. It is a case of reception through tradition, and through an oral tradition. This too is an important matter, that it should be oral and not by writing, that it should be a live proceeding in which the Word is communicated. Moreover, what is communicated, as Ranft also notices, is something not unknown to the Greeks: a λόγος θεοῦ.

The pagans were looking for the right thing; but they did not find its source, because they lacked true revelation. Only with Christ did the true Word of God enter the world. The apostle, surely, is setting up his mystery in clean contrast to the mysteries of the pagans; but in a sense, he is placing his along side the others, by using the terms, fulfilled and real here in Christ for the first time. We must emphasize this over again; the Word which the Thessalonians to whom this letter was written had received was a word of hearing; it is something live and capable of being received, it is not written down. This is the case with both St Paul and his community. Paul is in the middle; he has received the word from God and the community has received it from him. The Greek text makes this very pointedly by the position of the words: παραλαβόντες λόγον ἀκοῆς παρ' ἡμῶν τοῦ θεοῦ ... What St Paul is making emphatic is that the Word which the believers receive is nonetheless not his word but the Word of God. Nor is this word merely accepted and preserved in memory, but rather it is a live power of action which works and has its effects in man. Here once more and very clearly we meet the enthusiastic element in Christian *paradosis*.

Now it is just this note in *paradosis* which was also to be found in the tradition of the hellenistic mysteries, yet which was lacking in Judaism. In the latter what we find is a mere formal relationship between master and pupil, and a method of mere memorizing required. Bousset[1] gave a vivid picture of this in his quotation from the 28th Sukka. Here we read of a pupil in the school of the law:

> none came earlier than he to the lecture room; he never slept there, either by design or accident. He was the last to go, and no one ever saw him sitting silent when he ought to be repeating the lesson. He never spoke a word which he had not heard from his master's mouth, and he never mentioned that it was time to end the lesson.

In this portrait of the ideal pupil in a rabbinical school the Jewish way is characterized and exhausted by recital, memorization and repetition. The highest praise of a disciple is that he says nothing he has not heard from his master. Bousset says rightly that in late Judaism there is a terrible narrowing of the notion of wisdom and its transmission. First wisdom had been the mind of man open to the wisdom of God ruling all the world; in the later period it was confined exclusively to a knowledge of the law, after the time of Jesus and was thought of more and more as nothing but a cult of the law and a sum of ceremonial precepts. At first that was not so narrow; there had been en-

---

[1] Cf his book *Die Religion des Judentums im Späthellenistichen Zeitalter*, third edition, 1926, by H. Gressmann, p. 168.

thusiasm, at least in the old schools of the prophets. The later type, however, the teachers of the law, won out; and with them our Lord was always in conflict. They were the doctors of the law who bore the rabbinical tradition and handed it on in their schools from generation to generation.

By contrast the hellenistic school is much livelier. It too had the custom of handing on its content; but this *traditio* was carried out in rites, in the mystery rites themselves; here they were live experience, and the initiate was brought more and more into a living possession of them. This mystery aspect of the *paradosis* is essential to it in Christianity; here, as St Paul expressly says, we take up the word which we receive not as from man but from God, we give ourselves to it in obedience and thus we are to make it the deepest form of our minds; it is truly a tradition which we live. Of course St Paul does not mean that Christians are to imitate the pagan mysteries as such; but he is giving his converts forms built up among the pagans, which come alive in Christianity with a real content. Hence as Ranft says, St Paul makes use of the special language of the *traditio* which was current in the hellenistic mysteries; the formal expressions come of themselves to his dictation.

In Colossians 2, 6 we recognize how personal the *paradosis* is in Christianity: 'as you received the Lord Jesus Christ (παρελάβετε) so walk in him'. What is handed on and taken in by Christians is in the last instance not propositions but Christ himself, who becomes the most intimate possession of the believer; nor is he the Jesus of Nazareth 'of history' but the Lord, the Christ who has risen and is in the Spirit; it is he whom we hear, the Lord to whom we are joined by our inward faith and inward knowledge born of faith. It is this, the Lord in Spirit, who is the object of the Christian tradition. For this reason St Paul warns with such vehemence against a tradition which is not according to Christ, and which does not have him for its content. And again in Colossians 1, 26 he describes this the deepest content of Christian *paradosis* as 'the mystery which is Christ in you, the hope of glory'; in other words, the indwelling of the Lord, exalted in Spirit, in the church and in the soul. None of this is the product of human thinking, like modern anthroposophy for example, in which man produces his own God, which is really himself. No, here the true God has spoken, Christ has shown himself to the apostles so that they might give this faith to the chosen believers and they make it their own in faith and *gnosis*.

In this connection we may also look at Galatians 1, 8 where St Paul warns the Galatians against the judaising party who would turn away from the gospel of Christ. He tells them, 'but if an angel from heaven should bring another gospel than the one I preached to you, a curse upon him! I have said it and say it again now, if anyone bring a gospel which departs from that which you have received (παρελάβετε) a curse upon him!'

The gospel which the faithful have received through him, the apostle, from God is the one to which alone they must cling. It is the measure of truth. As it says, he is not 'apostle from a man, but through Jesus Christ and God the Father who awakened Jesus from the dead. .'
Later on he again gives divine authority to what he says in these words:

'I assure you, brethren: the gospel which I have made known is not after the fashioning of men. I did not receive it from a man (παρέλαβον) nor was I taught it, but rather through a revelation (ἀποκάλυψις) of Jesus Christ' (5, 11). Paul received his teaching by inward illumination from the Lord, the *Kyrios* himself. It is not, then, a human utterance but one from God which he gives over to the faithful.

Another passage of importance for this subject is 1 Cor 2, 1–5.

> For my part, brethren, when I came to you it was not to announce the mystery of God (a better reading than 'testimony') with the force of words or wisdom. No; I never wished to know anything among you save Jesus Christ and him crucified. In weakness and fear I came before you, and my word and preaching were not in convincing discourses of wisdom but in the showing of the Spirit and power; thus your faith was to have its foundation not in men's wisdom but in God's power.

This text gives a wonderful picture of the Christian *paradosis*. Paul places his preaching in conscious contrast with what he calls *logos* and *sophia*. He means the first term in a philosophical sense, the philosophical *logos* of the Greek philosophers, Aristotle for example. It is not, he is saying, this *logos* and this wisdom which I have brought, hellenic wisdom and science, but the mystery of God. With this notion taken from the cult life of the ancient mysteries Paul makes clear that the Christian truth is passed on because it is adapted to a ritual transmission. Human science and living worship are contrasted. Yet the content of the mystery which Paul proclaims is Jesus Christ, crucified and then glorified through the cross. Jesus is proclaimed not by science with some form of rational proof; the mystery is his announcement, the power of God at work in the resurrection of Christ. Therefore Christian faith rests not on words of human wisdom but on the rock of this power which reveals itself in the mystery. Ranft remarks that what Paul is saying to the Corinthians is, your *logos* and your doctrine have only sophistics, dialectics speculation on their side; what it lacks is *dynamis*, the power of action in the Spirit which is just what my word has from the cross; this is not its own possession but God's mystery hands it on. This is not the world's wisdom, it does not trace itself back to the princes of this world; it is God's wisdom. St Paul speaks of this in the following verses:

> Wisdom it is that we utter among the perfect, wisdom not of this age nor of them who are bound for destruction, its princes; no, we utter God's wisdom in mystery, the which was hidden and which God determined before the ages for our glory. None of the princes of this world has recognised it; if they had recognised it, they would not have crucified the Lord of glory. But, as it is written, 'eye hath not seen nor hath ear heard nor hath it entered the heart of man what God has prepared for those who love him'. For it is to us that God has made revelation through his Spirit (the Lord in glory, the *Kyrios*) has revealed; in him we have this knowledge now, not first in heaven. For the Spirit penetrates the whole, even the deep places of God. Who among men knows the things which belong to man except the spirit of man which is in him? In the same way no one knows what is of God save the Spirit of God. Now we have not received the spirit of this world, but the Spirit of God, so we are to know what God has given us. So we do not speak in words of wisdom from human instruction; we speak in what the Spirit has taught, interpreting things of the Spirit by the Spirit. The man of mere intelligence does not grasp what is of the Spirit of God; to him it is folly; he cannot understand it, for this must be known in the Spirit. But the man of the Spirit judges all, and he in turn is judged by none. Who indeed has the mind of Christ so as to teach him; but we do have the mind of Christ. (2, 6–16.)

This mind (*nous*), the Spirit of Christ gives us the strength and the capacity to receive the *paradosis* from God, to grasp its inmost meaning; it is not the wisdom of the schools of philosophy not men's wisdom, but wisdom which is God's immediate gift on the way of tradition.

Christ himself fought against the Jewish tradition, which with time had fallen to a mere external transmission of doctrines. We read in the gospel how he behaved towards the scribes and the Pharisees: 'why do you offend against God's command for the sake of your traditions?' (Mt 15, 3 and Mk 7, 13.)

In this false *paradosis* which Christ condemns we can see the danger for all religious institutions: that men will put their own requirements on a level with God's, and in the end these will seem to them more important than the commands God himself has given.

The pagan *paradosis* St Paul again characterizes as 'of men', according to the elements of this world and not of Christ (Col. 2, 8). These terms limit the Christian *paradosis* as the one which is according to Christ. Yet at the same time we may note that the pagan *paradosis* which is associated with Christian ideas at Colossai is not so externalized as the Jewish one; it is connected with the enthusiastic mystical element.

Both concepts of tradition play their part in the New Testament, yet the one which is formed by the mystery religions has the greater depth. The Jewish form is more external and doctrinal, while the hellenistic one in contrast is a true vital process. In it the master of the mysteries does not merely pass on some ideas for teaching; it is not a passive transmission but a lively awakening to truth: the tradition of the mysteries must rouse inner life. This takes place as the receiver makes the truth received his own; his own soul is renewed according to the pattern of what he hears; in other words, there comes to the external reception a kind of internal awakening.

The whole reaches its fulfilment in the form of a living mystery cult. We can see that the deeper Christian idea was in many ways better prepared for by Hellenism than by Judaism. It is unfortunate that modern theology is closer to this Jewish tradition with its simple transmission of knowledge; the true tradition resting on *gnosis* is an awakening of the mind which lives and experiences the truth. This conception has made itself felt in St John and St Paul, while in the synoptic writers the Jewish conception is more prominent. This Pauline and Johannine kind of tradition has an essential relationship to the mysteries. Baptism and eucharist are the means of *paradosis*; in it the truth is handed on in living, ritual form and so assimilated. On the one hand the paradosis is a thing in and of the spirit, on the other it is hierarchical.

Ranft goes on to say that the concept of tradition in the hellenistic mystery religions turns on the three terms: *paradosis*, *logos*, *mysterion*, tradition, doctrine, mystery. The first concept is related in the first place to the mysterious origin of the content, which is in God himself. In the pagan mysteries there is the appropriate cult god, while in the Christian rite there is the everlasting God the Father who makes the tradition through his Son the incarnate Christ. In the second place the *paradosis* means the passing on of the mystery's content. This takes place at the hands of men; but in spite of that it is not a human work. It is God who teaches; man is only the instrument by whom God acts. Thus, *paradosis* can mean both the hidden source of the mystery's content and more particularly its conveyance, the stirring of the inward man which can be bound up with cult acts.

The second term, *logos*, is really not to be translated; it means the content of the mystery, word, utterance, teaching. It is the living word which God gives for man's fulfilment. For Christians the *Logos* of the cross means the whole reality of the cross itself which, in this Word, comes before us.

The third notion, *mysterion*, expresses the contrast of God's revelation to his servants with philosophical methods of knowing. What this revelation gives is not a doctrine, something which the pupils get up, but an intimate knowledge. The priest brings man to divinity in order that it may work in the soul of man. Thus, the whole soul of man is aroused, new life is brought to birth in it; in amazement it lives and tastes divine reality and truth. This is no acquired truth which a man works out for himself by reasoning, but a knowledge which is infused. These are real, vital processes which take place in man; the initiate receives revelation, however, not directly, not before he has been prepared for it. This is done in suffering; it is pain which serves to purify and cleanse man, and make him fit for the higher knowledge. For Christians the cross is the way to the deep knowledge which is glory.

Thus, the term *mysterium* signifies that deep inward activity which is brought to fruition in the rites. It signifies the deepening of personal knowledge and experience which the initiate expects from the rites, as he did in the general view of hellenistic piety: here, a divine power was to be, which would lead him to such knowledge. This extraordinary union of the divine power which reveals and at the same time hides its object, the characteristic of all this type of religion, is what we mean when we speak of a *mysterium*. By the rites, the one to be inducted experiences the presence of his god in the secret ceremonies and actions; he is united to the god which is so shown to him.

One of the best texts for this is Luke 10, 21–24:

> At that moment Jesus trembled with joy beneath the Spirit and said, 'I bless thee, Father, Lord of heaven and of earth, for having hidden this from the wise and the clever and yet revealed it to the simple. Yes, Father, this has been your good pleasure. For all things

have been handed over (παρεδόθη) to me by my Father, and none knows (γινωσκει) who the Son is save the Father, and none knows who the Father is save the Son and him to whom the Son has been pleased to reveal himself'. Then turning to the disciples alone he said, 'Blessed are the eyes which see what you see, for I tell you that many prophets and kings have desired to see what you see and did not see it, and to hear what you hear and did not hear it'.

The Lord says that all things were entrusted to him; the Father gave him everything as he gave witness on his Son's behalf, and gave it to him for the elect. 'No one has seen God; God's only begotten Son who is in his bosom, it is he who has brought the news (ἐξηγήσατο) (Jn. 1, 18).

What is in God, only one has seen; the Son, the first of all initiates. He alone can convey it and he does so in the mystery (ἐξηγήσατο in a term proper to the mystery language). He does not do it in school wisdom but through revelation, acting as God incarnate upraised to *pneuma*.

The forward movement of the tradition of the mysteries in paganism from its first recipients is carried out in the chain of members, whose last member is the high priest. This too has certain parallels in Christianity; here the first recipient is Christ himself, appearing in the flesh in order to give us God's mystery. He hands it over to the apostles and they to the bishops, so that through the apostolic succession we have always our link with the source, Christ, who is God's immediate revelation. Thus there are two elements in the *paradosis*: external continuity and inward illumination by the Word made flesh.

Ranft goes on to say how the experiences and acts of God which form the content of the first revelation are brought together in prayers and formulae with the use of oral delivery. In Christianity too God's great acts, facts and events make up the content of the *paradosis*; and what we have received in the *paradosis* we perform in ritual, by setting out there the saving actions in a mystery presence. This is the sense of the liturgy; we speak the formulae which contain divine revelation, formulae which the church gives us, not as parts of a doctrine but as sacred prayers and rites for us to believe and live. Even where they are not fully understood rationally, these forms make up a real tradition which we preserve. Together with the dramatic forms of the deeds and acts of the godhead they form a sacred Word of the liturgical feasts, and rest on the conviction that the real Word about God, the primaeval *mythos* which contains the first revelation, events and deeds; this has come from God himself and has been passed on unchanged from member to member in the chain of initiates. This makes the notion of *paradosis* inseparable from that of the *mysterium* itself, and brings to fruition some of the most vigorous ideas which arise from the mystery. We may be reminded of a wall painting at Pompey where a woman initiate is shown receiving the sacred Word, which a boy reads from a roll. The Jewish Christians had a living tradition from the Old Testament which with its thousand years contains the sure foundation of faith for them, as Jesus pointed out; for the pagan Christians who knew the mysteries or were initiates this was made intelligible by the *paradosis* of these religions, the long succession of priests reaching back into the distant past and the cult god himself. At this point those who proclaimed Christ were able to make contact with the forms paganism had to offer, and to fill them with real, true content. They were able to show such men as these, from their own living experience that a *paradosis* was there, from God through Christ to them, and to oppose this one, true tradition to the false picture of the heathen mysteries. This was Paul's way. He warns the Colossians against the false traditions of men and in its stead will give them a true *paradosis* which is according to Christ. What he rejected then was only the content of those pagan forms; the forms themselves received confirmation from the truth which had come in Christ. How important these things are; they rule the whole of our lives. We ought not to think that we have, as it were taken up the tradition once, to possess it for all time; much more is it a living thing which must be continually fulfilled in us, a thing which has no end.

Of course St Paul looks back in the first instance to Jewish and Rabbinical thought; yet at the same time Hellenistic ideas do appear at many points in his letters. This is true particularly of those passages where St Paul is putting the absolute opposition between the old and the new Word, such as Colossians 1, 26. In this passage the whole manner of expression is in conformity with the language of the mystery religions. The same observation is true of what he says about the notion of the gospel, the *evangelium*. He makes use of the parallel between παραδιδόναι and παραλαμβάνειν *tradere* and *accipere*. He points out as well the mystical silence which surrounds the sacred rites. Yet throughout what Paul intends is to show to the pagan Christians the superiority of the mystery of God the Father and of Christ; it gives them the truth which until now they had only thought they possessed.

At first view there might seem to be some contradiction between the notion of *paradosis* and mystery, of tradition and inward mysticism. The one means the handing on of a doctrine, of definite knowledge; is this not the very opposite of mystical illumination? We have seen that in paganism the two elements did reach a unity. It was in fact only in Christianity that this unity was achieved. Judaism like Islam kept to a more academical kind of tradition, and this is the tradition which is still preserved in the schools of Islam throughout the Orient; the learning of the Koran by heart is the centre of muslim education. Of course in ancient Christian schools the same kind of thing had its role to play; we have only to think of the memorisation of Scripture, particularly of the psalms. Yet there is also an essential point of difference; in Christianity an element of enthusiasm enters the scene which was lacking in late Judaism as in Islam. This element played a great part, on the other hand, in the mysteries; in them the god himself was supposed to appear among the initiates; he fills them with enthusiasm and inspiration. In this the *paradosis* becomes a new religious experience, a personal experience of inward fulfilment, which gives to the initiate much more than scientific activity of the schools. This conjunction of enthusiasm and transmission which already exists in the pagan mysteries has come into Christianity and we see it in all clarity in early Christian practice. It is unfortunate that later there was a falling away from this fullness of the spirit.

In any case we can see the two extremes: Jewish traditionalism on the one hand and the mystical enthusiasm of the pagan mysteries, particularly of the Dionysiac line which is nothing but experience, together with the unity of the two which has been effected in Christianity; in the Christian *paradosis* both elements are to be found. Here is both the historical witness to the truths of faith and mystical contemplation of these truths, as well as their realization in the mystery action. We have already seen what Ranft wrote about the three terms *paradosis, logos, mysterium*. The first means a handing on from the part of the leader; to it corresponds the reception on the part of the initiate. In 1 Cor. 11, 23 there is a clear expression of this parallel: 'I received from the Lord (παρέλαβον) what I gave over to you (παρέδωκα)' The two concepts flow into one another. First St Paul speaks of an historical fact, the institution of the eucharist at the last supper. Although he was not himself present, he tells us about it; to the historical dimension of the event there comes a Spirital assimilation of the event. Paul received his *paradosis* from the Lord himself; in the way of the Spirit Christ taught him what had taken place, although there was an historical way of knowledge open to the same events. We see the two elements in one: Paul receives an historical event but in a spiritual fashion, through an immediate illumination from the Lord. He then hands on what he has received to the community of believers; there is a clear link from Christ to Paul, and from Paul to the community at Corinth.

The ancient Christians were very conscious of this aspect of the tradition. Clement of Rome in his letter to the Corinthians says, 'for this reason we do not wish to allow empty and useless notions to be abroad; we would keep to the great and venerable line of tradition (κάνων τῆς παραδόσεως) if we will see what is good, what is well pleasing and agreeable to him who made us'. (7, 2). Tertullian also mentions the chain of tradition, in his treatise *De Praescriptione Haereticorum* (37): 'truth is given out and we enter the rule (*canon*) which the church has of the apostles, the apostles of Christ and Christ of God (*tradidit*).'

In summary we can say this. The dramatic presentation of the experiences and acts of the godhead form a sacred word; this is the centre of a rite, which has artistic form; in the rite the high point of experience in the mystery proper is the *epoptie*, the ecstasy, personal experience of god. The sacred words are the liturgically fixed boundaries of the mystery piety; this piety rests on the certitude that the word has come from the god himself and has been kept unchanged from generation to generation of priests. The concept of *paradosis* is inseparable from the mystery itself, and gives expression to one of its most important aspects. The sacred word comes from the gods; they have given it to the priests who pass it on to the initiates. The chain of tradition gives the certainty that doctrine is from the gods.

It is only in Christianity and in a very deep way that this is all realized. Here is no mere myth which loses itself in the shadows of pre-history, but instead the appearance of the God-Man in the full light of time; in him history and what passes beyond it into eternity are brought together in unity.[1]

True and real community with Christ and his holy Spirit is the foundation of the church as a holy society; so, too, only one who is in the mystery communion of the church can really share in Christ.

When Christ was washing his disciples' feet on the evening before he suffered, and came to Peter, Peter refused the washing. He questioned, 'Lord, are you to wash my feet?' Jesus answered, 'what I do,

[1]From conferences on Colossians in January and February 1948.

you do not understand now; you will understand later'. There are deep things here. Peter says, however, 'you will never wash my feet', to which Jesus replied, 'if I do not, you have no part with me'. (οὐκ ἔχεις μέρος μετ' ἐμοῦ). Then Peter replies, 'not my feet alone, but my hands too and head'. Then Jesus replies, 'the one who is cleansed is cleansed entire, the feet are all that need be washed; you too are clean, but not all'. (Jn 13, 6–11.)

To have part in the Lord means something vast; Peter must give up his resistance and even offer to have his head and hands washed. At this point we hear the saying about having part in the Lord; Christ lifts a portion of the veil which covers this great matter.

We meet this phrase often in Scripture, and particularly in the liturgy too. There are a number of terms used for it: μέρος ἔχειν, κοινωνία *consortium, communio,* and others. St Paul says in 1 Cor. 10, 16: 'the chalice of blessing which we bless, is it not communion of the blood of Christ? The bread which we break, is it not communion of the body of Christ? One bread, one body, although we are many, for all have a share in the one bread. (μετέχομεν: *participamus.*)' Communion here clearly means a real sharing, a sharing which is of the order of being; to share in the one bread means that each of us makes himself part of the one bread, and the same is true of the wine. Yet bread and wine are signs, the *supposita* of Christ's body and blood. So the communion points to an achievement of union with the body and blood of Christ at a level of being. In his second letter St Peter writes, 'that you may be sharers in the divine nature' (ἵνα . . . γένησθε θείας κοινωνοὶ φύσεως) (II Peter 1, 4).

These passages show that real participation is of the order of being, not a distant copy or some merely moral relationship. The clearest example is in the eucharist, which we really do taste and eat. To have a share in Christ means to be united to him in all reality; to have a real part means that the being with which he is united gives a part of his very being.[1]

---

[1] The conceptual formulation of this great matter, given us in faith alone, is not easy. We really and truly eat and drink the body and blood of Christ in the Eucharist; thereby he is in us and we in him, as John 6, 56 says. The sharing in Christ which is thus accomplished is *wesenhaft,* of the order of being; it is real and actual, or ontic; it is not of a merely moral order, not merely thought or apparent.

Yet in all of this we must avoid anything which smacks of monism or would break down the distinction between persons or between God and creatures. This is what is meant by 'a gift of his own being'.

Hence we often find in the liturgy the word about participation. Each day in the Roman rite we pray at the mixing of the water and wine: *da nobis per huius aquae et vini mysterium eius divinitatis esse consortes qui humanitatis nostrae fieri dignatus est particeps: Jesus Christus.* 'Grant us through the mystery of this water and wine to become sharers in the godhead of him who deigned to become sharers in our manhood: Jesus Christ.' The prayer is taken from an old Christmas cycle; its theme is the wonderous exchange of that season which we sing in an antiphon for the feast of the circumcision. This is a share in being: Christ in our nature and we in his divinity.

Christ is our life: 'I am life; abide in me and I in you; he shall remain in me and I in him' (Jn 11, 25; 14, 6; 6, 56). Life means movement of the inmost being; if Christ is our life he must be within us in a real and vital way; we must touch him and he us. The Lord said to Thomas, 'bring your finger here and look at my hands and bring your hand here and place it in my side, and be not unbelieving but believing. The church makes this her song in the Communion of Low Sunday. The church too wants us to touch Christ, she gives us his body and blood. This means a share in being, not merely a moral mediation from afar by means of the soul's own powers; it is physical, through the immediate presence of the Lord and with him. If indeed Christ only worked upon us from a distance his religion would be a thing of the past; but it is more; it is the life of our own day and of eternity ever present. Christ is immediately present to us and always with us; he is our contemporary, as Steen has put it.[1] Because he is eternal, he is present to every age. It is for this reason that we are able to know him; we can only know something deeply if we touch it, become one with it by sharing in it. 'This is eternal life, that they may know thee, the one true God and him whom thou hast sent, Jesus Christ' (Jn 17, 3). This knowledge is a share in Christ, and through him in the Father.

By his death Christ passed over into new forms of life and being; he is no longer bound by human and temporal limits. Now he has power to put into play the divine, essential, power and activity, surpassing moral activity. Now that he has become Spirit, he can penetrate the deep places of our soul, give us a share in himself.

Participation means a most intimate touching and union of the participant in that in which he participates, in what has given him this sharing; yet at the same time it must imply an abiding state of reverence

[1] Source not found; perhaps Cornelius a Lapide.

and distance. Participation does not mean absolute union with the shared. The sharer receives from him, lives with him; but he remains what he is. A rose has its share in the beauty which belongs to the rose proper; but it has its own reality all the same. In this way the man who has a share in the Lord is not absolutely fused with him. He is formed anew in his image and becomes the offset of that original; but he remains the offset. Thus he is eternally dependent upon the Lord, eternally receptive, eternally mirroring what he receives and thereby eternally in love. Our sharing in Christ is no pantheistic fusion, not even an eternal, ecstatic vision of the first light and the first beauty; no, God is *agape*. His love never ends, not even, as is the case with eros, when it has found its goal. Hence there is no weakening of the participation, nor is there an absolute fusion. Rather, from the real participation which is ours, a love arises an unfading love.

Grace, therefore, raises us up to a participation in God's being, dignity and glory. *Agnosce, o Christiane, dignitatem tuam: et divinae consors factus naturae noli in veterem vilitatem degeneri conversationem redire. Memento cuius capitis et cuius corporis sis membrum.* 'Look at your own worth, man who bears the name of Christ; once you have been made a sharer in the nature of God, do not go back into your old ruin by the corrupt way you live; remember of what head and of what body you are a member' (Leo the Great, Second Sermon on the Nativity, 1, 3).

The Word did not assume an individual; if he had done so, this individual alone would have been redeemed, and the rest would have been able only to join at a moral level with this one man. No; the Word took up human nature; and the divine person which holds these two natures of God and man is the person of the *Logos*, the Son of God in the Holy Trinity. By this fact the *Logos* has found communion with the whole of mankind; all who possess human nature are called by God's Son to union with him, union in and about him, its head. The crucifixion carried the incarnation farther still; here the Son of God dies for our sins. Taking our nature, he took our lot as well and suffered for the evil we had done, killing them in his own body on the cross. Thus Christ dies for all sins, and redeems all men. 'Christ dies for all' (II Cor. 5, 15). He did not die for Peter or John or James alone but for all who have human nature and human guilt. Everywhere we see that the sacred community is essential to the work of salvation.

After he was taken into heaven and glorified, the Saviour sent his Spirit (*pneuma*). Within the Trinity this Spirit is the seal of community between the Father and the Son. In the bond of eternal generation, they both breathe forth the Spirit the bond of their community with one another, one in essence with them. The Spirit is this the seal of unity. Spirit is what the Son has sent us. Yet, because no one person of the godhead works outside their intimate life, the Spirit comes to us with the Father and the Son; all give us a share in their life together. The Spirit is a true gift of community; none of us receives it as isolated individuals; it is everywhere a bond of love, life and love together. This gift has created the church, has made it a holy community. 'This gift has been put into the church's trust, in order to fill that form with life and breath, to give life to all the members of this body; in this Spirit is communion with Christ; the Spirit is the pledge of undying life and strength for our faith and the way up to God.' (Irenaeus, *Adv. Haereses* III, 24, 1.)

When all are at one with the whole and the whole is carried by so many, then the service of God is a true *opus Dei*, a true *sacrificium Spiritale* and *hostia acceptabilis*; it is God's work, the Spirit's offering, a victim which God is disposed to accept.

Qui te fecit sine te, non vult te redimere sine te; 'he who made thee without thy will, will not redeem thee without thy will.'[1] He gives us the vision of his mysteries, he gives us a share in the action of these mysteries. Thus our own very prayer and service of him becomes in turn a mystery; it is a *participatio sancti mysterii*, a *consortium Dei*: a share in the sacred mystery, a community with God. The bride receives the secret things of her spouse, full of reverence and fear. Day by day the church has the right to touch the body and drink the blood of Christ; she stands next to his cross, not a dumb onlooker, but a living co-offerer and priest. She dies his death with him; she goes with him to the Father. For this is what she does in the sacred mystery of worship beneath the veils of the rites; it is reality and truth for the eye of faith to see. The church rests in the heart of Christ; his blood is hers, his pulse is hers. Here the sharing comes to its last possibility. Christ does not work upon us from afar off; he does not convey his grace to us from heaven; he is in our midst, he is within us, he is us. *Vivo ego, iam non ego, vivit*: 'I live, no longer do I live, but Christ lives in me' (Gal. 2, 20). The *communio* becomes *unio*. As Chrysostom says, 'the bread which we break—is it not the community of the body of Christ (κοινωνία)? Why then does he not say sharing (μετοχή)? Because he wanted to reveal

---

[1] St Augustine Sermo 169. M.L. 38, col. 923.

still more and show us a deeper bond (συνάφεια). For we are in community (κοινωνοῦμεν) not merely by sharing (μετέχειν) and participating (μεταλαμβάνειν) but by becoming one with him (ἐνοῦσθαι).'[1]

What God does daily in the liturgy must become our daily life; it must work itself out in our life, become our own work. The share we have in the exalted Lord, his deeds, his pain, his death and resurrection and glorification must be turned to the shape of our daily existence.[2]

Sharing in Christ is the aim; the way is, through sharing in his sufferings, to share in his glory which hides behind them.

'But if you are children, you are heirs as well; if heirs, then joint-heirs with Christ. If we suffer with him, it is so that we may be exalted with him. I hold that the sufferings of this age are nothing in comparison with the glory that is to come, the glory that is to be revealed in us.' (Rom. 8, 17).

From the sonship which God's children have, comes their heirship with Christ, (5, 17). To be a joint-heir with Christ means to have a share in God with him. God himself is our portion, and glory is our share in him.

The last stage in our becoming members of Christ is not that we should share his pain, but that we should be taken up into his glory. As Scripture insists over and over this is the real content of the Christian faith and hence of monastic life. Cf II Cor 4, 10: 'we bear the killing of Jesus about in our body, so that the life of Jesus may be revealed in our body too. For we who live are continually being given to death for his sake, so that the life of Jesus may be revealed in our mortal flesh.' And Galatians 6, 17: 'I bear the wounds of Jesus in my body'; or II Cor 13, 3: '. . . because you would have evidence that Christ speaks in me, Christ who is not weak but strong for you. For he was crucified in weakness, but he lives in the power of God. So, too, we are weak in him, but we shall have life with him in the power of God.' Phil. 3, 10: 'so that I may recognize him and the power of his resurrection and the communion of his pains; fashioned like him in his death, so that I may perhaps also attain the resurrection from the dead.' Phil. 2, 8: 'Christ became obedient to death, the death of the cross. Therefore God raised him up and gave him a name which is above all other names.'

---

[1]Homily 24, 2 on I Corinthians 10, 16, M.G. 61, 200.
[2]From a retreat for 1936.

In all of these passages we see the two typical aspects of Christian life: without, there is human weakness, and within, the power of God's Spirit is alive and working. So then the church is full of power and of light, even though for the most part she seems reviled and persecuted.

The aim of our suffering with Christ is that we should have a share in his glory (Romans 8, 17). Romans 8, 8 tells us that the passion and the glory which grows out of it are of such different levels that they can in no way be compared. The passion is not an end in itself; it aims beyond to what is higher, and the glory which is there. The passion's place is here, in this age, while glory lasts. Hence, the purpose of our sharing in the mystery is not the passion alone, but the glory which it hides. The thoughts of verse 17 and following culminate in verse 30 which says clearly how we who have a share in Christ's sufferings are by that fact already sharers in his glory. 'For those whom he foresaw he chose out beforehand, that he would fashion them in the shape of his own Son so that this Son might be the first among many brothers. Those whom he foresaw, he called; and those whom he called he made just; and those whom he made just he glorified.' The idea of δόξα glory- and its verb δοξάζειν is not moral: honour and glory before the world; it means the very being of God as revealed and communicated to us. We do not gain a share in this glory first at some future date; by the promise of the Spirit we have it now. Verse 30 expresses this by using the Greek aorist, the tense of an already finished action: 'whom he justified, he glorified as well'. The First Epistle of St John 3, 1 depicts the state of glory as something present: 'look what the Father's love has given us; we are called the children of God, and this we are. For this reason the world does not know us, because it has not known him. Beloved, we are God's children now, and it is not yet revealed what we shall be. We know that when he will be revealed, we shall be like to him, for we shall see him as he is. Everyone who has this hope within him sanctifies himself, as that other one is sanctified.'

In the song about the glory to come (Romans 8, 19 ff) St Paul combines present aorist and future in a similar way, just as he had formerly done with indicative and imperative. He speaks of our glory as something future (19–25) and present, something already attained (30). The explanation of this is that with Christ we have in fact already attained our glorified being; yet we are not yet within its fullness; this wholeness of glory lies ahead of us. The gift of glory with Christ is already ours, but it has not yet appeared. Externally the suffering alone is there for us to see; but, in the vision of the Spirit, it recedes before the glory to which it leads, of which it is another aspect. For as long as we are subject to sin we live subject as well to the laws of time and space; we must wait for the fullness of glory when Christ comes; then all will have its fullness, and all barriers will fall away.[1]

'Sharing in the divine nature', the bold phrase of second Peter is clarified by a comparison of Christian and hellenistic attitudes.

In the hellenistic mysteries man considers himself called to gain a sharing in godhead in such a fashion that by it he becomes the god of the cult. This view occurs again and again in the piety of those mysteries; they talk continually of some sort of divinisation.

In Christianity the divinisation takes place; in humbleness we attach ourselves to the *Logos*, live a life in imitation of him, and so become Spirit. Thus Christianity gives recognition to the drift of pagan piety, and lifts it onto God's own level. St Peter in his Second Epistle (1, 4) recognizes the good that is here by his use of expressions proper to the mysteries.

But where is the difference? In the hellenistic mysteries everything takes place in the individual, and yet the individual gradually recedes; by different methods it seeks to pass over into the whole. Against all this, the mysticism of Christ rests on humility, the cross, the passion, unconditional gift of self to Christ the Lord. The Christian comes, at a later stage, to what the Greek aimed at; but they did not know the cross and they sought to divinise themselves. At one point the initiate cries out, 'I am in the earth, I am in the water, I am in the air, I am in the things which grow, I am in the womb of the mother';[2] he becomes one with Pan.

We see here, in spite of all the likeness in word and tendency, the great difference of hellenistic from Christian piety; the Christian begins with faith, with humility. He must be joined to a God-made man, and only in this way will he come to a vision of the mysteries. The first direction of the heathen mysteries is given recognition nonetheless, and this is the reason and cause why Christianity was able to find better soil in hellenism than among the Jews.

The main point in the first sentence of the second letter of St Peter is, that by this 'you may become sharers in the divine nature'—a phrase

[1] From Conferences on Romans, 1935–42.
[2] Cf the Prayer of the mystes, *Hermes Trismegistus* XIII (XIV), 17.

like many met with in the hellenistic literature of mysticism. Yet this
entry into a share in God's life takes place now, in this life. What the
apostle teaches about the divine nature and sharing in it is very closely
related to spiritual begetting, birth out of God. Peter, John, and Paul all
speak of it very frequently. We must take literally the things they say.
It is only begetting which can bring to life one being out of another of
the same nature. We have in fact God's own nature, but our share in it
is not to be understood as if we have passed into him entirely. This was
the hellenistic notion. If it were true, we should be unable to love him
any more and it would be an end to all creaturehood. But this is not so;
we cannot take on God as a sort of incident to our being. It is the other
way round; through the grace which comes forth from him we gain a
life and being which is his alone, a communion which is completely
inward and holy. The Fathers often use this image: when a piece of
iron lies among refuse it is ugly and unseemly; but when held in fire it
glows and gives light. Although still iron, it gains another kind of being.
The iron which burns is the light of divinity which glows within us; the
iron which gives heat is the love of God which acts within us. Yet if we
take the iron out of the fire it takes on its old appearance once more. The
diamond gives another analogy. In a case it is like all the other stones;
but in the sun's light it has a being which gives it a name.

St Cyril of Jerusalem says that divinisation is completed in the
Eucharist. The child in his mother's womb has its own life yet it lives
by the same blood as which passes through the mother's veins; so too
the Eucharist means a real community of life for us. St Cyril says[1] by
this receiving of the Eucharist we become Christ carriers; his blood
and flesh are in our own members. In St. Peter's words, we are made
partakers of the divine nature.[2]

*The first foundation of the share in the mystery of Christ's saving act
is faith and the deep knowledge, the gnosis, which is born of faith.*

The vision the mystery gives awakens our longing for the whole of
vision, and at the same time is the pledge of this vision. We pray, therefore, in the old octave of Epiphany:[3] *caelesti lumine quaesumus Domine
semper et ubique nos praeveni, ut mysterium cuius nos participes esse
voluisti, et puro cernamus intuitu et digno percipiamus affectu*: 'May the
divine light go everywhere and always before us; thus, may we gaze

[1] Catecheses Mystagog, 4, 3.
[2] From conferences on II Peter 1929–30.
[3] Postcommunion for 13 January.

with pure sight upon the mystery of which you have willed to make us members, and receive it with a worthy disposition'.

Again, the deep phrase about sharing in the mystery. It is not a mere effect of the mystery which we are to receive, a fruit of it, an application; no, what we have is the mystery itself. What then does this sharing consist in? In the first place, in a vision. We see the mystery in knowledge born of faith, in *gnosis*. Yet this is no idle and ineffectual knowledge; this vision is at work transforming us, as St Paul says, 'we look with face unveiled on the glory of the Lord as in a mirror, and we are transformed from glory to glory, for this is what the Lord of the Spirit does' (II Cor 3, 18). But if we are transformed, then we are ourselves co-actors, co-workers of the mystery. We do not merely look at the glory of the Son of God; we are ourselves through him and with him made the sons and the daughters of God. What took place in Christ takes place in us; he is the first-born among many brothers.[1]

By making use of the analogies of hellenistic mysteries it should be possible for us to make clearer what the vision of God means in the Christian mystery: the vision of faith, of God's making which transforms man.

There is one thing in the ancient mysteries to which we ought to pay particular attention. The vision which stands at the centre of them is a vision which acts, which makes a man what he is looking at. Man is transformed in likeness to God, not of his own power, but through the very vision of God. This is the deepest mysticism. The ancients had some notion of it; it is a great objective fact in the Christian mystery. Here God appears in bodily form, when the Eucharist is celebrated. So too the initiate Lucius, in Apuleius' book the *Metamorphoses*[2] becomes the sun-god by a vision, and appears the next day and receives a god's honour. The Christian too can say, I am Christ.[3]

The all important thing in the mysteries is vision. The entrant himself does nothing; he is taken up by a higher power. What happens is a παθεῖν a suffering.[4]

[1] From a conference on Epiphany 1935.
[2] Book XI, 23–24. For his glorification of the service of Isis, also P.W. 2/1 246–258.
[3] From a conference on Ephesians from 1947. Cf II Cor. 3, 18; 1 Jn. 3, 1; II Cor. 4, 6 and Gal. 2, 20.
[4] From a conference in 1945 where he also cites the wonderful fragment of Aristotle preserved in Synesius, that the initiate is not a learner but a sufferer. (*Fragments* ed. Ross, Oxford, 1955, p. 84).

We emphasize once more that, in the real sharing in Christ and his saving acts, Christ is the doer and the giver; only when he has given me what is his, when I am really and actually bound to him and then open myself to him, does that marvellous exchange take place which is the only way to salvation.

We have seen how the mysteries afford us the way to pass with Christ through his death; the all important thing is that it is Christ who acts here; it is not a man, not the priest as a man, but Christ himself who takes us into his death. He is present at the mystery and he accomplishes the saving act. He dies the death which he suffered for us, the death of the cross which was the killing of the sinful flesh he had taken up. By this death he redeemed that sinful flesh. After this death he went to the Father in his risen body, freed from all the burdens of sin, which he had of his own will taken up for love of us and in obedience to the Father. As he was the offerer on the cross, Christ is the actor too in all the church's mysteries. He does not take us into his death alone. He did not remain in death; we do not remain there either. Every man who dies with Christ rises with him too and receives his life, his Spirit.

When Christ stretches his death out over us the whole man dies. The entire old manhood disappears and a new man appears in his place. Mystical death means more than the death of the body. I can undergo the second and fall into hell; my own death has no power to change me into a new man. Only the death in Christ can change me; the death of my body has no finality to it. By dying to it I am no different than I was, I am not transformed. So the mystic death is more important; it means a death of the whole man with Christ and it is this which brings the transformation. For the mystical death it is essential that the entire being, body and soul, be brought to nothing that a new man arise in its stead. The sign of this death is the rite of baptism: a rite of dying. The candidate is plunged into the water, which signifies that he is killed: water is the death of man. As the Lord died so must we die too, in order to be transformed as he was transformed in his resurrection.

To die with Christ is to gain a share in his immortal life. It is of this sharing that the postcommunion of the twenty-third Sunday after Pentecost speaks: 'we beg thee, almighty God to grant that those who have joy in participation of thee according to thy will may not fall victim to earth's dangers.' The contrast here is between *divina participatio* and *pericula humana*: participation in God and the threats of earthly dangers due to our human constitution. God makes us a gift of the one, and we attain it through the mystery. When we have come to share in God's life, when we have eaten from God's table we are no longer subject to the *pericula*, the dangers of what is purely human, as the Postcommunion says. Who ever has done all this no longer is mere man; hence he is placed outside the dangers which arise from the merely human. Of course he experiences the dangers just as he did before he knew the mystery; but now his attitude towards it is different, his daily life is in heaven. He—all of him—is with God and filled with the power of God. The merely human has its power over any of us, over all of us. We read in Philippians, 'our rights as citizens are in heaven' (3, 20). For us to have such rights means that we have already and on earth all the rights which the saints have in God's presence. Among them is participation in God's life. It is a real, not a merely moral one, as the Latin term *participatio* indeed implies; *participatio* means taking part in some whole. Hence anyone who shares in God must share in the whole; for God cannot be divided. To possess a share in God is to possess the whole; for God is always whole. As we have said, this sharing is physical; it is of the order of being. Opposed to that is moral participation, but that would not require union. It can be content with merely striving to follow the words and teachings of the master. In such a matter the subject seeks by his own power and in his own power to fashion his life; but he has no such power.

When we attain participation in God something flows out from his inmost being to us; the light and life of God flow over to us. Hence, only one can truly see God who has a share in his light. The psalmist says, 'in thy light we see light' (35, 10). God must give us his life, must let his light flow in upon us, if we are to know him. Still we must accept the light he sends; we must allow the light of God to enter and to penetrate us. The inward eye must become like the sun through him; then we shall see the light which shines upon us. Our talk of doing as God did, of following Christ, means nothing. By our own strivings we attain nothing of a share in him. It is God who must first come to us, he who must first give us a share in his inmost being.

The Son is the light from the author of all light, the Father, who carries in him all the power of the first light. The world's light comes from the Son and it is therefore an image of the Son; it has a share in the light which the Son is.

So, then, we can only share if we are really bound to him in whom we are to share; this in turn means that he in whom we are to share must give himself, give his life. If I receive something from God I enter into communion with him, very God. In all that he gives me, he gives something of his own life; he gives me a share in his own being.

Christ is God and man, and all who join with him through faith and the mysteries are joined into his divine nature and person. Free love led him to take a share in our manhood so that we might have a share in his godhood. This is the saving plan of his love. God has carried through this plan in Jesus Christ, in order to bring us help. We have only one thing to do; we must join ourselves to the Son.

At every mass this exchange is expressed by the mixing of the wine and water. A little water is mixed in the wine and united with it; the water is a sign of us, the wine of Christ and his godhead. Still the mixture is only an imperfect sign; for the mystery of the incarnation does not so bring us up into the godhead that we are mixed with it; we are united with it, and in this uniting each being remains what it was.

God is happy beyond all measure. In that love of his, he wills to give us his creatures a share in that happiness, through a sharing in his own godhead; this sharing he gives through Christ. Only through the God-Man do we reach a share in God. In order to attain that end we must go to him who has the two natures in himself. We cannot go immediately to God; this way is closed off to us by sin. The church knows this, and so she closes every prayer with the words, 'through Jesus Christ our Lord, thy Son'.

God calls his people home; he redeems this people by giving them a share in his divinity. God has taken our nature, as the priest says when he mixes water and wine before the sacrifice of the mass; he did so in order to give us a share in his own nature. What takes place is an exchange between God and mankind. The everlasting God takes up our being, not in its first flower and glory as he made it, but in the lowliness into which we have brought it by sin. Only in this way could he give us a share in himself. This unutterable exchange is our way to healing, our way to God. Without him we are a nullity, and in him alone is health, in union with him alone.[1]

[1]From a conference of the period 1947–48.

THE EDITOR'S NOTES TO PART I

p. 4. Generalizations about the history of spirituality always involve a certain risk. They are, so to speak, long range shots, and do not have the same measure of validity for every individual phenomenon. What is said in depreciation here and on the following page is meant in the first instance only for those schools, above all the Christian ones, which gradually estranged themselves from the church. It cannot, then, be applied without any modification to legitimate developments within the theology and piety of the Church, after the Renaissance. But at the same time we may not overlook the great complexity of give and take in such movements; hence, it is possible for the criticism expressed here, if a sharp one, to have its justification, even of matters within the church.

p. 13. The great theme of Casel's presentation is the oneness and uniqueness of the sacrifice of the New Testament. The Lord sacrificed once; he does not sacrifice again. But in her sacramental ritual action the church is so taken into the one sacrifice of Christ that in every new action of hers that one sacrifice of his is present. This corresponds wholly and entirely to the teaching of the church as expressed in the encyclical *Mediator Dei* of Pope Pius XII, even though there is, nonetheless, room for disagreement about the kind and manner of this presence. Pius XII wrote: 'in order that individual sinners may be washed in the blood of the lamb, the cooperation of the Christian faithful is required. For although Christ, speaking in general, has reconciled mankind, the whole human race, to the Father by his bloody death, he willed that they should come, should be drawn, by the sacraments and the eucharistic sacrifice, to his cross, in order to obtain the fruits of redemption won by him through it. As we have already explained, Jesus Christ dying on the cross, endowed his church with an immeasurable treasure of redemption, to which she contributed nothing at all; but where it is a question of the distribution of this treasure, he not only gives his chaste bride a share in the work of sanctifying human beings, but wills that this work should, in a manner, arise from her action. The august sacrifice of the altar is as it were a most precious instrument by which the merits of the redeeming cross are distributed to those who believe: "as often as the commemoration of this victim is celebrated, the work of our redemption is fulfilled" (Secret of the 9th Sunday after Pentecost). Far from this detracting from the value of the bloody sacrifice of the cross, it underlines and makes clearer its necessity and greatness, as the Council of Trent emphasizes. For as it is offered daily, it reminds us that there is no other salvation except in the cross of our Lord Jesus Christ, and that God wills the continuation of his sacrifice . . .', (second 99.) (Encyclical Mediator Dei ASS 1947 p. 551 seq.)

p. 15. St Paul's teaching on baptism has been in the forefront of interest in the last few years. Cf the brief bibliography in the editor's preface to this volume, particularly note seven. Here we would recall only the paper by Victor Warnach, '*Die Tauflehre des Römerbriefs in der neueren theologischen Diskussion*' (A.L.W. V/2, 1958, pp. 274–332).

p. 15. The words of Cyril and their use are disputed. Casel translates and discusses the passage in A.L.W. I (1950), 140–142. He says in the course of this exposition, 'Cyril here contrasts the (natural or historical) reality with the sacramental imitation of the saving act; the one is the model, the other the image. By the presentation of the image, the believer takes a share in the original; through the one he reaches the reality of the other, yet without again posing its natural reality, which is, of course, unique . . .' (140). See the next comment on p. 39.

p. 16. To determine more precisely the degree of reality which this medial thing has is the thorny task of theology in our day. The first fully scientific labour, under Casel's stimulus, as it were an inaugural study, was G. Söhngen's *Symbol und Wirklichkeit im Kultmysterium* (1937). It was followed by Victor Warnach's article in *Liturgisches Leben* 5 (1938): '*Zum Problem der Mysteriengenwart*', and Casel's own articles in J.L.W., particularly 15 (1941), 253–269. The latter works are critical of Söhngen. In the last-named article Casel formulated his point of view in these words: 'In the knowledge born of faith we see in the sacramental image its original, the saving work of Christ. We see it in faith and *gnosis*, that is to say, we touch it, make it our own, are conformed to it through participation and re-formed after the likeness of the crucified and risen Christ . . . Sacrament and original saving act are not two separated things, but one; the image is so filled with the reality of the original deed that it may rightly be called a presence of it' (op. cit. p. 268). A valuable contribution to the explanation of the mode of this presence has been made recently by J. Betz and his proposal of 'commemorative actual presence' (cf the work by him cited in note 9 of the preface). P. Polycarp Wegenaer in his book *Heilsgegenwart* has emphasized the Thomist concept of the *contactus virtutis divinae*; the contact of original saving act and sacramental activity, whereby the power of God is conveyed.

p. 17. The expression which we may find harsh, 'the Lord became Spirit *pneuma*)' is formed in a way consonant with the usage of Scripture: Cf 1 Cor. 15, 45 and Jn. 7, 39. The adequately correct formulation in our language would be, 'the Lord, raised up, became Spirit, that is to say, was exalted to God in his humanity as well, having his throne at God's right hand . . .' Cf Neunheuser 'Der Hlg Geist in der Liturgie': *Liturgie und Mönchtum* 20 (1957) 11–33, esp 29 ff.

p. 17. This must of course be understood to mean that baptism itself, even without subsequent confirmation is a beginning of communication of the Holy Sprit. Cf Neunheuser, *Taufe und Firmung* in the new Herder *Handbuch der Dogmenschichte* IV/2, p. 39 ff, esp p. 40 and 57.

p. 18. The unusual formulation as it may seem to us once again corresponds to the usage of scriptural language: the passage cited before, 2 Cor. 3, 17 ὁ δὲ κύριος τὸ πνεῦμά ἐστιν. Casel himself gives an interpretation a few lines below of the equivalence: Christian = other Christ = Spirit which is wholly in keeping with the usage of present-day dogmatic theology.

p. 21. The teaching on sacrifice here and in the pages which follow corresponds wholly and entirely to the requirements of the Council of Trent in the XXIInd session (Denzinger 937a ff) and the encyclical *Mediator Dei*. To the extent, however, that they pass beyond those requirements (it is well-known that these pronouncements of authority did not seek to solve the questions in controversy among theologians) their particular aim, in Casel's mind, was the presentation of the numerical unity of Christ's act (Cf. J.L.W. 6 (1927), 193, where he speaks of the identity of the act of sacrifice in mass and cross); in the historical act of Christ's sacrifice in its temporal moment and in the act which the church is always performing, there is but one single sacrificial act of Christ. Because the church presents this sacrifice by her action, she makes the sacrifice of Christ; she shares in it through her sacramental service, and beyond that she is bound to join herself to the one offering which is present by her own wholly personal activity.

p. 30. The Old Testament of course knew no mysteries if we understand the term in the full sense of the NT; it is in this sense that the following lines use the word. But this does not prevent us from speaking in concert with e.g. Hebrews, 10, 1 and the majority of the fathers about mysteries or sacraments in an imperfect sense. Thus St Thomas answers the question whether there had to be sacraments after the fall yet before Christ (III, 63, 1), in other words, under the Old Testament: 'The first sacraments to be celebrated and observed by the law were heralds of Christ to come, and it was necessary that the coming

of Christ should be announced; hence it was necessary that there should have
been sacraments to prepare the way for this coming of his. . . . These sacraments
were certain sensible signs of invisible things by which man is made holy . . .
signs by which man gave testimony of his faith in the coming of the redeemer;
such signs were called sacraments.'

p. 31. Earthly salvation and earthly goods: long life, daily bread, the continuance of the people in its land flowing with milk and honey, etc. These must
however be seen very much as a symbol of things beyond this level; as their
promise and foundation. They were in fact a means for the Israelite who faith-
fully performed his duties towards God of obtaining everlasting salvation.

p. 32. Of course the world of the Old Testament failed when faced with the
greatness of the revelation of God's merciful love in the New Testament. But it
failed less because this revelation was of a different spirit from its own than
because God's revelation had *not yet reached such final possibilities*. Not even the
forms of the Indo-germanic peoples reached this highest stage of divine revelation. This does not mean that some elements of their achievement were not to
have a special meaning, thanks to God's providence, in a later time; that is
surely what Casel means. There is still much to be done concerning the details
of this matter; we may mention Padberg's article (Note 14 of the preface above)
and one by Victor Warnach: A.L.W. V/2 (1958), p. 331 ff.

p. 34. It is most important to keep this in mind. The all-important fact is
that Christianity is a mystery religion in virtue of its own very nature and the
liturgy of mysteries is the central and essential activity of this religion. Cf above
p. 52. The question of the concrete manner in which the mystery terminology
was brought into the church, particularly the development from hellenistic
mysterion to Latin *mysterium* and *sacramentum* in profane and Christian use is
a matter of special interest and not a closed question. Of interest is A. Kolping's
review of Fittkau's book on the mystery in Chrysostom: *Theolog. Revue* 51
(1955), 24–28.

p. 35. It is certainly correct that in the heart of the Christian Middle Ages
with its new Northern peoples and their formative influence upon that age,
a new climate of thought arose, one at first tempestuous and excessive, as in
Abelard for example. But it was very largely taken in hand by the great figures
of the golden age of the universities, and placed at the service of a new and
different but nonetheless truly Christian synthesis. The evil consequences which
Casel names here and on the following pages are phenomena of a markedly
later age, in which the synthesis had come apart. To the extent that the attitudes
of modern anthropocentric thought remain within the church's circle of influence
they can constitute a real value, even in these forms of piety; where the church is,
there is the mystery as well. Casel's judgment on this development is perhaps
too negative.

p. 37. The proper thing here would be to list all the work done in the last
decade; I content myself with recalling Filthaut's book and the other notes
on more recent work in the A.L.W. Cf supra, notes 1–7, page x, and 1–2, page xi.
Not least is it important to realize that there is a difference in Casel's great
work between elements which are simply exegesis of the plain if somewhat
structured teaching of faith, and those which are his own conclusions, a further
development of the traditional data. Casel sought only to work in the first way;
but he may well have underestimated his own work in the second genre.

p. 38. It is well to compare Casel's definition with that of liturgy given in the
encyclical *Mediator Dei*: 'Sacra igitur liturgia cultum publicum constituit, quem
Redemptor noster, Ecclesiae Caput, caelesti Patri habet; quemque christi-
fidelium societas Conditori suo et per ipsum aeterno Patri tribuit; utque omnia
breviter perstringamus, integrum constituit publicum cultum mystici Iesu
Christi Corporis, Capitis nempe membrorumque eius.' (ASS 1947, p. 528–9).

p. 51. The fact of a change in the form of piety cannot be denied; but in
judging it we must in any case remember that its beginning in modern times
even if centred on the self, anthropocentric, must by no means therefore stand

opposed to a truly liturgical and church-oriented piety. Pope Pius XII says in *Mediator Dei* 'If the private and personal piety of the individual neglects holy mass and the sacraments, withdraws from the saving influence which flows from head to the members it will without doubt become a reprehensible and fruitless thing'. But this does not need to be. When modern forms of piety are rightly integrated in the spirit of the church, in proper and organic relationship, made 'theocentric', to use the word of the encyclical, they can be of great value for the liturgical service itself.

p. 52. In order to evaluate properly what is being said here, we must remember that the 'communal mysticism of antiquity' which is praised can be preferred to the mysticism of modern times only in the form in which Christianity gave it. The dark adumbrations of hellenistic cults could in no way be preferred to modern Christian mysticism. Casel's picture here is of ideal types.

p. 55. Casel has advanced on what he says here in the article which was published in A.L.W. I/1 on the mystery language of St Paul. A good introduction to the whole problem is to be found in the book of Victor Warnach: *Agape*, Patmos 1951 (a translation is to be published by Darton, Longman & Todd). Chapter: *Die Agape als Mysterium*. The question of mysterion is treated (German), on pages 372-374, and the extent of the mystery presence, (German) on pages 389-91. A good survey of the latest state of the question of St Paul and the mystery religions of his environment is to be found in Warnach's article 'Die Tauflehre des Römerbriefes', A.L.W. V/2 (1958) p. 329 note 117. Among other things, Bornkamm's article in Kittel's *Wörterbuch* should also be mentioned: IV (1940), 809-834. None of these questions have found final answers; but the fruitfulness in discussion of Casel's original stimulus should not be overlooked. It has made possible a truly Christian explanation of the healing Christ has brought, realized in the church and its sacramental, liturgical actions; it has made possible as well a reasonable explanation of the wide use of the words *mysterium* and *mysteria*, *sacramentum* and *sacramenta* in the language of the classical Rome liturgy. Through it too is made possible an historical picture which holds pre- and non-Christian cults in their proper relationship to the salvation which God has accomplished, salvation which is not without its witnesses outside the realm of revelation.

p. 60. Cf the note on page (37) and the literature mentioned there.

p. 63. One might mention the additional material in 'Beiträge zur Theologie des Kirchenjahres' in *Liturgie und Mönchtum* 1950, No. 5 and 'L'Année liturgique selon Dom Casel' in *Questions liturgiques et paroissiales* 1957, p. 286-298.

p. 90. A book by Dom Casel's disciple Aemiliana Löhr has further developed these thoughts in an admirable way: *Abend und Morgen*, Pustet, 1955.

BIOGRAPHY OF ODO CASEL

ODO CASEL was born in Koblenz, on 27 September 1886, and attended schools there. In 1896 he was at the progymnasium in Malmédy and from 1899 to 1905 at the Gymnasium at Andernach where he sat for his examinations. After half a year of classical study at Bonn, he entered the Abbey of Maria Laach, and was professed on 24 February 1907. He studied at Maria Laach and Rome, and in 1913 took his theological doctorate with a thesis on the eucharistic teaching of Justin Martyr. Returning to Laach, he went back to Bonn, where, in 1919 after a brilliant examination, he took the degree of D.Phil. His thesis, *De philosophorum Graecorum silentio mystico*, appeared in the series *Religionsgeschichtlicher Versuche und Vorarbeiten*. At Laach once more, he continued his studies, especially concerning himself with liturgy and its mystery character. In the following years, he developed the idea of ritual as the sacramental presence of Christ's saving work; it had been hinted at in the dissertation on Justin, and the small book which had appeared in 1919, *Das Gedächtnis des Herrn in der altchristlichen Liturgie*, and was presented in full form for the first time in his book *Die Liturgie als Mysterienfeier* (1922). The scientific groundwork and defence of the thesis was carried on particularly in the *Jahrbuch für Liturgiewissenschaft* (1921–1941 Aschendorf, 15 vols.).

Dom Odo became chaplain to the Abbey of Benedictine nuns at Herstelle in Westphalia in 1922, and remained there until his death on Easter morning, 28 March 1948.[1] A published bibliography is to be found in *Vom Christlichen Mysterium*, a book of studies on the Mystery by scholars of all nations; it includes 110 items of Dom Odo's own work, 211 reviews and 17 translations into foreign languages. Dom Odo's last work, unfinished at his death, *Das Christliche Opfermysterium*, is being prepared for publication.

INDEX